The Millennium Development Goals and Beyond

Rethinking International Development Series

Series Editors:

Andy Sumner, Fellow of the Vulnerability and Poverty Research Team, Institute of Development Studies, UK.

Ray Kiely, Professor of International Politics, Queen Mary University of London, UK.

Palgrave Macmillan is delighted to announce a new series dedicated to publishing cutting-edge titles that focus on the broad area of 'development'.

The core aims of the series are to present critical work that:

- is cross disciplinary;
- challenges orthodoxies;
- reconciles theoretical depth with empirical research;
- explores the frontiers of development studies in terms of 'development' in both North and South and global inter-connectedness;
- reflects on claims to knowledge and intervening in other peoples lives.

Titles include:

Simon Feeny and Matthew Clarke
THE MILLENNIUM DEVELOPMENT GOALS AND BEYOND
International Assistance to the Asia-Pacific

Andy Sumner and Meera Tiwari
AFTER 2015: INTERNATIONAL DEVELOPMENT POLICY AT A CROSSROADS

Rethinking International Development Series
Series Standing Order ISBN 978–0230–53751–4 (hardback)
(*outside North America only*)

You can receive future titles in this series as they are published by placing a standing order. Please contact your bookseller or, in case of difficulty, write to us at the address below with your name and address, the title of the series and the ISBN quoted above.

Customer Services Department, Macmillan Distribution Ltd, Houndmills, Basingstoke, Hampshire RG21 6XS, England

---

The Millennium Development Goals and Beyond

International Assistance to the Asia-Pacific

Simon Feeny
Senior Lecturer, School of Economics, Finance and Marketing
RMIT University, Australia

and

Matthew Clarke
Associate Professor, School of International and Political Studies
Deakin University, Australia

First published 2009 by
PALGRAVE MACMILLAN

Palgrave Macmillan in the UK is an imprint of Macmillan Publishers Limited, registered in England, company number 785998, of Houndmills, Basingstoke, Hampshire RG21 6XS.

Palgrave Macmillan in the US is a division of St Martin's Press LLC, 175 Fifth Avenue, New York, NY 10010.

Palgrave Macmillan is the global academic imprint of the above companies and has companies and representatives throughout the world.

Palgrave® and Macmillan® are registered trademarks in the United States, the United Kingdom, Europe and other countries.

ISBN-13: 978–0–230–22443–8 hardback
ISBN-10: 0–230–22443–1   hardback

This book is printed on paper suitable for recycling and made from fully managed and sustained forest sources. Logging, pulping and manufacturing processes are expected to conform to the environmental regulations of the country of origin.

A catalogue record for this book is available from the British Library.

A catalogue record for this book is available from the Library of Congress.

10   9   8   7   6   5   4   3   2   1
18   17   16   15   14   13   12   11   10   09

Printed and bound in Great Britain by
CPI Antony Rowe, Chippenham and Eastbourne

Contents

List of Boxes, Tables and Figures

Figures

Acknowledgements

This book is an outcome of a research project generously supported by the Australian Research Council (ARC) and World Vision Australia. The views expressed in the book are those of the authors and not necessarily those of the funding organisations. The authors are grateful to a number of people for helpful advice and comments including James Cox, Brett Parris, Garth Luke, Kirsty Nowlan, Suzi Chinnery, Grant Hill, Tim Fry, Mark McGillivray, Tony Addison, Lindsay Rae, John McKenzie and Chitra Thumborisuthi.

Preface

This book reflects the insights into the global development challenge gained from three years of broad and innovative research by Simon Feeny and Matthew Clarke. World Vision Australia, part of the world's largest privately-funded international development agency, has been an enthusiastic partner in this research. Our support grows from a strong belief that the Millennium Development Goals (MDGs) represent the best framework yet conceived for measuring and driving progress in tackling world poverty. The research results in this book have helped to confirm the validity of the MDGs and to identify and refine ways in which they can be applied to greatest effect.

Indeed, this work, supported also by funds from the Australian Research Council, has strengthened our view that a stronger knowledge base is a critical need in addressing several challenges faced by organisations seeking to reduce global poverty.

First, global poverty cannot be reduced unless it is understood. While national governments, the UN, the World Bank and numerous official agencies provide a wealth of statistical and qualitative information about aspects of poverty, the tasks of analysis and application remain complex, and constantly in need of new thinking. All those concerned with action on poverty need a clear sense of the context in which we work in order to understand how our programme activity can contribute to the global project.

Specifically, development agencies need to become more effective learning organisations, able to adapt and change approaches in the light of new knowledge and greater experience. Too often situations are analysed, or programmes evaluated, yet the insights gained fail to promote changed thinking or behaviours.

Further, an expanded knowledge base is required to address three specific challenges which development organisations already face, and which will certainly become more intense in the decade or so ahead.

The first of these is the changing nature of accountability. In the past agencies have primarily seen the accountability issue in terms of financial accounting. As they have grown they have become increasingly aware that donors expect, and regulators will demand, that agencies should demonstrate that development funds have been used appropriately, and the promise to donors has been kept. This has led agencies to focus on quantitative measurement of outputs – being able to show the quantity of goods and services provided to poor communities, or the number of activities undertaken, or the number of individuals or families receiving a benefit.

This has now changed, partly because poor communities themselves, as well as a more sophisticated donor community has come to reject the 'charity' model of development assistance as direct benefit, especially beyond the context of humanitarian emergency responses. Increasingly the development sector needs to work on demonstrating effectiveness in advancing and sustaining community wellbeing rather than merely reporting outputs. This is difficult, in the first place because of the problems associated with identifying appropriate indicators of wellbeing, capturing baseline data and then monitoring progress. But beyond this are difficulties of attribution – even if strong progress can be identified, it is not always simple to explain what causes, in what combination, were responsible.

A second challenge is developing the human and intellectual capital that will maximise the effectiveness of those working in the field. As the scale and intensity of global development initiatives grow, it will become increasingly difficult to ensure we can attract, retain and develop the skilled people needed to manage and deliver programmes. This applies not only to international non-government organisations, but to all those working in the field, including governments, local civil society organisations, the education and health sectors and the business community. It also emphatically applies to leaders within communities. What is required is not merely more and better education and training, but a rethinking of how people work and relate within and between organisations, and within and between communities. This will be an impossible challenge unless accurate, timely and useful knowledge and analysis is widely available, and the idea of the development worker as knowledge worker is advanced.

The third challenge is embodied in Millennium Development Goal 8 – building a global partnership for development depends on growing public support for development, which is entirely knowledge dependent. Goal 8 reflects a clear understanding that the kind of development needed to meet the ambitious targets of the MDGs cannot be achieved unless everyone plays their part. The main agents of development will continue to be poor communities themselves. But governments, international agencies, civil society organisations, businesses, the media and the formal education sector all have critical roles to play.

For Non-Governmental Organisations (NGOs) in the development field it is critical to maintain public confidence and support. NGOs can only generate the resources they need if the public respects and appreciates their work. It is no longer sufficient merely to have an honourable cause or noble aspiration – the public expects that NGOs will be creative, innovative and effective in their responses to poverty. Similarly, one of the ways in which NGOs can contribute most effectively is through policy influence. Again, political leaders and other decision-makers are disinclined to respond to mere 'wish lists', but rather expect NGOs to mount credible, well-argued cases for particular policy directions.

For these reasons World Vision and other development organisations highly value the work of scholars such as Matthew Clarke and Simon Feeny, especially in both confirming the value and validity of the MDGs, and in suggesting some ways in which these Goals need to be further explored and refined.

The world is now more than halfway from the adoption of the MDGs to the target date for their achievement. Yet it is still a priority for advocacy groups in development to promote awareness and commitment to the Goals among the public and by governments. This book is a positive sign that the pursuit of knowledge can contribute powerfully to social change, as well as a reminder that the years ahead will demand an ever greater commitment from scholars within the great global partnership working for the end of poverty.

Lindsay Rae
Research and Education Manager
World Vision Australia

Part I

1
The Millennium Development Goals in the Asia-Pacific: An Introduction

1 Introduction

At the United Nations (UN) Millennium Summit in September 2000, 191 UN member states committed themselves to the achievement of the Millennium Development Goals (MDGs). These goals emanated from a number of international conferences during the 1990s, which themselves drew on pre-existing goals and targets dating back to aspirations espoused by the international community before World War II. The MDGs are a set of eight internationally agreed goals to improve the well-being of the poor in developing countries. They are designed to address many of the multidimensional aspects of poverty and include: (1) eradicating extreme income poverty and hunger; (2) achieving universal primary education; (3) promoting gender equality; (4) reducing child mortality; (5) improving maternal health; (6) combating HIV/AIDS, malaria and other diseases; (7) ensuring environmental sustainability; and (8) developing a global partnership for development. In addition to the eight goals, there are 18 targets and 48 indicators which are listed in the appendix to this chapter. Using 1990 as a baseline, both developed and developing countries have pledged to meet the MDGs by 2015.

The achievement of the MDGs will require considerable effort and commitment from both developed and developing countries. This is recognised by the eighth MDG of developing a global partnership for development. Developed countries have obligations to increase the level and quality of their foreign assistance, provide greater access to their domestic markets and reduce the debt burden of their development partners. At the same time, responsibility for achieving the MDGs rests largely with the governments of developing countries and requires a strengthening of their own commitment to poverty reduction. The governments of developing countries must therefore work to combat corruption and improve governance, undertake important policy reforms and ensure that additional aid funds are used effectively if the goals are to be achieved by 2015.

In some respects the Asia-Pacific region is making good progress towards the MDGs. There are some well-performing economies already achieving large reductions in poverty and making good progress towards other development targets. Further, as a whole the region is on track to achieve the first MDG of reducing by half the proportion of people living in poverty. This is due to remarkable progress made by the regions two largest developing economies: China and India. However, the Asia-Pacific region is extremely diverse and analysis at the regional level often masks important differences between countries at a national level. Other Asian countries have not made good progress towards the goals and countries in the Pacific have, in general, not performed as well. In particular the Melanesian countries of Fiji, Papua New Guinea, the Solomon Islands and Vanuatu need to make much faster progress if the MDGs are to be achieved by 2015. The Pacific includes a number of Small Island Developing States (SIDS), which face a number of specific constraints to development and therefore the achievement of the MDGs.

The focus of this book is how international foreign (government) aid donors and Non-Governmental Organisations (NGOs) can assist with the achievement of the MDGs. International donors and NGOs have important but very distinct roles to play. International donors have started scaling up their aid flows and for many countries they will be an important source of additional resources to fight poverty in its many forms. While NGOs will have considerable fewer resources at their disposal, they will play an important role in ensuring basic services reach the poor, monitoring progress towards the goals and holding governments and donors accountable for their actions. As part of civil society, NGOs must work to combat corruption, strengthen community and civil institutions, undertake important community-focused development interventions and advocate to ensure that additional funds are used effectively.

As noted, countries within the Asia-Pacific region are diverse in terms of their economic circumstances, geography, natural resource endowments, demographic conditions and political institutions. Countries in the region are also diverse in terms of their starting points in achieving the MDGs. However, there are some general themes that cut across these countries and a better understanding of these themes can assist with determining the role that international assistance can play in achieving the MDGs. This book therefore provides four country case studies which focus on these different themes. The case studies clearly demonstrate the need to tailor the goals to individual country contexts. They also demonstrate distinct country-specific issues faced by donors and NGOs in assisting with MDG achievement: improving governance in Papua New Guinea; increasing the efficiency of aid in Cambodia; dealing with a post-conflict environment in the case of the Solomon Islands; and helping a well-performing middle-income country in the case of Thailand. The international community face these important issues in a number of other developing countries throughout the world. The book highlights the fact that different country contexts require different MDG targets and different responses from international donors and NGOs.

This introductory chapter provides an overview of the issues regarding the achievement of the MDGs in the Asia-Pacific region. Although the MDGs represent an important commitment to reducing poverty in developing countries, the support for them is not universal. The reasons are discussed in section 2. Section 3 examines whether the goals are feasible and the need to tailor some of the MDG targets in some countries given their specific circumstances. Section 4 examines the progress towards the MDGs that has already been made in the Asia-Pacific at an individual country level. The section highlights the importance of widely reported and reliable data in order to track MDG progress and improve accountability and identifies those countries most at risk of not achieving the goals. While the focus of the book is the role of international aid in assisting with the MDGs, section 5 discusses some of the other factors which will also be important for their achievement.

2   Critiques of the MDGs

The MDGs are not the first set of international development targets, although they are more comprehensive than previous targets and have received unprecedented support from around the world. Declarations of achieving universal primary education, for example, date back to the League of Nations in 1934. The importance of the MDGs though lies in clarifying the objectives of development policy and providing a strong case for additional funding from the international community during an era of aid fatigue. Moreover, by committing to the MDGs international donors and developing country governments have made themselves more accountable to taxpayers and voters. However, enthusiasm for the MDGs is not universal. Some critics argue that the goals are too ambitious while others argue that they are not ambitious enough. Others argue that the existence of the MDGs is unlikely to lead to any change by donors due to a persistent problem of donor accountability. Other critics argue that they prioritise quantitative indicators over qualitative indicators and mask reality by relying on averages. These critiques are discussed in turn. Whilst there are a number of reasons to be cautious in embracing the MDGs and in evaluating country progress in 2015, the case to reject the goals outright is arguably weak.

The United Nations Millennium Project Report (UN, 2005) clearly argues that the MDGs can be achieved albeit with great effort from developing country governments and the international community. The report argues that 'the starting assumption should be that they are feasible unless technically proven otherwise' (UN, 2006, p.55). Vandemoortele (2002) also argues that the MDGs remain feasible and affordable even though at the current rate of progress only the MDG target of halving the proportion of people without access to safe water will be met globally by 2015.

However, not everyone agrees that they are feasible. Radelet (2004) outlines three reasons why the MDG targets might be unattainable in some countries. The first is that they could be technically unattainable – even if resources are adequate and the domestic environment is favourable, reaching the very high growth rates necessary to reduce poverty, for example, is simply not possible. Secondly they could be fiscally unattainable where a country has inadequate financial resources to reach them. Thirdly MDGs could be unattainable because of other constraints such as trade policies, a lack of institutional capacity or due to cultural values and norms (such as a tradition of keeping girls at home rather than sending them to school). The latter constraint suggesting that the MDGs were developed within a *western* paradigm.

Clemens *et al.* (2007) also argue that the MDGs are impossible to meet because of how they were designed. They argue that achieving the goals would imply a rate of progress in many countries which has not previously been experienced by many successful industrialised countries. For example, referring to World Bank studies, they argue that African countries will have to experience economic growth rates in excess of 7 per cent over 15 years to halve poverty. However, during the period 1985 to 2000, only five countries managed to sustain 7 per cent growth. Moreover, the average rate of growth for African countries was just 2.4 per cent for the past 15 years and nearly half of them have experienced negative per capita growth resulting in a higher level of income poverty. Although studies have argued that policy changes and higher levels of aid could foster unusually high levels of growth, Clemens *et al.* (2007) argue that the role of policy in determining growth rates is likely to be only modest. Moreover there is also a limit to how much progress towards the MDGs can be accelerated through increased aid due to questions over its impact in countries with poor policies and diminishing returns to aid at high levels. This issue is discussed further in Chapter 2. Similar arguments apply to the health and education goals since improvements in indicators usually occur only slowly through time and are only tenuously linked to higher levels of financial resources.

Others argue that rather than being too ambitious, the MDGs are not ambitious enough. Rather than halving global poverty, they argue that the international community should be trying to eradicate poverty completely. The MDGs should though, not be seen as an end in themselves but as a way of benchmarking progress towards the eventual eradication of global poverty widely defined (UNESCAP, 2003). It is also asserted that the goals are not broad enough and neglect a number of aspects of well-being which are at danger of being ignored by governments as they strive to achieve the goals by 2015. It is true that the goals fail to address directly issues of rights, empowerment, citizenship, freedom and security all of which are widely regarded as being fundamental to development. At the same some time many of these issues will be addressed indirectly if the MDGs are achieved. Improving health and education for example, will improve rights and empowerment.

White and Black (2006) outline a problem of accountability. Although all public sector bodies should be accountable for their actions, it is difficult to envisage how development agencies could be held accountable for failure in reaching the MDGs. Firstly, attributing failure directly to agencies would be very difficult but secondly, donors are accountable to their electorates in their own countries rather than to the poor in developing countries which they seek to help.

The MDGs are also criticised at a technical level as many of the MDG targets relate to averages that can mask inequality in development across and within countries. For example, China and India are likely to achieve the goal of halving poverty in the near future. Yet income poverty for many in these countries is not improving. This is particularly true for those living in rural isolated areas. Vandemoortele (2006) argues that a good assessment of progress towards the MDGs must go beyond aggregates and averages. Within countries, progress towards the MDGs is likely to be very different for people of different gender, ethnic and social backgrounds. For example, large reductions in child mortality do not necessarily mean that child mortality has been reduced for certain disadvantaged groups. For example, internally displaced people or illegal migrants are often excluded from data collection processes, yet it is these groups that are most vulnerable and most likely to experience poverty. Reducing inequality between different groups within countries should therefore be a priority for policy-makers in striving to achieve the MDGs by 2015.

A final criticism of the MDGs is that some of the targets rely on quantitative rather than qualitative targets. They focus on the provision of activities without any analysis of the quality of outcomes. For example, although enrolments in schools and access to health care might be improving, the quality of education and health care might actually be deteriorating. This issue is particularly relevant for Pacific countries where educational standards are often deemed to be low. In some cases therefore, donors and developing country governments will need look beyond the MDG targets and ensure, for example, that children receive a valuable, relevant education with access to textbooks, classrooms and teaching resources once they are enrolled at school (Feeny and Clarke, 2008).

3 Tailoring the targets

Notwithstanding the criticisms discussed above, the international community is committed to MDG achievement. However, it is becoming increasingly clear that some countries in the Asia-Pacific region are not going to achieve the MDGs by 2015 – even with large increases in foreign aid and improvements in governance. The goals are simply too ambitious. This is particularly true for many of the countries referred to by the international community as 'fragile states' which are discussed in detail in Chapter 2. The governments of these countries either lack the commitment and/or the capacity to reach the MDGs. Some have little chance of progressing towards the goals due to conflict or civil unrest. In some, poverty levels have actually increased since 1990 rather than fallen. It is difficult (and not always sensible) to work towards achieving the MDGs as they stand in these circumstances and there are serious doubts over the capacity of these countries to absorb even higher levels of aid. About one-third of the world's poor live in fragile states. There are a number of countries in the Asia-Pacific that are often referred to as fragile.

In 2015 it is very likely that the governments of these countries together with international aid donors will be heavily criticised for a lack of success. This will further weaken the support for aid and any important reforms undertaken by developing countries could be undermined – an outcome which must be avoided (Clemens *et al.*, 2007). It is sometimes asserted that the goals be abandoned in these countries. This book, however, argues that development goals are important and rather than abandon the MDGs, the answer lies in tailoring them to specific country contexts. The United Nations Development Program (UNDP) has taken the lead on this issue with developing country governments. What matters is the existence of appropriate, mutually agreed upon targets that governments and the international community can work towards. This will lead to greater action to achieve them. Goals need not be the same for China and Tonga for example. They should reflect countries different situations and development constraints.

In tailoring the MDG targets, it is important that the revised targets are ambitious but achievable. If they are not ambitious, they are unlikely to induce any significant policy reform or warrant additional financial resources. If they are overly ambitious though, they are unlikely to gain widespread support and there will be little genuine effort to achieve them. Given the importance of ownership for successful development, tailored goals and targets should be devised by developing countries themselves and incorporated into their national development strategies. The goals should then become the focus of foreign aid donor activities, being explicitly incorporated into their policies and programmes. The international community should have no excuse for not backing country-owned, ambitious but achievable development targets.

Some countries in the Asia-Pacific, discussed in this book, have tailored the original MDG goals and targets. Papua New Guinea, the subject of Chapter 4, experienced very poor rates of economic growth during the 1990s and made little development progress. The country has subsequently tailored the goals, making some MDG targets less ambitious but more achievable by 2015 which, arguably, has led to broader support for the goals. Conversely Thailand is expected to achieve all of the goals before 2015. It has therefore tailored the goals to be more ambitious. Thailand's tailored goals include reducing poverty to less than 4 per cent by 2009 and achieving universal secondary (as well as primary) education by 2015. These are discussed in Chapter 7. Not only might the goals need to be tailored but additional goals might need to be added. Cambodia, (examined in Chapter 5), has amended some of the MDG targets and also included a goal for zero impact from landmines. In contrast though, the Solomon Islands (examined in Chapter 6), has not begun to fully incorporate the MDGs into a coordinated national framework. Devising appropriate MDG targets in this post-conflict country remains a challenge.

The year 2015 is inevitably going to be a year of finger pointing and blame allocation when some countries fail to achieve the MDGs. However, unless countries are working towards realistic goals, there is risk that improvements in development will not be given their due recognition and too much discussion will be devoted towards ineffective aid and poor levels of governance. Tailored goals for some countries that are ambitious but realistic could help resolve this problem – and lead to far greater action to achieve them.

4 Tracking progress in the Asia-Pacific

The timeframe for achieving the MDGs is 2015 using 1990 as the baseline year. It is important though to monitor progress towards their achievement before this date to ensure that current activities, interventions and policies are indeed being effective and for identifying areas needing priority attention. Unfortunately, tracking progress towards the achievement of the MDGs in the Asia-Pacific region is hampered by the lack of available and reliable data. This is particularly true for Pacific countries. Data in the Pacific are rarely collected and compiled in a timely manner and using different sources of data sometimes makes comparability difficult. Further, data for Pacific countries are often not made widely available (Feeny and Clarke, 2008).

The data relating to many of the MDG targets for the baseline year of 1990 do not exist for many Pacific countries. Questions then arise as to how the achievement of the MDGs will be assessed in 2015 for such countries. For example, given no data relating for the number of people in poverty in the baseline year 1990, it is impossible to assess whether such countries have halved the proportion of people living on less than $1 a day between 1990 and 2015. This also makes it difficult to devise development policies in support of the goals. Moreover, given that Pacific countries are characterised by high levels of inequality, data would ideally be disaggregated within countries to identify large regional differences as well as differences across gender and ethnic groupings. In fact some countries have devised different MDG targets for different provinces and regions. Unfortunately such data are not readily available in the Pacific and many countries in Asia.

Reliable and widely accessible data is crucial not only for tracking progress towards the MDGs. It is necessary for identifying areas of priority, conducting MDG needs assessments and devising Poverty Reduction Strategies and National Development Plans. Accurate and widely available data and statistics are vital for evidence-based policy-making. Adopting evidence-based policy-making ensures that decisions are transparent and that governments can be held accountable.[1]

Tracking progress towards the MDGs for Asia-Pacific countries is complicated further by some countries having already tailored the targets (while others are in the process of doing this). Tables 1.1 and 1.2 only provide an indication of the progress made by countries towards some of the original MDG targets. However, the tables are useful to provide indications of which targets and countries are progressing well and which are faring poorly. Progress is tracked for all low and middle-income countries in Eastern, Southern and South-East Asia and Pacific countries of Oceania. Progress towards eight MDG targets relating to the first five MDGs and a further MDG target relating to Goal 7 is examined. Progress towards the MDG of combating HIV/AIDS, malaria and other diseases is not assessed as data are only available for recent years. Goal 8 calls for a global partnership for development and includes a further seven targets. However, progress towards this goal is subjective and is not examined. Further details are provided in the notes to the tables (see also, Feeny and Clarke, 2008).

For the analysis of progress towards the achievement of the MDG in the Asia-Pacific region, this paper utilises the Millennium Development Goal Indicators Database from the United Nations. The database is compiled using data from a number of different sources including the World Bank, the Food and Agricultural Organisation (FAO), the World Health Organisation (WHO), the United Nations Educational Scientific and Cultural Organisation (UNESCO) and the United Nations Children's Fund (UNICEF). The data for each particular target are collected from just one of the sources identified above. Although it might be possible to supplement the data from national sources, this would introduce problems of consistency and comparability.

---

[1]The importance of statistics for development is highlighted by Scott (2005). The report identifies the following important uses of statistics: (i) to help identify issues; (ii) to inform the design and choice of policy; (iii) to forecast the future; (iv) to monitor policy implementation; and (v) to evaluate policy impact.

Table 1.1 Progress Towards the MDGs – Asian Countries

	Goal 1 Poverty and Hunger Target 1	Target 2	Goal 2 Education Target 3	Goal 3 Gender Targets 4, 5 and 6	Goal 4 Child Health Target 5	Goal 5 Maternal health Target 6	Goal 7 Environment Target 10	Overall progress
Afghanistan	–	–	–	–			–	Insufficient Data
Bangladesh							–	At Risk
Bhutan	–	–	–	–			–	Insufficient Data
Cambodia	–						–	At Risk
China								At Risk
India								Severe Risk
Indonesia								On track
Iran	–							At Risk
Korea PDR	–			–	–			Severe Risk
Laos							–	Severe Risk
Malaysia								On track
Maldives	–	–						At Risk
Mongolia								Severe Risk
Myanmar	–							At Risk
Nepal	–							At Risk
Pakistan								Severe Risk
Philippines								At Risk

Table 1.1 Progress Towards the MDGs – Asian Countries – *continued*

	Goal 1 Poverty and Hunger		Goal 2 Education	Goal 3 Gender	Goal 4 Child Health	Goal 5 Maternal health	Goal 7 Environment	Overall progress
	Target 1	Target 2	Target 3	Targets 4, 5 and 6	Target 5	Target 6	Target 10	
Sri Lanka	Off-track	On-track	Off-track	Insufficient Data	On-track	On-track	On-track	At Risk
Thailand	On-track	On-track	On-track	On-track	On-track	On-track	Off-track	On track
Timor Leste	Insufficient Data	Insufficient Data	Insufficient Data	Insufficient Data	Off-track	On-track	Insufficient Data	Insufficient Data
Vietnam	On-track	On-track	On-track	On-track	On-track	Off-track	Off-track	On track

On-track — (white box)
Off-track — (dark box)
Insufficient Data — (light grey box)

Source: Feeny and Clarke (2008).

Notes: Targets are defined in the chapter appendix. Countries are classified as 'on-track' if their current rate of progress (calculated using available data) is sufficient to achieve the MDG target if maintained. The final column provides an indication of countries overall progress towards the MDG targets. A country is classified as 'at risk' of not achieving the MDGs if it is off-track to achieve at least one-third of the MDG targets (for which data are available). A country is classified as at 'severe risk' of not achieving the MDGs if it is off-track to achieve at least two-thirds of the targets (for which data are available). A country is classified as having insufficient data if data are available for less than three MDG targets. Progress towards MDG 3 of promoting gender equality is assessed by examining the average progress towards three MDG targets of eliminating gender disparity at primary, secondary and tertiary levels of education.

Table 1.2 Progress Towards the MDGs – Pacific Countries

	Goal 1 Poverty and Hunger		Goal 2 Education	Goal 3 Gender	Goal 4 Child Health	Goal 5 Maternal health	Goal 7 Environment	Overall progress
	Target 1	Target 2	Target 3	Targets 4, 5 and 6	Target 5	Target 6	Target 10	
Cook Islands	–	–	–	–		–		Insufficient Data
Fiji	–	–					–	On track
Kiribati	–	–	–	–		–		Insufficient Data
Marshall Islands	–	–		–		–		At Risk
Micronesia	–	–		–		–		Insufficient Data
Nauru	–	–				–	–	Severe Risk
Niue	–	–			–	–		On track
Palau	–	–				–		At Risk
P. New Guinea	–	–						At Risk
Samoa	–	–						At Risk
Solomon Islands	–	–		–			–	Severe Risk
Tokelau	–	–	–	–	–	–	–	Insufficient Data
Tonga	–	–				–		On track
Tuvalu	–	–	–			–		At Risk
Vanuatu	–	–						On track

Table 1.2 Progress Towards the MDGs – Pacific Countries – *continued*

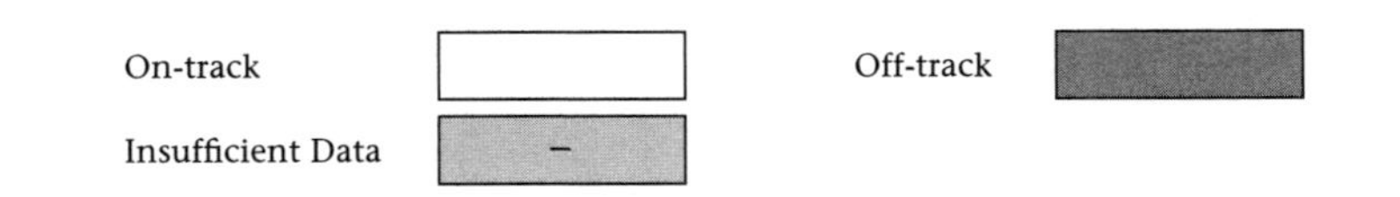

Source: Feeny and Clarke (2008).
Notes: Targets are defined in the chapter appendix. Countries are classified as 'on-track' if their current rate of progress (calculated using available data) is sufficient to achieve the MDG target if maintained. The final column provides an indication of countries overall progress towards the MDG targets. A country is classified as 'at risk' of not achieving the MDGs if it is off-track to achieve at least one-third of the MDG targets (for which data are available). A country is classified as at 'severe risk' of not achieving the MDGs if it is off-track to achieve at least two-thirds of the targets (for which data are available). A country is classified as having insufficient data if data are available for less than three MDG targets. Progress towards MDG 3 of promoting gender equality is assessed by examining the average progress towards three MDG targets of eliminating gender disparity at primary, secondary and tertiary levels of education.

Table 1.1 summarises the progress of Asian countries towards the MDGs. As a region, the Asia-Pacific has made some good progress towards the achievement of the MDGs by 2015. However, there are large variations in progress across both countries and goals. Four countries are on track to achieve the MDGs: Indonesia, Malaysia, Thailand and Vietnam. However, there are five countries at severe risk of not achieving them: India, North Korea, Laos, Mongolia and Pakistan. There are insufficient data to assess the progress made by Afghanistan, Bhutan and Timor-Leste. The other countries in Asia are classified as at risk of not achieving the MDGs. The MDG target most at risk of not being achieved is that of universal primary education. While many Asian countries have high primary school enrolment rates, insufficient progress is being made to fulfil this target. Poor progress is also being made towards the targets of reducing hunger and child and maternal mortality rates.

Table 1.2 highlights the poor availability of data for Pacific countries which makes tracking progress towards the MDGs for this region very difficult. The Cook Islands, Kiribati, Micronesia and Tokelau are countries which do not have enough data to meaningfully evaluate their progress towards the MDGs. According to the data used, Fiji, Niue, Tonga and Vanuatu are classified as being on track to achieve the MDGs. Table 1.2 also indicates that Nauru and the Solomon Islands are at severe risk of not achieving the MDGs by 2015 with five other Pacific countries classified as being 'at risk' of not achieving the MDGs. Far greater progress at reducing child and maternal mortality and improving access to safe water is required in the Pacific region. Overall both tables indicate that unless there are good reasons to believe that much faster progress will be made towards the MDGs in coming years, many countries in the Asia-Pacific will fail to achieve them by 2015 – unless they are suitably tailored.

The tables highlight that the role of the international community in assisting with achievement of the MDGs will differ markedly in each of these countries depending on their progress and specific development constraints and priorities. While China has made remarkable progress on reducing poverty and hunger and increasing access to education the country has experienced a rapidly increasing level of inequality. Inland provinces have not experienced the development gains experienced by the coastal provinces. Priorities will include the targeting of the poor in rural areas, improving health services, providing the required infrastructure to cope with rapid urbanisation and targeting a number of environmental concerns associated with its rapid progress. While Malaysia, Thailand and Vietnam are also making good progress towards the achievement of the MDGs, Cambodia, Indonesia, Laos and Myanmar are performing less well and priorities include rural development and improving access to social services. These will also be priorities for India despite its remarkable recent economic record and progress at reducing poverty (UN, 2005).

Many of the Small Island Developing States (SIDS) of the Pacific require interventions aimed at improving governance, increasing rural incomes and ensuring greater access to social services. These countries are also vulnerable to natural disasters and to climate change. This requires interventions that address climate change adaptation and mitigation, disaster preparation and also rapid responses when extreme climatic events occur.

4   Conclusion

While this book focuses on the role of foreign aid donors and NGOs in achieving the MDGs, it is important to emphasise that most responsibility for the goals lies with the developing country governments. They are responsible for mobilising and allocating resources for development. This can be achieved by undertaking policy reform and improving institutions and the level of governance. Governments must provide business environments for a flourishing private sector and must take the lead on social sector delivery and infrastructure. If the goals are to be tailored, this must involve the private sector and civil society. Effective progress towards the MDGs requires them to be incorporated into a comprehensive development strategy or plan. Development plans and strategies should be closely linked to their annual budgets and results frameworks developed and evaluated.

Moreover, in addition to the provision of foreign aid, the international community can play an important role through its other policies. Importantly, international donor countries must adopt other policies which support their development efforts rather than undermine them. This refers to a concept known as policy coherence. The Organisation for Economic Cooperation and Development (OECD) defines policy coherence as the systematic promotion of mutually reinforcing policy actions across government departments and agencies creating synergies towards achieving agreed objectives (OECD, 2003). There are potential trade-offs (and synergies) between development policies and trade, security, migration and environment policies. For example, providing aid to increase a recipient's ability to trade while at the same time maintaining high trade barriers against the recipient are contradictory and incoherent policies. Policies in these sectors should support the attainment of development objectives or they will undermine the effectiveness of foreign aid.

This book consists of three parts. This chapter has highlighted some of the criticisms of the MDGs and the need to tailor some of the MDG targets in some countries to maintain or increase support for their achievement. It has demonstrated that progress towards the original goals varies considerably by country but overall faster rates of progress are required in most countries for the MDGs (as they stand) to be achieved by 2015. Chapter 2 considers the role of foreign aid in achieving the MDGs whilst Chapter 3 considers the role played by non-governmental organisations. Part II of this book consists of four case studies. These case studies were selected on the basis that they represent particular (and important) themes that the international community faces in developing countries throughout the world. Papua New Guinea (PNG) highlights the importance of governance to the achievement of the MDGs, while Cambodia emphasises the importance of improving aid efficiency. The Solomon Islands is an example of a post-conflict environment whilst Thailand represents the unique circumstances of a middle-income country. Lessons learnt from these themed country case studies will also apply to a number of other developing countries. Part III concludes the book with a summary and a way forward.

Chapter 1 Appendix: The Millennium Development Goals, Targets and Indicators

GOAL 1: ERADICATE EXTREME POVERTY AND HUNGER

Target 1: Reduce by half the proportion of people living on less than a dollar a day

Indicators

1. Proportion of Population Below $1 (PPP) per Day (World Bank)
2. Poverty Gap Ratio, $1 per day (World Bank)
3. Share of Poorest Quintile in National Income or Consumption (World Bank)

Target 2: Reduce by half the proportion of people who suffer from hunger

Indicators

4. Prevalence of Underweight Children Under Five Years of Age (UNICEF)
5. Proportion of the Population below Minimum Level of Dietary Energy Consumption (FAO)

GOAL 2: ACHIEVE UNIVERSAL PRIMARY EDUCATION

Target 3: Ensure that all boys and girls complete a full course of primary schooling

Indicators

6. Net Enrolment Ratio in Primary Education (UNESCO)
7. Proportion of Pupils Starting Grade 1 who Reach Grade 5 (UNESCO)
8. Literacy Rate of 15–24 year-olds (UNESCO)

GOAL 3: PROMOTE GENDER EQUALITY AND EMPOWER WOMEN

Target 4: Eliminate gender disparity in primary and secondary education preferably by 2005, and at all levels (including tertiary) by 2015

Indicators

9. Ratio of Girls to Boys in Primary, Secondary, and Tertiary Education (UNESCO)
10. Ratio of Literate Women to Men 15–24 years old (UNESCO)
11. Share of Women in Wage Employment in the Non-Agricultural Sector (International Labour Organisation)(ILO))
12. Proportion of Seats Held by Women in National Parliaments (IPU)

GOAL 4: REDUCE CHILD MORTALITY

Target 5: Reduce by two thirds the mortality rate among children under five

Indicators

13. Under-Five Mortality Rate (UNICEF)
14. Infant Mortality Rate (UNICEF)
15. Proportion of 1 year-old Children Immunised Against Measles (UNICEF)

GOAL 5: IMPROVE MATERNAL HEALTH

Target 6: Reduce by three quarters the maternal mortality ratio

Indicators

16. Maternal Mortality Ratio (WHO)
17. Proportion of Births Attended by Skilled Health Personnel (UNICEF)

GOAL 6: COMBAT HIV/AIDS, MALARIA AND OTHER DISEASES

Target 7: Halt and begin to reverse the spread of HIV/AIDS

Indicators

18. HIV Prevalence Among 15–24 year-old Pregnant Women (UNAIDS)
19. Condom use rate of the contraceptive prevalence rate and Population aged 15–24 years with comprehensive correct knowledge of HIV/ AIDS (UNAIDS, UNICEF, UN Population Division, WHO)

20. Ratio of school attendance of orphans to school attendance of non-orphans aged 10–14 years

Target 8: Halt and begin to reverse the incidence of malaria and other major diseases

Indicators

21. Prevalence and Death Rates Associated with Malaria (WHO)
22. Proportion of Population in Malaria Risk Areas Using Effective Malaria Prevention and Treatment Measures (UNICEF)
23. Prevalence and Death Rates Associated with Tuberculosis (WHO)
24. Proportion of Tuberculosis Cases Detected and Cured Under Directly-Observed Treatment Short Courses (WHO)

GOAL 7: ENSURE ENVIRONMENTAL SUSTAINABILITY

Target 9: Integrate the principles of sustainable development into country policies and programmes; reverse loss of environmental resources

Indicators

25. Forested land as percentage of land area (FAO)
26. Ratio of Area Protected to Maintain Biological Diversity to Surface Area (United Nations Environment Programme (UNEP))
27. Energy supply (apparent consumption; Kg oil equivalent) per $1,000 (PPP) GDP (World Bank)
28. Carbon Dioxide Emissions (per capita) and Consumption of Ozone-Depleting CFCs (ODP tons)

Target 10: Reduce by half the proportion of people without sustainable access to safe drinking water

Indicators

30. Proportion of the Population with Sustainable Access to and Improved Water Source (WHO/UNICEF)
31. Proportion of the Population with Access to Improved Sanitation (WHO/UNICEF)

Target 11: Achieve significant improvement in lives of at least 100 million slum-dwellers, by 2020

Indicators

32. Slum population as percentage of urban population (secure tenure index) (UN-Habitat)

GOAL 8: DEVELOP A GLOBAL PARTNERSHIP FOR DEVELOPMENT

Target 12: Develop further an open, rule-based, predictable, non-discriminatory trading and financial system. Includes a

commitment to good governance, development, and poverty reduction – both nationally and internationally

Target 13: Address the special needs of the least developed countries Includes: tariff and quota free access for least developed countries' exports; enhanced programme of debt relief for Highly Indebted Poor Countries (HIPCs) and cancellation of official bilateral debt; and more generous Official Development Assistance (ODA) for countries committed to poverty reduction

Target 14: Address the special needs of landlocked countries and small island developing States

Target 15: Deal comprehensively with the debt problems of developing countries through national and international measures in order to make debt sustainable in the long term

Target 16: In cooperation with developing countries, develop and implement strategies for decent and productive work for youth

Target 17: In cooperation with pharmaceutical companies, provide access to affordable essential drugs in developing countries

Target 18: In cooperation with the private sector, make available the benefits of new technologies, especially information and communications

Indicators

Official development assistance

32. Net ODA as percentage of OECD/Development Assistance Committee (DAC) donors' gross national product (targets of 0.7 per cent in total and 0.15 per cent for Least Developed Countries (LDCs))
33. Proportion of ODA to basic social services (basic education, primary health care, nutrition, safe water and sanitation)
34. Proportion of ODA that is untied
35. Proportion of ODA for environment in small island developing States
36. Proportion of ODA for transport sector in landlocked countries

Market access

37. Proportion of exports (by value and excluding arms) admitted free of duties and quotas
38. Average tariffs and quotas on agricultural products and textiles and clothing
39. Domestic and export agricultural subsidies in OECD countries
40. Proportion of ODA provided to help build trade capacity

Debt sustainability

41. Proportion of official bilateral HIPC debt cancelled

42. Total number of countries that have reached their HIPC decision points and number that have reached their completion points (Cumulative) (HIPC) (World Bank-IMF)
43. Debt service as a percentage of exports of goods and services (World Bank)
44. Debt relief committed under hipc initiative (HIPC) (World Bank-IMF)
45. Unemployment of 15–24 year-olds, each sex and total (ILO)
46. Proportion of population with access to affordable, essential drugs on a sustainable basis (WHO)
47. Telephone lines and cellular subscribers per 100 population
48. Personal computers in use and internet users per 100 population

Source: UN (2008).

2
The Role of Foreign Aid in Achieving the MDGs

1 Introduction

Progress towards the achievement of the MDGs is largely determined by developing country governments. Strong government commitment to the goals, policy reform and political leadership are crucial for success. However, it is widely agreed that international aid donors also have an important role to play and this is recognised by the eighth MDG, calling for a global partnership for development. It is also recognised by the Monterrey Consensus, emanating from the United Nations Conference for Finance and Development in 2002 (see Box 2.1). Many developing country governments do not have the domestic resources to fund the interventions necessary for MDG achievement. This is particularly true for low-income countries in the Asia-Pacific with low domestic revenues bases and which are unable to attract significant private capital flows.

As outlined in Chapter 1, an important way for donors to assist with the achievement of the MDGs is to help developing countries appropriately tailor the goals to their specific country circumstances. Further, in very general terms, donors need to support a recipient-owned development strategy which is aligned to the MDGs and agree to fund a set of mutually agreed upon development activities. Donors though, should recognise that development plans have greater chance of being achieved if they are devised by developing country governments, rather than being externally driven. Difficulties can arise if countries do not have well-formulated strategies or government commitment to development targets is weak. Moreover, the international donor community has reservations over increasing aid to some countries due to concerns over how much aid they can use effectively. Such concerns are supported by the aid effectiveness literature which finds that there are diminishing returns to aid at high levels. There is a danger, therefore, that providing large amounts of foreign aid to some recipients might hamper its effectiveness and have only a limited impact on the MDGs.

The specific role that foreign aid will play in assisting with MDG achievement will vary greatly with each individual Asia-Pacific country. Donors (and recipients) face important decisions regarding the most appropriate levels of aid, how it should be distributed across the different economic and social sectors and what is the most suitable manner for it to be delivered. In some Asian countries foreign aid flows from international donors constitute a relatively minor source of development finance. Domestic revenues and private flows are more important than foreign aid for many developing countries. This is particularly true for China, India and Indonesia. Foreign aid will play only a very minor role in progress towards the MDGs in these countries. However, other countries in the Asia-Pacific region receive some of the highest levels of aid in the world (relative to their populations and size of their economies) and foreign aid remains a very important source of finance for many low-income developing countries. Low-income countries include Afghanistan, Cambodia, Laos and Timor-Leste in Asia and Kiribati, Papua New Guinea, Samoa, the Solomon Islands and Vanuatu in the Pacific. Foreign aid will usually need to fund a diverse range of activities but there are likely to be some areas of greater need requiring most attention. In some countries, the education sector will take priority, while in others, support for improving governance will need to receive the lion's share of assistance. Further, to maximise its impact on MDG achievement, foreign aid should be provided to a recipient government in the form of general budget support in some countries while channelled though NGOs and other service providers in other countries where the capacity of the recipient government is believed to be weak.

While it is generally accepted that scaling up aid flows from existing levels will be necessary to assist many developing countries make progress towards the MDGs, there is also a consensus that the quality of foreign aid needs to increase if it is to have any substantial impact on their achievement. Often donors work in isolation leading to a duplication of their development efforts. The way their aid is delivered can impose high administrative burdens on recipient country officials although sometimes aid is provided independently of the recipient government which can reduce ownership and is unlikely to support their own development plans and strategies. International donors have

Box 2.1   The Monterrey Consensus

The Monterrey Consensus is an outcome from a United Nations International Conference for Finance and Development held in Monterrey, Mexico, March, 2002. Conference participants recognised the need for scaling up aid flows to help low income countries achieve the MDGs.

Heads of state and government committed themselves to

(i)   mobilising domestic resources,
(ii)   attracting international flows,
(iii)   promoting international trade as an engine for development,
(iv)   increasing international financial and technical cooperation for development,
(v)   sustainable debt financing and external debt relief, and
(vi)   enhancing the coherence and consistency of the international monetary, financial and trading systems.

Sound policies, good governance and the rule of law were emphasised as essential pre-requisites to development (UN, 2003).

showed recent signs of both scaling up levels of aid and improving the way it is delivered, although many argue that this progress has been too limited.

This chapter proceeds by examining what constitutes foreign aid and how it is defined in section 2. Section 3 discusses how foreign aid can assist with MDG achievement, based on what we know about its effectiveness. Estimates of how much aid is required to achieve the MDGs by 2015 are explored in section 4 followed by an examination of how much aid is currently allocated to the Asia-Pacific region in section 5. Section 6 looks at how donors should allocate aid across countries in the region in order for their aid to be most effective. Section 7 discusses how the quality of foreign aid can be improved before the chapter concludes with a number of policy implications in section 8.

2   What is foreign aid?

Foreign aid relates to assistance provided to developing countries. An official and the most widely used definition of foreign aid, provided by the Development Assistance Committee (DAC) of the OECD is Official

---

Box 2.2   Official Development Assistance

The most commonly used measure of foreign aid is Official Development Assistance (ODA) which is defined by the Development Assistance Committee (DAC) of the OECD. To qualify as ODA, flows to developing countries must consist of grants or loans which are: (i) undertaken by the official sector; (ii) with promotion of economic development and welfare as the main objective; and (iii) loans must be provided at concessional financial terms (with interest rates below market rates). In addition to financial flows, technical cooperation is included in aid. Technical cooperation consists of grants to nationals of recipient countries receiving education or training. It also includes payments to consultants, advisers, teachers and administrators serving in recipient countries. Assistance for military purposes is excluded (OECD, 2007a).

Development Assistance (ODA) (see Box 2.2). This book adopts this measure, referring to ODA when it considers foreign aid. Although this includes emergency and humanitarian aid, it is actual development aid which is the focus of the book. Foreign aid is provided in many forms including grants, loans, technical cooperation, food and emergency assistance. It includes bilateral and multilateral aid. Bilateral aid relates to assistance from one government to another. Multilateral aid is assistance provided by a government to an international institution for disbursement such as the United Nations, the World Bank and the Asian Development Bank. Foreign aid is usually provided directly to a recipient government or channelled through NGOs.

3   How can foreign aid help with the achievement of the MDGs?

Proponents of foreign aid argue that aid budgets need to increase dramatically in order to assist many developing countries achieve the MDGs. Yet not everyone believes that foreign aid is effective and will assist with MDG achievement. Critics of foreign aid argue that it could even be harmful, asserting that it is wasted on unproductive activities and prevents necessary policy change. Jeffrey Sachs and William Easterly represent well-known commentators at either end of the polarised debate (see Sachs, 2005 and Easterly, 2006). This chapter argues that while it is true that in some instances, foreign aid has failed to have its desired impact and might have assisted in keeping corrupt leaders in power, on average aid has been effective at reducing poverty (McGillivray *et al.*, 2006). At the same time it is clear that the international community has much to do in order to improve its effectiveness. There is now an extensive literature which has examined the issue of foreign aid effectiveness which can help reveal how aid can assist with progress towards the MDGs. This section examines this literature, starting with studies which investigate its impact on economic growth. This is the most heavily scrutinised area of aid effectiveness. However, foreign aid can play very important roles in assisting with MDG achievement other than by increasing growth. The section therefore proceeds by examining the impact of aid on human well-being more directly.

The impact of foreign aid on economic growth

The debate regarding the effectiveness of foreign aid is as old as foreign aid itself. It has centred on its impact on economic growth rates in recipient countries. As noted earlier in this chapter, there are many different purposes of foreign aid. Although poverty reduction is viewed by donors as the ultimate objective of aid, economic growth is widely perceived as an important means of achieving this goal and growth will play the major role in the first of the MDGs concerned with halving income poverty.[1] It is generally agreed that it should lead to higher economic growth in recipients by funding investment or increasing productivity. For example, donors supporting or funding infrastructure such as roads, ports and airports will increase the flow of goods and services and spur income earning opportunities. Foreign aid in the form of appropriate policy advice can also help recipient governments create a domestic environment conducive to the private sector and foreign investment which will raise employment and spur economic growth. Further, increasing the level of human capital should also lead to higher growth rates.

A large body of recent work suggests that, on average, aid works. That is, the vast majority of recent studies find that aid is effective at spurring growth in developing countries. The implication is that economic growth would be lower in developing countries in the absence of foreign aid (see McGillivray *et al.*, 2006 for a recent review of numerous

---

[1]Economists have long recognised that poverty reduction is the main objective of foreign aid programmes. However, a paucity of reliable data relating to poverty has prevented studies from examining the relationship between aid and poverty directly.

studies). However, controversies remain. Some studies dispute this finding, concluding that aid has no impact on economic growth (Easterly *et al.*, 2004; Rajan and Subramanian, 2005a). Further, some are critical of the literature, arguing that studies using cross country data suffer from results being sensitive to the data employed and the estimation technique used. Most studies are also criticised for not recognising that aid supports a diverse range of activities, not all of which will impact directly on growth and which will have different impacts over time periods (Clemens *et al.*, 2004). While accepting some of the criticisms concerning the approach of these studies, the aid effectiveness literature still provides a number of important potential insights into how aid should assist with the MDGs in the Asia-Pacific region.

The policy community has long known that the impact of foreign aid varies greatly by recipient country and this is supported by the empirical literature. There are likely to be numerous different factors which are important for determining the effectiveness of aid. Recipient government ownership and commitment to development are widely believed to be by far the most important factors determining foreign aid's impact. Unfortunately, these factors are very difficult for empirical studies to measure. The literature does, however, confirm that foreign aid works better in some countries or environments than in others. For example, researchers find aid works best in politically stable countries (Chauvet and Guillaumont, 2002), more democratic countries (Svensson, 1999; Islam, 2003), countries outside the tropics (Dalgaard *et al.*, 2004) and when it is allocated in a predictable manner (Clarke *et al.*, 2007). Aid is also found to be effective at mitigating the impacts of trade shocks and natural disasters (Collier and Dehn, 2001; Guillaumont and Chauvet, 2001).

However, the factor determining aid effectiveness which has received by far the most attention relates to the importance of macroeconomic policies and institutions in recipient countries. Well cited World Bank studies find that aid works best in countries with good macroeconomic policies (most notably, Burnside and Dollar, 1997, 2000). These studies define good policies as low rates of inflation, balanced budgets and openness to trade. While a number of other studies have found this to be a very weak empirical result (Hansen and Tarp, 2001; Dalgaard and Hansen, 2001), there is a general consensus that there are some policies which will enhance the impact of aid in recipient countries. Arguably it is policies which relate to raising the level and efficiency of investment and social sector expenditures which will complement foreign aid inflows rather than those proposed by the World Bank studies.

The importance of the World Bank studies should not be under-stated. Partly as a consequence of their findings, some international donors have adopted policies of selectivity whereby more aid is provided to countries with perceived better policies and stronger institutions. The studies concede that previous policies of conditionality, whereby aid is tied to recipients undertaking policy change, have not worked. Therefore donors should provide more aid to those countries with desirable polices already in place. The merits of such policies for achieving the MDGs are discussed in section 6 below. In particular, the international community has grave concerns regarding the impact of aid in countries with policies that are widely perceived to be very poor. Such countries are often referred to as fragile states. Other terms referring to the same group of countries include failing states, weak states, poorly performing countries, Difficult Partnership Countries (DPCs), and Low-Income Countries Under Stress (LICUS). Countries in which the government has virtually ceased to function are sometimes referred to as failed or collapsed states.[2]

Fragile states include countries suffering from a fairly diverse range of problems. Some are engaged in civil war or conflict, some are run by corrupt or undemocratically led governments, and some are small countries with limited resources which are highly vulnerable to natural disasters. In general, the governments of these countries lack the cap-acity and/or the commitment to effectively reduce poverty making the achievement of the MDGs in fragile states a formidable development challenge. Given the international community's concerns regarding the capacity of fragile states to use aid flows effectively, scaling up aid to these countries is not always considered to be viable. According to the World Bank definition, Afghanistan, Cambodia, Laos, Myanmar, and Timor-Leste are countries in Asia which have recently been class-ified as fragile. In addition, Bangladesh, Indonesia, and Nepal have also been classified as fragile at some point since 1999. Iraq and North Korea are other Asian countries often referred to as fragile. In the Pacific, Kiribati, Papua New Guinea, the Solomon Islands, Tonga

---

[2]While there is no one strict definition of a fragile state, the World Bank class-ifies a country as fragile if it is a low-income country belonging to bottom two quintiles of Country Performance and Institutional Assessment (CPIA) scores. The CPIA has 20 equally weighted components divided into the following four categories: macroeconomic management and sustainability of reforms; struc-tural policies for sustainable and equitable growth; policies for social inclusion; and public sector management. Low-income countries are also classified as fragile if they have not been rated in the CPIA exercise.

and Vanuatu have all been recently classified as fragile according to the World Bank definition, while Nauru is another country that could be included.

Another important (and consistent) finding from the aid effectiveness literature, is that the aid-growth relationship is subject to diminishing and eventually negative returns. The finding implies that foreign aid is effective at spurring economic growth up to a certain threshold of aid but past this threshold, its impact diminishes or becomes smaller.[3] It demonstrates that there are likely to be limits to the amounts of foreign aid inflows that an economy can efficiently absorb. This has very important implications for the scaling up of foreign aid to help achieve the MDGs, particularly in Pacific countries which already receive very high levels of aid.

There are a number of explanations as to why high levels of aid will have diminishing impacts on growth. One explanation relates to diminishing returns to capital or investment (which aid often funds). Another explanation is that high levels of aid place a large administrative burden on recipients. At higher levels of aid, they face negotiation, management and reporting requirements for an increasing number of projects but also with an increasing number of donors. Officials spend extensive time dealing with aid bureaucracy rather than on their core functions. The Paris Declaration on Aid Effectiveness seeks to address these issues and is discussed below (see Box 2.3). Another explanation for diminishing returns is that high levels of aid induce so-called Dutch Disease effects whereby aid inflows have an adverse impact on the export competitiveness of developing countries by causing an appreciation of the local currency (Rajan and Subramanian, 2005b).

Estimates of the level of aid at which its incremental impact on growth diminishes vary, but it typically seems that this occurs at around 20 per cent of recipient GDP. So should the diminishing returns to aid restrict the scaling up of aid being embarked upon by donors? Feeny and McGillivray (2008) demonstrate that aid budgets can increase dramatically without inducing diminishing returns on per capita income growth if the allocation of aid across countries is appropriate. This is true with a doubling of aid and even if donors provide aid at levels equal to the well-known target of 0.7 per cent of their Gross National Income (GNI). Getting the allocation of aid right would imply that countries receive aid up

---

[3]See for example, Hansen and Tarp (2000, 2001), Lensink and White (2001), Dalgaard and Hansen (2001), Hudson and Mosley (2001), Dalgaard *et al.* (2004) and Clemens *et al.* (2004).

Box 2.3   The Paris Declaration on Aid Effectiveness

Ownership: There is a broad consensus that aid programs are less effective when they are donor-driven. The PD concept of ownership involves recipient country governments exercising strong and effective leadership over their development policies and strategies. Evidence of ownership is often represented by a National Development Strategy or Poverty Reduction Strategy. The responsibility for ownership rests with recipient countries.

To ensure that development is truly owned, the MDGs must be customised or tailored to individual country circumstances. They should be built into the nationally owned development strategies and poverty reduction strategies. Although donors might have some concerns over the quality and priorities of a strategy, the importance of ownership is paramount.

Alignment: There are two components to alignment. Firstly donors should align their aid programs with the development strategies of partner countries. Secondly, donors should use the existing systems and procedures in recipient countries. This involves increasing the amount of aid which is recorded in the budgets of partner countries, using their partner country procurement and public financial management systems, reducing parallel implementation units and ensuring aid is disbursed in the year in which it is scheduled.

Harmonisation: Donors need to harmonise their actions by (i) establishing common arrangements, (ii) simplifying procedures and (iii) sharing information. Increasing the use of programme based approaches to aid delivery in believed to be necessary in establishing common arrangements. Harmonisation activities will also include conducting joint missions, developing joint assistance strategies and donors undertaking joint analytical work.

Managing for Results: Countries should establish transparent and monitorable performance assessment frameworks which can be used to improve decision making.

Mutual Accountability: Donor and partner countries should undertake mutual assessments of progress in implementing agreed commitments on aid effectiveness.

Source: Based on OECD (2007c).

to the threshold level of 20 per cent of their GDP. Therefore a 'big push' in foreign aid levels can lead to important increases in economic growth and reductions in poverty if a sensible allocation strategy is followed.

The impact of foreign aid on human well-being and the MDGs

From a MDG perspective, it is disappointing that so much of the aid effectiveness literature has focused on evaluating its impact on economic growth. Foreign aid can help achieve MDG targets in numerous ways other than through increasing the rate of economic growth in recipient countries. For example, assistance for rural development and raising agricultural productivity will increase food security and reduce hunger (MDG target 2). To achieve universal primary education (MDG target 3), donors should help fund the construction of schools and the infrastructure required for people to have access to schools. They can also assist with the provision of school materials, the development of school curriculum and the training of school teachers. By helping to fund the education sector, donors can assist with the elimination of school fees which is likely to be very important in getting children to school in many Asia-Pacific countries. Achieving universal primary education will assist with eliminating gender inequality in Asia-Pacific countries (MDG target 4). In many countries there are large disparities between the sexes and donors should also target projects which improve the economic participation of women and which are likely to improve their health and education status (Feeny and Clarke, 2008). There is widespread support for such interventions despite a relatively sparse literature examining their impacts.

Foreign aid can play very important roles in achieving the health related MDGs (Goals 5, 6 and 7) and their associated targets. Foreign aid has already demonstrated a significant impact on health outcomes. Levine and the What Works Working Group (2004) demonstrate that foreign aid played an important role in the global eradication of smallpox, controlling tuberculosis in China, eliminating polio in the Americas, reducing maternal mortality rates in Sri Lanka, controlling river blindness in Africa, preventing infant deaths from diarrheal disease in Egypt through oral rehydration programmes, controlling trachoma in Morocco, reducing guinea worm disease in Africa and Asia and eliminating measles in southern Africa.

Foreign aid donors should fund further research into new vaccines to assist with the health goals. Further they can assist with the construction of hospitals and medical centres, undertake immunisation programmes and promote health awareness and health education. Foreign aid can also contribute to the MDGs by funding HIV/AIDS prevention programmes. Donor funded HIV/AIDS programmes have had notable success in Thailand and Cambodia. Even foreign aid's strongest critics often concede that foreign aid can play an important role in improving health outcomes. Moreover, there is an increasing body of evidence from Randomised Control Trials (RCTs) that aid projects, particularly in the health and education sectors, have beneficial outcomes (Banerjee and He, 2003). RCTs are widely regarded as the most effective method of project evaluation and while they have their limitations, there is scope for donors to undertake more evaluations of this type to determine what works best in different environments (Banerjee, 2007).

To assist with the goal of environmental sustainability (Goal 7), donors should assist recipient countries with the management and sustainable use of their natural resources. This is particularly important in the Asia-Pacific region since a large proportion of the populations of these countries rely on agriculture, forestry and fishing for their livelihoods. Interventions in certain sectors will assist in the achievement of more than one MDG. Improvements in education are likely to improve health, for example, and improvements in health are likely to lead to higher incomes. Further by donors assisting countries provide clean water and improved sanitation will not only help achieve MDG targets associated with Goal 7, but will lead to improvements in health (Feeny and Clarke, 2008).

In summary, foreign aid can assist with MDG achievement in many different ways. Just a few examples are provided above. Foreign aid will assist the MDG target of reducing by half the proportion of people living in income poverty, predominantly though spurring economic growth. However, the impact of aid will vary according to the recipient and donors need to recognise the factors which impinge on the effectiveness of aid at very high levels. Foreign aid can also assist with MDG achievement through numerous ways, other than through impacting on economic growth. Given the importance of ownership for aid effectiveness, donors should seek to work with and through the central recipient government when at all possible. Aid programmes need to be designed with recipient governments and aligned with their development strategies.

4 How much aid should be provided to achieve the MDGs?

Although it is widely accepted that foreign aid levels need to increase to assist with the achievement of the MDGs, it is difficult to estimate with any precision, just what level of assistance is appropriate. The UN Millennium Project calls for dramatic increases in the foreign levels from their existing levels. It asserts that the world's poor are trapped in a cycle of poverty, with saving rates that are too low to fund the required investments for development. 'The role of aid is therefore to push the elements of the capital stock – infrastructure, human capital, public administration and so forth…. above the threshold needed for self sustaining growth' (UN, 2005, p.50). The report argues for a big push since 'if aid amounts are so small that a country's infrastructure and human capital are persistently insufficient, growth will never take off in a self sustaining manner, and aid will remain a handout rather than a solution to a poverty trap' (UN, 2005, p.52).

In 2006, ODA from members of the Development Assistance Committee (DAC) accounted for 0.30 per cent of their Gross National Income (GNI). At the International Conference on Financing for Development held in Monterrey, a number of governments reasserted the commitment for donor countries to achieve an ODA to GNI target of 0.7 per cent. This level of aid has been a long-standing development target, originally committed to back in 1970. But is this level of aid high enough to achieve the MDGs? A number of other studies have attempted to estimate how much foreign aid is required to achieve the goal by 2015. This is a very difficult exercise and studies have needed to make a number of heroic assumptions. Clemens *et al.* (2007) provide a comprehensive evaluation of these studies while three well-known reports are briefly discussed below. Studies have estimated levels of aid to achieve the MDGs globally rather than specific levels for their achievement in the Asia-Pacific region.

The Zedillo Report (Zedillo *et al.*, 2001) estimates that an extra US$50 billion per year of foreign aid would be required to achieve the MDGs (in comparison to 2001 levels). Similarly, Devarajan *et al.* (2002) estimated that annual aid flows would need to increase by US$54 to 62 billion in order to achieve the goals (depending on whether policies improved in recipient countries). Further, the UN Millennium Project estimates that aid flows (for direct MDG support) need to increase to US$135 billion by 2015 for the achievement of all the MDGs.

Although these estimates are some way short of the level of aid that would equate to 0.7 per cent of donors GNI, it is important to note that these studies are likely to yield underestimates for a number of reasons. The UN Millennium Project Report estimate for MDG achievement (in countries with adequate governance) corresponds to an estimated 0.54 per cent of OECD countries GNI. However, the report argues that additional resources are likely to be required since the estimates only cover investments that contribute directly to MDG achievement. The level of ODA does not include resources to combat climate change or protect global fisheries. The cost of combating climate change in developing countries is likely to require many more billions of ODA annually. Further, the estimate of Devarajan *et al.* (2002) is based on what's called a financing gap. The level of investment required to achieve the growth rates necessary to halve poverty by 2015 is calculated. Domestic savings are subtracted from this calculated level of investment leaving the amount of external assistance or foreign aid required to make up the shortfall. However, a large body of research demonstrates that not all aid is used for investment. Although investment increases in response to aid, it is not a one for one relationship with some aid being used for non-investment expenditures (McGillivray and Morrissey, 2001).

All three studies report estimates of the level of aid required based upon assumption regarding the conditions in developing countries. For example, the Zedillo *et al.* (2001) estimate requires developing countries to play their part by improving the level of governance, adopting sensible macroeconomic policies and expenditure patterns and building effective institutions. The Devarajan *et al.* (2002) study notes that the amount of additional aid will depend on growth, policies and the efficiency of aid allocation. However, favourable conditions will not always prevail.

Studies also employ unit costs to estimate the cost of achieving many of the goals. They use the average cost of those already receiving education (for example, a child enrolled at school), as an estimate of the cost of enrolling additional children. Although there may be some economies of scale in social service provision, the costs of reaching those in isolated rural communities will be far higher than average unit costs. It is also important to note that the relationship between public spending and health and education outcomes is found by many studies to be very weak. Additional spending on health, for example, by no means guarantees better health outcomes. Therefore increasing the efficiency of public expenditures is likely to be very important for progress towards the MDGs.

Finally estimates do not incorporate the costs of any expected shocks. Examples of shocks include natural disasters, wars and conflicts and the impact of climate change. Such shocks can seriously derail a country on its path to MDG achievement and additional resources will be required to mitigate the impact of such events. In summary, the amounts of aid that studies have estimated are required to achieve the MDGs are likely to be insufficient. The UN Millennium Project estimate of US$135 billion by 2015 should be regarded as a minimum. Moreover aid flows only provide a necessary but not sufficient condition for MDG achievement. Recipient countries must improve policies and governance in addition to large increases in foreign aid if the goals are to be met by 2015.

5   How much aid is provided to the Asia-Pacific?

At a global level, donors are scaling up their foreign aid programmes. ODA increased to a record high of over US$106 billion in 2005 before declining slightly in 2006 to $103.9 billion. The decline is largely explained by large amounts of debt relief granted to two countries: Iraq and Nigeria in 2005. Debt relief is expected to decline in subsequent years.[4] Moreover aid from non-DAC members is also increasing dramatically. Further, given a number of recent pledges by countries to increase aid, ODA from DAC members is estimated to increase to US$130 billion in 2010 (OECD, 2007a). The simulations are based on the recent pledges by DAC Donors.

Figure 2.1 provides trends in the value of ODA to Asia and the Pacific. The figure shows that the value of aid to Asia increased steadily from 1997 to 2004, before spiking in 2005 to over US$45 billion. The very high value for 2005 is partly explained by large increases in aid

to Iraq (in the form of debt relief) and Afghanistan due to concerns over security and the war on terror. Another part of the explanation is the high levels of assistance provided in response to the 2004 Indian Ocean Tsunami. This assistance was crucial for reconstruction in the countries affected. However, it was not aid provided with the explicit objective of the achievement of the MDGs (even though any achievement in the tsunami-affected areas would have been extremely unlikely without reconstruction occurring (Clarke, 2008a).

Foreign aid flows to the Pacific amounted to around US$2 billion per year between 1990 and 1999 before plummeting in 2000. The main explanation for this large decrease in the value of aid to the Pacific is that

---

[4]Aid provided in the form of debt relief is often criticised since it does not lead to any additional transfer of resources. Debt relief is expected to fall over the next few years, implying other forms of aid will have to increase substantially (OECD, 2007a).

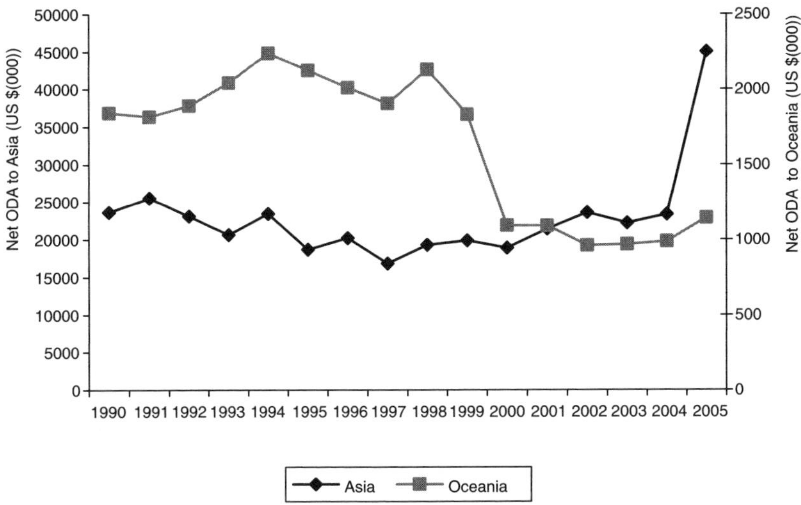

Figure 2.1   Trends in Net ODA to Asia and the Pacific ($US000, 2005 prices)

French Polynesia and New Caledonia graduated from the OECD list of developing countries and therefore became ineligible to receive aid. These two countries received considerable amounts of assistance from France. Since 2000, foreign aid has remained fairly steady at approximately US$1 billion per annum. Figure 2.1 does not demonstrate a recent dramatic rise in foreign aid that many believe is required to achieve the MDGs.

Relative to the Pacific, it is clear that Asia receives a far larger amount of foreign aid. However, Pacific countries are some of the largest aid recipients in the world, relative to the size of their populations and economies. Figure 2.2 provides the ratio of ODA to GNI for countries in Asia and the Pacific. The figure demonstrates that using this measure Pacific countries are far larger recipients of aid than Asian countries. In 2005, aid accounted for 13 per cent of the Gross National Income (GNI) of Pacific countries but less than 1 per cent of the GNI for Asian countries. Further, Pacific countries received US$142 of aid per capita compared to just US$13 for the case of Asian countries.

Both of these figures show that despite the large increase in aid to Asia in 2005, (predominantly accounted for by debt relief to Iraq), there is little evidence to suggest that the international community has increased aid levels in the Asia-Pacific region since the Millennium Declaration was signed in 2000. This may change if donors honour the pledges they have recently made. However, unless this happens soon,

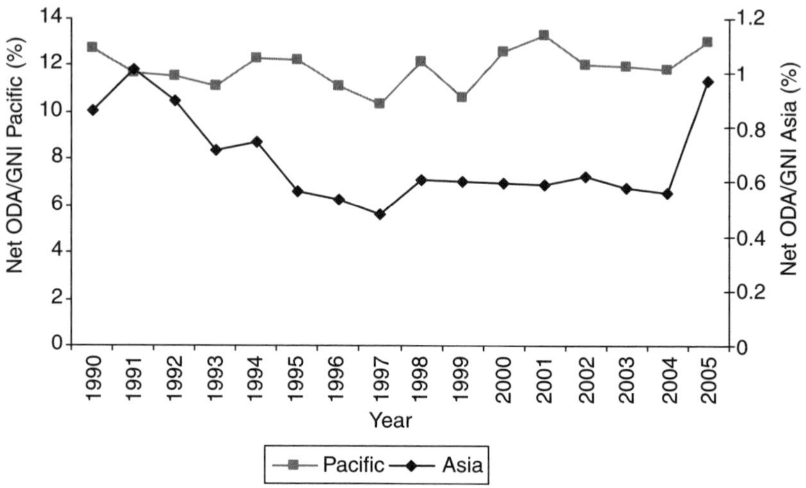

Figure 2.2   Trends in Net ODA/GNI to Asia and the Pacific (%)

many developing countries are unlikely to speed up their progress towards MDG achievement and donors will be heavily criticised in 2015 when the goals are not achieved. This outcome is also likely to weaken support for aid in the future.

6   How should foreign aid be allocated to assist with the MDGs?

Even with increasing aid budgets, international aid agencies are forced to make decisions regarding how to allocate their limited aid budgets across developing countries to maximise progress towards the MDGs. Government aid agencies also face questions over how much of their aid budgets to channel through multilateral aid agencies and how much to provide through NGOs. Further decisions are required regarding how to allocate their aid across different sectors within recipient countries, although these decisions should largely be dictated by country's development strategies. These challenges are discussed in turn.

Allocation across country

How foreign aid is allocated can have important implications for the achievement of the MDGs. Arguably, greater assistance should be provided to those countries which are most off-track to their achievement. However, it can also be argued that most aid should go to those countries that use aid most effectively. These countries were identified in section 3 and might include countries with good policies and strong institutions. In 2006, DAC members of the OECD provided almost US$104 billion in ODA. Over 40 per cent of this ODA was allocated to Asia, a greater share than any other continent. Asia also accounted for six of the largest aid recipients in 2005: Iraq, Afghanistan, Indonesia, Vietnam, China and India. While Pacific countries receive relatively small amounts of foreign aid in absolute terms (about 1 per cent of the global total), as outlined above, the region accounts for many of the world's largest aid recipients relative to the size of their populations and economies.

So why do particular countries receive very large amounts of foreign aid relative to others? How do international donors decide how much to provide to individual developing countries? An extensive body of literature has sought to answer these questions. Motives for the provision of foreign aid are often classified into three groups: commercial, political or strategic and humanitarian. While humanitarian concerns can partly explain the pattern of international aid giving, they do not provide a complete picture (Alesina and Dollar, 2000; Alesina and Weder, 2002; Berthélemy and Tichit, 2004). International donors are also found to favour former colonies, important trading partners and developing countries within their region. It is also clear that political and strategic motives play a major role in the provision of aid. This was particularly true during the cold war era, with the US and former Soviet Union providing large amounts of foreign aid to their political allies, sometimes using their aid to influence the political ideology of a recipient country. It is no surprise that studies conducted during the 1970s and 1980s usually found that such motives dominated foreign aid agendas (McKinlay and Little, 1979; Maizels and Nissanke, 1984). Political motives are believed to have played less of a role during the 1990s but they are beginning to gain prominence once again since the 2001 terrorist attacks in the US. This (at least partially) explains the very large amounts of aid currently provided to Iraq, Afghanistan, and Pakistan.

Moreover, international donors have recently started adopting policies of 'selectivity', whereby larger amounts of aid are provided to countries that are perceived to use aid best.[5] As the empirical literature

---

[5]Dollar and Levin (2004) find some empirical support of the increasing selectivity of foreign aid although Radelet (2004) argues that donors aren't really becoming more selective with large amounts of aid still going to middle-income countries and countries with poor governance.

on aid effectiveness discussed in section 3 highlights, the impact of aid varies according to the recipient. Some studies find that aid works best in countries with better macroeconomic policies and stronger institutions. Although this finding has been shown to be empirically weak, there is still a strong belief in the policy community that aid effectiveness is higher in such environments.[6]

The policy of aid selectivity is exemplified by the US's Millennium Challenge Account (MCA) development fund, created in 2004 whereby eligible low-income countries are rated according to a number of criteria relating to governing justly, investing in people and promoting economic freedom. The rationale for the policy is that these criteria are essential conditions for development. The World Bank also adopts a system of Performance-Based Allocations for its aid distributed to low-income countries. This is largely based on its Country Performance and Institutional Assessment (CPIA) ratings. CPIA ratings are based on 16 indicators relating to economic management, structural policies, policies for social inclusion and public sector management and institutions. The Asian Development Banks has a similar system in place.

Unfortunately, countries with better policies and institutions are often those that need less aid. If strict policies of selectivity are pursued by the international community, far less aid will go to poorly governed countries, in far greater need of assistance. This is particularly important given that many Asia-Pacific countries are characterised by poor policies and weak institutions. Aid donors need to find appropriate levels in poorly governed countries and find appropriate ways of providing aid in these settings. It is encouraging that most aid donors continue to engage with poorly performing countries. Despite concerns regarding the effectiveness of aid in fragile states, there is a consensus in the international community that donors should continue to engage with them. Disengagement is likely to exacerbate poverty in these countries and there are dangers of cross-border spillovers leading to regional or global instability. These spillovers can include the spread of conflict, humanitarian crises and refugee flows, organised crime, terrorism, illegal drugs and

---

[6]Collier and Dollar (2002) derive a poverty efficient allocation of aid – aimed at maximising poverty reduction for a given amount of aid. They find that aid budgets could triple and a poverty-efficient allocation of more aid to countries with better policies would double the number of people lifted out of poverty.

epidemics.[7] The risk of return to conflict in post conflict countries is high. Examples in the Asia-Pacific region include Afghanistan, Iraq, the Solomon Islands and Timor-Leste. Declining states have a deteriorating commitment to and/or capacity for development.

Further, donors can assist developing countries with improving policies and strengthening institutions. Old style conditionality, whereby donors only provide aid if donor-driven policy reform is undertaken in recipient countries has been shown to be ineffective. However, if proposed policy reform is recipient owned and led, it is likely that donors can assist with its implementation through aid support. Donors can also seek to improve policies and institutions through capacity building in recipient public sectors, improving financial and economic management, strengthening the legal and judiciary system, improving human rights and democracy and strengthening civil society. This is why fragile states often receive a high proportion of their aid programmes in the form of technical assistance.

Further, section 3 highlighted some of the concerns that donors need to be wary of when providing very large amounts of aid to recipients. These concerns related to absorptive capacity constraints and possible Dutch Disease impacts of aid and provide further considerations for donors in allocating their aid budgets. In summary, the challenge for donors is to evaluate existing levels of need in recipients, the progress they are making towards the MDGs, how effectively they currently use aid and whether they will be able to use additional amounts effectively. Allowing political and strategic criteria to influence decisions will prevent MDG efficient allocations. Donors also face decisions regarding the type of aid to provide to different countries.

Allocation across types

Government donors can provide aid bilaterally (directly to another government) or multilaterally where funds are pooled from multiple donors and distributed through an international agency. Little is known about

---

[7]Further, standard approaches to aid delivery are unlikely to work in fragile states due to a lack of political stability, commitment, weak administrative capacity and low levels of competence in economic management. The standard prescription for engaging with fragile states is that they should receive low levels of assistance, provided in the form of aid projects rather than budget support. Aid should be disbursed through non-state actors such as NGOs rather than central government and projects should have a short time horizon. Technical assistance should be provided to assist with improved policy formulation (Leader and Colenso, 2005).

the relative effectiveness of each although, arguably, by channelling aid through multilateral agencies there is less risk that its allocation is subject to the political strategic and commercial motives of donor governments. Aid donors can also contribute directly to a number of global funds. These include the Education For All Fast Track Initiative (EFA-FTI), the Global Fund to Fight AIDS, Tuberculosis and Malaria (GFATM), and the Global Alliance for Vaccines and Immunisation (GAVI). Table 2.1 indicates that over 25 per cent of aid allocated to Asia has been provided through various multilateral agencies although this proportion has fallen in recent years. However, the vast majority of aid provided to the Pacific has been bilateral aid and there might be scope for donors to provide greater amounts using multilateral agencies.

Donors are often criticised for providing their aid in the form of concessional loans. If recipient countries fail to use loans productively they are left with a higher debt burden and fewer resources for development. The Meltzer Report (2000) recommended that multilateral agencies should provide their support to developing countries in the form of grants instead of loans. However, there can be complementarity between the two. Repayments on loans can be used for financing subsequent loans, and they should exert discipline on resource allocation. Loans can also improve countries credit ratings and if donors provide only grants it can restrict a country's future financial market access (OECD, 2006). It is clear that if donors are to provide foreign aid in the form of concessional lending, they must be convinced the loans are put to good use. Table 2.1 indicates that the proportion of aid provided in the form of loans to Asia has fallen in recent years although still remains high at over 21 per cent. However, providing aid in the form

Table 2.1   Total Net Disbursements of ODA by Type (%)

	Asia		Pacific	
	1990–99	2000–05	1990–99	2000–05
DAC Bilateral	65.8	71.1	91.9	88.9
Multilateral	31.0	25.1	7.7	10.8
Grants	60.3	78.5	95.4	100
Loans	39.7	21.5	4.6	–
Technical Cooperation	24.6	24.0	42.3	46.4

Source: OECD (2007b).

of loans has been phased out in Pacific countries, possibly due to concerns over their use.

Technical cooperation involves the transfer of skills to increase capacity within developing countries. It also includes advice and services required for the implementation of aid projects. It is criticised on the grounds that it is costly, inappropriate and often does not lead to any genuine transfer of skills. Table 2.1 demonstrates that Pacific countries receive a very large share of their aid in the form of technical assistance. Donors need to make sure that this form of assistance is leading to genuine capacity building in these countries. The merits and drawbacks of providing aid in other forms are discussed in section 7 below.

7 Improving the quality of foreign aid to assist with the MDGs

While increasing the quantity of foreign aid will be important for achieving the MDGs, it is widely accepted that increasing the quality of aid must accompany the scaling up of aid. Initiatives to improve the quality of aid generally seek to reduce the transaction costs of delivering aid. Such costs relate to aid recipients dealing with donor missions and coping with reporting requirements such as the monitoring and evaluation of aid projects and programmes. The more donors operate in the country, the more time is spent dealing with their requirements and each donor will have their own requirements and procedures which exacerbates the problem. Further, many aid donors might result in a large number of fragmented aid projects that are uncoordinated and can often lead to duplication of aid interventions. All of these issues are becoming increasingly important as donors scale up their aid programmes.

A consensus has emerged that foreign aid is effective when it is recipient led, are aligned with local priorities and use the recipients existing systems and procedures. This led to an international agreement to improve the quality of aid known as the Paris Declaration on Aid Effectiveness (see Box 2.3). The Paris Declaration (PD) is an international agreement to improve the quality of foreign aid. It was signed in March 2005 by over one hundred government ministers and heads of agencies. The PD commits countries and organisations to continue increasing efforts in improving key areas based around five principles: (i) ownership; (ii) alignment; (iii) harmonisation; (iv) managing aid for results; and (v) mutual accountability. The DAC have devised 12 indicators in order to monitor progress in achieving results.

It seeks to strengthen the relationship between donors and recipients, ensure that development resources are used effectively and that donors and recipients are mutually accountable for development progress. The PD also involves donors and recipients undertaking periodic surveys at a country level in order to monitor progress on a number of indicators relating to the PD principles. The first survey was conducted in 31 selected countries in 2006 with subsequent surveys to be carried out in 2008 and 2010.

Monitoring progress against the PD principles is difficult. Many of the principles are difficult to measure. The 2006 survey was the first and was therefore largely responsible for collecting baseline data on which to compare future surveys. However, the results from the 2006 survey point to a number of areas in which donors clearly need to improve on. In most countries there is considerable discrepancy between the aid funds disbursed by donors and the funds that are actually recorded in recipients' budgets. Aid flows also need to become more predictable with the amounts disbursed by donors becoming more in line with the amounts committed. It is also clear that coordinating activities requires a far greater time commitment from donors (OECD, 2006). The OECD (2007c) finds that donor practices are slow to change. In particular technical cooperation continues to be donor-driven and greater visible progress on untying aid is required.

One way donors are trying to increase the quality of their aid is to increase the use of Program Based Approaches (PBAs) rather than provide aid in the form of projects. Project aid is assistance which is tied to a distinct investment or activity such as building a bridge or a road. Programme aid relates to funding to support a particular sector such as education or health and is not tied to specific projects. PBAs include aid provided in the form of direct budget support and Sector Wide Approaches (SWAps). Direct budget support involves providing aid funds directly to a recipient's national budget to supplement domestic expenditures on agreed priorities using their own financial management systems. A SWAp is a method of funding and coordinating the actions and resources of government and aid donors within a particular sector.

PBAs and SWAps arose out of a dissatisfaction with the project approach to aid delivery. Often donors providing project aid establish Project Implementation Units (PIUs) which operate outside recipient government ministries and fail to build capacity of public sector staff and institutions in developing countries. SWAps seek to overcome this weakness by improving government ownership, increasing government accountability and strengthening existing government systems and processes. They can also reduce the transaction costs of aid, improve coordination among donors and reduce fragmentation of aid projects.

However, SWAps will not provide a universal solution to aid effectiveness. They require strong government leadership to manage and implement programmes. In countries with weak public sector financial management systems, high corruption and ineffective monitoring systems SWAps are not likely to yield desired results. SWAps are also not useful for cross-cutting sectors such as gender, rural development and the environment and in some circumstances could be just as demanding of recipient public sector officials time and resources than aid projects. Improving coordination and harmonisation and the development of mechanisms for dialogue, monitoring, reporting and evaluating could actually increase the transaction costs of aid that SWAps are designed to reduce (Killick, 2004). A further mechanism for proving aid to recipients is through NGOs. Providing aid through NGOs can assist with service delivery and relieve absorptive capacity constraints of recipients. The role of NGOs in delivering aid is discussed further in Chapter 3.

8   Conclusion and policy recommendations

The need for country specific strategies makes general conclusions on how international donors can help achieve the MDGs in the Asia-Pacific difficult. Moreover, the region consists of a very diverse group of countries. Aid will play a relatively small role in the Asian giants of China and India. However, the impact of aid in the small island states of the Pacific will potentially be high. What is clear is that foreign aid can play an important role in MDG achievement and the challenge for donors is to find what interventions work best in different countries.

This section draws on the information provided in this chapter and Chapter 1 to outline a number of general policy recommendations that donors should follow in the Asia-Pacific region to assist with the achievement of the MDGs.

(i) Support tailored MDG targets and national development plans
Ownership and government commitment to the goals is vital for their achievement. The goals should be tailored to individual country contexts and be ambitious but achievable. The process of tailoring the targets should be participatory, involving civil society and the private sector to ensure they are truly owned by recipient countries. Revised

MDG targets should be incorporated into national development plans. The MDGs should be accurately costed and poverty reduction strategies and development plans should detail exactly how the targets are to be achieved. MDG targets should be the focus of donor activities and be explicitly incorporated into all aspects of their policies and programmes.

(ii) Donors should gradually and predictably scale up their foreign aid flows

To assist with the achievement of ambitious development targets, donors will need to increase their level of support to recipient countries. Aid levels should account for absorptive capacity constraints in recipient countries and aid programmes should consist of untied predictable flows. Long-term aid commitments should be made to assist with planning and MDG progress. Where donors have concerns regarding the capacity of recipients to absorb more aid they need to improve the capacity of recipient governments to absorb more aid or find alternative channels for its distribution.

(iii) Improve the allocation of foreign aid

To maximise the impact of foreign aid on progress towards the MDGs, it is important that foreign aid flows to countries which need it most as well as those that can use it best. It is crucial that political and strategic concerns of donor governments do not constrain aid agencies from adopting allocations of aid which will maximise their impact on poverty reduction and the achievement of the MDGs in developing countries. Foreign aid should be reallocated from middle-income countries to countries that need it most, as well as to those which can use it best. Aid should be scaled up quickly to poor developing countries with well devised strategies and the willingness and capacity to use extra resources wisely.

(iv) Adhere to the Paris Declaration principles and improve the way aid is delivered

International donors should continue working towards the Paris Declaration principles of ownership, harmonisation, alignment and managing for results. Donors also need to employ different forms of aid in different recipient environments. However, they should increasingly use PBAs to lower the transaction costs of aid. Foreign aid in the form of budget support in support of poverty reduction strategies that support the MDGs is likely to be the most effective form of aid delivery in countries with strong governance. Radelet (2004) argues that donors should provide most of their support in the form of long-term commitments for budget support or programme aid to central government in well governed countries. Programme aid rather than project aid will allow greater responsiveness to shocks. However, smaller short-term projects delivered through NGOs are more appropriate in poorly governed countries.

(v) Aid for statistical capacity building
International donors need to provide considerably more assistance to some countries for the collection and analysis of accurate and reliable statistics. This is particularly true for Pacific countries. While it is an expensive exercise in such fragmented rural-based economies, it is a very important one. The lack of data for many Asia-Pacific countries makes tracking progress towards the MDGs virtually impossible. Further, the absence of reliable and widely accessible data makes it hard for civil society to hold governments accountable for their actions. It also makes it difficult to identify the geographic areas and groups of the population in most need.

(vi) Focus on rural areas
One common characteristic among many countries in the Asia-Pacific is a strong rural-urban divide. Often the very poor are located in rural areas dependent upon agriculture for their livelihoods. This is true of the region's largest countries like China and India as well as many of the Pacific islands. Therefore to effectively assist with the achievement of the MDGs, rural areas should be the focus of the activities of international aid donors and NGOs.

People in isolated rural communities are often difficult to reach. Improving transport infrastructure in rural areas will help to make aid programmes more cost effective at reaching such communities. Countries cannot achieve the universal primary education until schools are accessible in all areas of the country. Moreover, progress towards the MDGs can sometimes be more cost effective in rural areas. High child and maternal mortality rates in rural areas can be due to easily preventable diseases.

(vii) Development education
International donors should more effectively communicate the difficulties in working in many of its partner countries to ensure that public expectations of foreign aid are realistic and that public support for aid

does not wane in the future. It is important to emphasise that development is a long and complex process. Training teachers and doctors and building schools and hospitals takes a long time. Moreover, results from aid interventions will vary greatly. Although our knowledge of aid effectiveness has increased greatly in recent years, far more understanding regarding what works, what doesn't and why it is needed and will take time to develop.

(viii) Support policy coherence

International donor countries should ensure that other policies relating to trade, security, migration and the environment support their development efforts rather than undermine them. If this is not the case any benefits from arising from increasing aid levels could be reduced and sometimes mitigated by other policies that will hamper progress towards the MDGs. Greater efforts to assist countries with climate change adaptation and mitigation are required, in addition to scaling up aid to achieve the MDGs.

3
The Role of Non-Governmental Organisations in Achieving the MDGs

1 Introduction

The term Non-Governmental Organisation (NGO) obfuscates more than it illuminates those agencies to which it is referring. It is an imprecise term that by definition includes all organisations that are not within the government sector. Therefore, all organisations free from government control could be labelled NGOs, but this does not assist us in seeking to understand the role of NGOs in achieving the MDGs.

It is necessary, therefore, to expressly define the NGOs being discussed in this chapter. Consideration of their general characteristics can assist in defining more accurately which organisations are best described as NGOs. Four general characteristics of the organisations we are interested in include being: (1) independent; (2) not-for-profit; (3) voluntary; and (4) 'not for the immediate benefit' of its members (or altruism) (Ball and Dunn, 1996). Moreover, our interest is in NGOs that both display these characteristics and specifically seek to improve the circumstances of the poor in developing countries.

Identification of NGOs can be further refined by contrasting international NGOs (INGOs), local NGOs (LNGOs) and Community-Based Organisations (CBOs). The distinction is largely the locale in which these organisations are based and where they undertake their development activities. INGOs are based in developed countries and often work in a variety of developing countries. LNGOs are based in a developing country but may work in a wide range of geographical locations within that country. CBOs are normally based and work in their own communities within developing countries. These organisations often partner together so that CBOs and LNGOs implement the *on-the-ground* development interventions funded by (or funded through) INGOs. However, this demarcation is becoming increasingly fuzzy as LNGOs and CBOs grow in size and expertise and begin to work across national boundaries (Lewis, 1998). Fowler (1997) emphasises the importance of *values* in such poor-focused organisations. Therefore, for the purposes of this chapter, discussion of NGOs will allow incorporation of INGO, LNGOs and CBOs with the overriding determinant of inclusion being if the organisations' *raison d'être* is improving the lives of the poor in developing countries. Thus NGOs for purposes of this analysis include internationally regarded organisations such as World Vision, Oxfam, Save the Children and Médecins Sans Frontières in addition to relatively unknown and small community-based groups such as Industry Kiik Feto Timor, Afghan Women Network, and the Solomon Islands Development Trust.

From the outset, it is important to note the question of whether NGOs should be working to assist in the achievement of the MDGs. As noted in Chapter 1, while the MDGs provide a fairly comprehensive list of development targets, this list is not exhaustive. There are may aspects of development and well-being which are not included in the goals. For example, the MDGs include a target for achieving using primary education but not for secondary education. Moreover, there are no explicit targets for the mentally ill or the disabled. Nor is women's reproductive health explicitly considered within the current MDGs. Therefore NGOs might decide to focus their activities on these neglected areas rather than (or in addition to) the MDGs. The focus of their activities should depend upon the strengths of the NGO, the priorities of the country and the commitment and effectiveness of the government and other overseas aid agencies to the MDGs.

This chapter proceeds by briefly examining the NGO effectiveness literature in the next section to help determine their role in achieving the MDGs. Section 3 examines the growth in NGOs. The evolution of NGOs over the past five decades is discussed in section 4. Section 5 focuses specifically on how NGOs can impact on the achievement of the MDGs in both their programming and advocacy interventions as well as providing some brief case studies to illustrate this impact. Some policy recommendations on how NGOs might increase their impact on achieving the MDGs are outlined in section 6.

2   A brief overview of the NGO effectiveness literature

NGOs are often viewed as participatory, democratic and cost effective organisations which work directly with the poor. Arguably, they can be effective at a number of activities including strengthening civil society, improving democracy, and strengthening governance. However, some studies dispute their effectiveness while others argue that their effectiveness is diminishing with their increasing reliance on governments for funding, which arguably has led to increasing accountability to donor governments rather than to the poor (Zaidi, 1999).

The effectiveness of NGOs is often assessed against the effectiveness of the State in improving the lives of the poor (Edwards and Hulme, 1995). Yet, this criteria places NGOs at an immediate disadvantage as they are being assessed within an environment of failure that has largely necessitated their existence. For it is precisely the failure of the State to improve the lives of the poor, that has resulted in NGOs being called upon to rectify and remedy this dismal situation. NGOs are thus at risk of being poorly evaluated for failing in the same way the State initially failed. The pressure to be successful is also intensified by the high expectations attached to NGOs, often by their own supporters. Promoters of NGOs suggest that they are 'more cost-effective in service delivery, have a greater ability to target poor and vulnerable sections of the population, demonstrate a capacity to develop community-based institutions and (are) better able to promote the popular participation needed for sustainability of benefits' (Fowler, 1991, p.56). In addition, NGOs are considered to have intrinsic characteristics 'such as strong grassroots links; field-based development expertise; the ability to innovate and adapt; [a] process oriented approach to development; participatory methodologies and tools; long-term commitment and emphasis on sustainability; [and] cost-effectiveness' (World Bank, 1995, p.15). Thus it is not surprising that NGOs are harshly judged given these high expectations.

Evaluating the effectiveness of NGOs is also difficult due to their heterogeneity. As has been discussed, the term *non-governmental organisation* is a broad church under which many distinct and possibly conflicting agencies are grouped. With often little in common apart from the desire to improve the lives of the poor, judging these disparate agencies as a whole is potentially very misleading. As Kaimowitz (1993, p.1139) argues, 'when dealing with as heterogeneous and complex a phenomena as the NGOs, one is forced to make generalizations that may not apply to each individual case and to present general tendencies more schematically than they occur in practice'. Therefore, while some NGOs do not positively impact on the poor because of their approach or because of the mitigating circumstances in which their interventions take place, others will be more effective.

Evaluation of NGO effectiveness must therefore proceed at the general level. The World Bank (1999b) found that whilst NGOs were often more effective than state agencies in delivering development interventions, they themselves often failed to reach the poorest of the poor and their impact was limited in terms of direct beneficiaries. These results reflected other studies (see Riddell and Robinson, 1995; Intrac, 1999). However, alternative studies have found that 'most NGO projects were achieving, or likely to achieve, their stated objectives and outputs... All projects had made some positive impacts on the lives of the intended beneficiaries' (AusAID, 2000a, p.viii; also see AusAID, 2000b). Thus, the evaluation of impact by NGOs is mixed.

NGOs can be effective across a range of development issues. Improvements in the lives of the poor can originate at the community level, regional or province level, and at the national or international level. NGO activities may include both service provision and advocacy. Work with communities, or *grassroots* programmes, account for a significant proportion of NGO activities. This includes activities such as the provision of education services, care and support for those with HIV or malaria, feeding programmes to improve child nutrition, agricultural extension programmes, or micro-finance schemes. Depending on the nature of the activity, NGOs will include men and women, local leaders, youth representatives, religious leaders and local government officials in decision-making. Because they work closely with those receiving their services, NGOs are better able to target those most in need. NGOs have also recently begun to increase their advocacy work. Advocacy is particularly important in fragile states and where governments are corrupt and are failing to deliver essential services to their citizens. Advocacy programmes aim to directly address those responsible for the weak policies that are contributing to poverty. NGOs may work independently or in collaboration with other NGOs. They will identify key policy issues affecting the country and put pressure on both the national government and the international community to address these issues. They may seek additional funds to support better education and training outcomes, or they may focus on increasing participation in the political process by calling on national governmentsto allow greater freedoms in various public spheres. Their advocacy work is vital to developing transparent and effective governments with strong democratic foundations.

3   The growth of NGOs

The numbers of NGOs seeking to improve the lives of the poor are increasing rapidly, but despite this recent surge in organisations being established, it is important to remember that such organisations are not new. At the international level such organisations date back to the Anti-Slavery Society established in 1839 and the International Committee of the Red Cross formed in 1864. A decade later there were 32 registered INGOs and just prior to World War I over 1,000 INGOs were registered (Chatfield, 1997). Figure 3.1 shows that growth occurred throughout the twentieth century with nearly 9,000 INGOs being registered in 1990 and increasing to nearly 12,000 in 1999 (Anheier *et al.*, 2001). Growth continued into the twenty-first century with there now being over 13,600 registered INGOs in existence (UIA, 2007). Estimates of LNGOs and CBOs are more difficult to make with any accuracy as they can be established and dissolved with little formal recognition. It is accepted that the number of LNGOs and CBOs is many times that of INGOs. For example, it is estimated that there are 1.5 million CBOs in India alone (IndianNGOs, 2007).

The growth in the number of NGOs raises some important questions over the coordination of their activities. In many developing countries, several hundred NGOs will be operating and unless they share information and coordinate their activities, there will be a lot of duplication in their development efforts. Many NGOs will operate in the same areas undertaking similar activities. To assist with MDG achievement it is vital that NGOs become more efficient by coordinating their

Figure 3.1   Number of INGOs 1956 to 2006

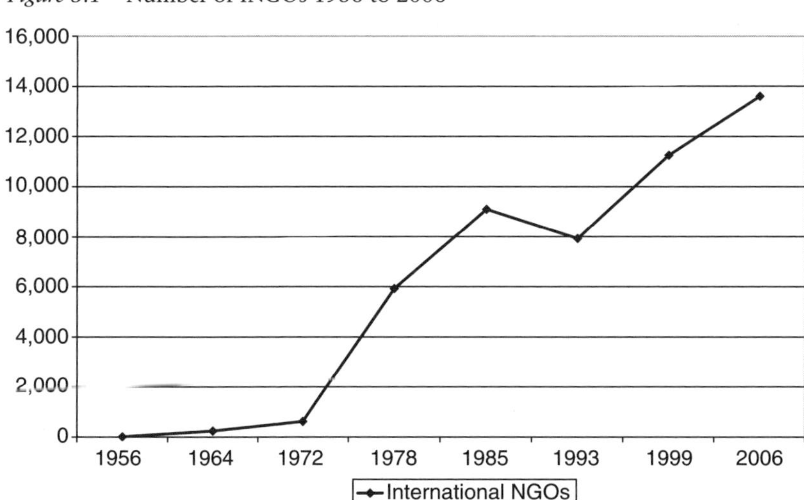

Source: Anheier *et al.*, 2001 and UIA, 2007.

Figure 3.2   Receipts of ODA by NGOs 1976 to 2005 (US$ 2005 prices)

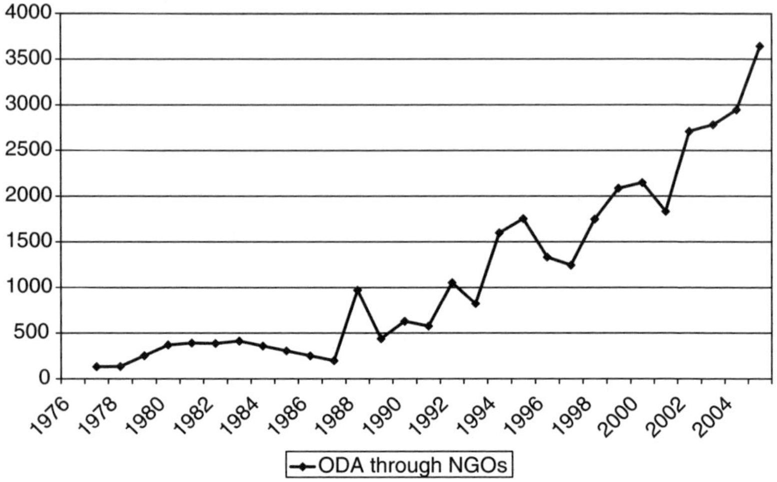

Source: DAC statistics available online at www.oecd.org/dataoecd/50/17/5037721.htm, accessed in September 2007.

activities and ensuring that the multiple needs of all communities are being addressed effectively.

Funds flowing to and through these organisations have also grown rapidly in recent years. Figure 3.2 indicates the growth in the amount of ODA from government aid agencies received by NGOs over the past three decades. In real terms, NGO receipts of ODA have grown over 27 times during this period. NGOs also receive funding directly from private donations. Agg (2006) also suggests an increase in private donations to NGOs generally over the past decade, but the lack of a centralised data collection agency makes it difficult to accurately analyse this data: 'data illustrating NGO activity is notoriously unreliable ... (as) OECD data has many limitations, with complex reporting requirements differently interpreted by individual governments' (p.16). It is clear though that the public do respond very generously to some appeals launched by NGOs for humanitarian emergencies (Feeny and Clarke, 2007) and that events such as the 2004 Indian Ocean Tsunami generated significant public responses to NGOs (Clarke, 2008a).

4   Evolution of NGOs

Development is a contested term, with meanings differing depending on time, place and vantage point (see McGillivray and Clarke, 2006).

Given this lack of consensus therefore and the large number of NGOs in existence, it is unsurprising that the approaches to development undertaken by these organisations vary greatly. It is therefore inappropriate to speak of the NGO approach to development or the NGO conceptualisation of development. The impact on achieving the MDGs by NGO will depend partly on how different NGOs undertake development interventions. However, whilst being cautious of overstatement, there is value in seeking some loose classification of the different approaches.

Korten (1990) has suggested that there are four typologies of NGO assistance: 1) relief and welfare; 2) community development; 3) sustainable systems development; and 4) people's movements. A fifth classification of 'domestic change agents' is added by de Senillosa (1998). Korten posits these classifications as 'generations' along a continuum of best practice – moving from relief and welfare through to people's movements (and as de Senillosa suggests, through to domestic change agents). Practice however suggests that NGOs move between these classifications depending on circumstances, funding and programming needs. Further, the impact and effectiveness towards achieving the MDGs will differ between these typologies (see Table 3.1).

Given the very specific focus on the MDGs, development interventions must occur at the grassroots level but in most instances this will only be possible with appropriate national policy support in place. For example, achieving universal primary education requires infrastructure and teaching staff to be available at the community level throughout an entire country. However such provision will generally only occur if national policy and budget support exists at the national level. Likewise, seeking to reduce the number of those living in poverty may in part rely on NGO sponsored micro-finance schemes but without a functioning national economy it is unlikely that micro-enterprises will be sustainable or effective into the future. It is also necessary that the international community continue to support the achievement of the MDGs through increased aid provision, fairer trade and debt relief. In this regard, achievement of the MDGs will be assisted by the range of NGOs typologies being implemented simultaneously in both developed and developing countries.

NGOs as the third sector

The existence of NGOs is precisely related to the necessity of the MDGs. Both the market and state have failed to deliver a quality of life to all deemed sufficient by the international community (Makoba, 2002).

Table 3.1   Classification of NGOs and Impact on MDGs

Generation	Description	Potential Impact on MDGs
Relief and Welfare	NGOs provide goods and services to communities NGOs make the decisions as to what goods and services are to be provided and how the distribution will take place and how long they will remain working with that community. The role of the community is limited to recipient only.	Impact is achieved through the provision of services (such as feeding programmes for malnourished children or provision of education). This may be needed in the short term to assist the poorest of the poor build their own capacity.
Community Development	NGOs animate local communities in relation to local issues and concerns. The role of communities is more active and they participate in agenda setting and decision-making at the local level.	Impact at the local level across all MDGs may be sustained.
Sustainable Systems-development	NGOs focus more on national or regional concerns – such as environmental on trafficking and begin to focus more on lobbying and advocacy rather than actual programming. The role of communities is again limited due to the larger geographic focus of these campaigns. However representatives of communities are included as key stakeholders.	Impact on national and regional policy may result in increased funds. Implementation at local level will differ between communities based on local capacity.

Table 3.1   Classification of NGOs and Impact on MDGs – *continued*

Generation	Description	Potential Impact on MDGs
People's Movement	NGOs begin to link disparate communities together around common goals and development objectives. Activities are largely advocacy-based more so than programming based. Representatives of communities are included as key stakeholders with communities encouraged to work directly together.	Impact on national policy may change. Implementation at local level will differ between communities based on local capacity.
Domestic Change Agents	NGOs (with an emphasis on International NGOs) begin to educate their domestic communities on issues of development and seek international change through changing behaviours in developed countries. The role of communities are to be partners to communities in developed countries.	Impact on international awareness of MDGs may elicit some change at the international level, such as increased aid flows. Impact at local level will depend on local capacity.

These twin failings have brought about a need for the third sector (in which the NGOs are part) to become active in remedying the situation of low development (as espoused by the MDGs).

NGOs are able to address state and market failures through their close connection to their constituent communities (see Weisbrod, 1975; Hansmann, 1987; Brinkerhoff and Brinkerhoff, 2002). This ability is linked to the four characteristics discussed earlier in this chapter. For example, where it may be unfeasible for the market to provide health care due to high costs associated with sparse or isolated populations, NGOs are better placed to access local communities and provide these services at lower cost as they require less infrastructure. Likewise, NGOs are also able to provide services in contexts of states failing to provide services. Illegal Burmese migrants in Thailand provide an example of both the market and state failing to provide basic health services to these non-citizens (Clarke, 2007b). These migrants have no access to privately provided health services due to their inability to move freely within townships without fear of harassment and deportation. If they were able to avoid arrest and attend a private medical clinic they would normally be unable to afford this private treatment earning on average less than US$3 a day. Should they be able to avoid arrest and afford the cost of private medial care they would then face the difficulty of locating a medical professional with whom they could effectively communicate due to language barriers. The Thai state is unable to provide health services to these migrants due to their illegal status. Treating illegal Burmese migrants would place public health officials outside of Thai law. Further, the illegal status of these migrants also means that public health departments are not allocated funds for their treatment by either national or provincial governments. It is therefore left to NGOs to provide services to these individuals. For example, World Vision Foundation of Thailand (WVFT) has worked with illegal Burmese migrants for many years in various locations throughout Thailand (WVFT, 2007). Due to their ability to form trusting and long-term relationships with these communities and offer health services at negligible or no-cost to the patient. World Vision Foundation of Thailand are financially supported to undertake these interventions by various international donors.

It is important to note that NGOs can improve the lives of the poor without reference to the achievement of the MDGs. NGOs play a second important role as third sector agents. They provide an 'alternative model of development' (Wallace, 1996). NGOs have neither commercial nor political interests, rather they espouse and practise a different set of objectives and priorities to mainstream development models. By and large, NGOs emphasise participation, project a pro-poor focus, advocate fair distribution of resources, seek sustainability, promote gender equality and pursue environmental protection (Makoba, 2002; also see Hearn, 2000; McIlwaine, 1998; Ottaway and Carothers 2000 for further discussion of this role of NGOs). These principles as an alternative are often communities' first experience of democracy and participation. The importance of improving the lives of poor in this regard should not be understated. So whilst this chapter explicitly considers how NGOs can assist in achieving the MDGs, it is acknowledged that much of their work and impact lies outside the specific boundaries of the MDGs.

5   NGOs and the MDGs

While the type of interventions implemented by NGOs vary widely in scope, size and approach, over 85 per cent of NGOs are involved in activities that are aimed at promoting or achieving the MDGs (Foster and Wells, 2004). These activities may include programming interventions or advocacy activities. To achieve the MDGs, development interventions must occur at different levels of society (see Figure 3.3). Improvements in the lives of the poor can be effective at the community (micro) level, regional or province (meso) level, at the national (macro) level, or at the international (supramacro) level. As previously stated, interventions may include both programming and advocacy activities. NGOs have the greatest capacity to impact on achievement of MDGs through programming at micro- and meso-levels and through advocacy at all levels. This section will consider the role that NGOs can play at each of these levels in both programming and advocacy to assist the various MDGs being achieved.

Those interventions that occur at the community or grassroots levels are called micro-interventions and these account for a significant proportion of NGO activities. Such micro-interventions would include a range of activities, such as provision of education services, care and support of those with HIV or malaria, supplementary feeding programmes, agricultural extension programmes, or micro-finance schemes. Activities at the micro-level specifically focus on particular target groups.

Micro ⟷ Meso ⟷ Macro ⟷ Supramacro

Figure 3.3   Continuum of Development Interventions

Key stakeholders will include, for example, local leaders, youth representatives, religious leaders, and local government officials. These stakeholders will also likely be involved in decision-making and programme management. Working closely with recipients, NGOs can assist in achieving the MDGs directly with those in need.

Interventions undertaken by NGOs at the regional or provincial level are called meso-interventions. At this level, NGOs are often given responsibility to address state or market failure in order to deliver certain services to entire communities or certain cohorts within those communities. This occurs as NGOs are seen to have greater ability to access these communities and are understood to have the flexibility to deliver services to communities that often are excluded by mainstream delivery mechanisms. Such services may include provision of health care, HIV/AIDS awareness campaigns, or water and sanitation programmes. As with micro-interventions, these meso-interventions still directly address the needs of communities' members and may also include key stakeholders within the planning and management aspects. However, the breadth and scope of the project requires a higher level of oversight and control. NGOs undertaking meso-level interventions may sub-contract some programming activities to a number of smaller community-based NGOs.

At the national level, NGO interventions are called macro-interventions. At this macro-level, NGOs are more likely to be focusing on influencing government policy around certain development issues rather than actually delivering actual goods and services. NGOs, either working independently, but more commonly working together, will identify certain needs affecting the wider nation and seek to pressure the national government to address these needs in a more effective manner. At the national level, NGOs may seek additional funds to support better education and training outcomes or they may focus on increasing participation in the political process calling on national governments to allow greater freedoms in various public spheres.

Interventions that cross national borders also occur and these are called supramacro-interventions. It is unusual for these macro-interventions to involve NGOs working directly with communities. Rather these are interventions aimed at changing policy or increasing financial support for needs that affect more than a single nation. The most effective examples of NGOs undertaking supramacro interventions involve a number of NGOs acting in concert. Due to the coordination and sophisticated requirements of undertaking these transnational interventions, local communities are often used to illustrate the need being highlighted and are less likely to be drivers of these campaigns.

As with Korten (1990) and de Senillosa' (1998) typologies of NGOs discussed above, NGOs may find themselves undertaking different levels of interventions along this continuum simultaneously. Whilst they may be participating as one of a consortium of NGOs pressuring the international community to provide debt relief, they may also be implementing supplementary feeding programmes at the village level. The roles undertaken by NGOs will depend again on the values that underpin their existence and the expertise and experience they have and the public funds they have raised to finance these activities. While some NGOs will prefer to focus on programming interventions, and others may see greater impact through advocacy, many will see programming and advocacy activities as complementing one another and equally necessary to achieve the MDGs.

NGO programming and the MDGs

Since their inception, NGOs have primarily been concerned with initiating development programmes. Practical, on-the-ground assistance to communities (whether through Korten's (1990) welfare or community development typologies), was how NGOs began their existence. Implementing development interventions is most effective when NGOs are able to work closely with the targeted community. The further a NGO (or any implementing agency for that matter) moves away from those it is seeking to serve, the less effective the intervention will be. NGOs are therefore more effective in implementing programming interventions at the micro- and meso-levels.

NGOs work directly with targeted communities within the micro- and meso-levels. Within this proximity they are best able to provide services to those in real need, but also discern changing needs over time. As NGOs move away from direct beneficiaries and begin to work at the macro-level (or beyond) they lose that intimacy with the communities and face the same difficulties faced by government organisations around the blindness of bureaucracy and deceit of distant. When circumstances change without being noticed, it is likely that increasing numbers of those in need fail to be reached.

Figure 3.4   Effectiveness of MDG Programming Interventions

NGO advocacy and the MDGs

NGOs have only recently begun to increase their advocacy interventions (see Hudson, 2000; Chapman and Wameyo, 2001, Clark, 2003). Advocacy is a particularly important intervention in terms of achieving both MDGs and other non-MDG improvements in the lives of the poor (Foster and Wells, 2004). NGOs can assist communities in pressuring local governments to improve or provide services for which they have responsibility at the micro-level. The provision of medical care was provided to illegal Burmese communities in a single province in Thailand following significant lobbying by a local NGO. Previously, illegal migrants could not access government provided health clinics. After this lobbying, the NGO was provided with government medical supplies and granted permission to offer health care to these illegal migrants (Clarke, forthcoming). At the macro- or supramacro-levels NGOs can lobby those responsible for the national and international policy environment.

Effecting change requires certain skills and knowledge. It is more likely that NGOs will need to work cooperatively in order to advocate at the macro- and supramacro-levels to achieve positive outcomes (Collins *et al.*, 2001; Chapman and Fisher, 2000). Within developing countries, the major impediment in achieving positive change in favour of the poor is that it often challenges the *status quo*, and this inevitably (at least in the short term) threatens the position of the dominant elite. This elite wields significant political power. Advocacy requires gaining access to those in decision-making positions but also raising public awareness and public support in order to shift the balance of power. In this regard, advocacy requires both internal (private) and external (public) pressure. It is unlikely that smaller NGOs or even larger NGOs acting in isolation will be able to effect this change by acting alone. Rather, coalitions such as those seen recently advocating for debt relief through the *Jubilee 2000* and *Making Poverty History* campaigns, are able to gain public support and gain private access to key stakeholders at the national and international levels (see Grenier, 2003; Edwards and Gaventa, 2001). There is a cost though associated with working together. For NGOs this cost is the loss of direct connection with the communities for whom they are advocating. So while the *Live 8* concerts were being performed as part of the *Make Poverty History*

Figure 3.5   Effectiveness of MDG Advocacy Interventions

campaigns there was very little evidence of participation and ownership of these campaign events by poor community members. This is not to say that local grassroots NGOs are not included, but the direct representation of community members is weakened as the advocacy campaign grows.

Examples of NGOs assistance with MDG achievement

There are numerous ways in which NGOs will be able to assist with the achievement of the MDGs (though again it is noted that NGOs do improve the lives of the poor outside the boundaries of the MDGs). The following discussion will however limit itself to discussing the most practical and common methods in which NGOs can assist with the achievement of the MDGs. Often, both advocacy and programming interventions will be required for the most effective response. For a country to achieve any of the MDGs, there requires effort from the international community, national governments and local communities as well as NGOs. Not one of these stakeholders will be able to achieve the MDGs in isolation. NGOs will play an increasingly important role in nations in which the government delivery of services is poor and where NGOs have themselves become the de-facto primary deliverer of development services and interventions. NGOs will also play an important role through advocacy and placing constant pressure at both the national and international level to place more resources in these areas that will enhance the achievement of the MDGs (Prasad and Snell, 2004; Micklewright and Wright, 2004).

Goal 1: Eradicating extreme poverty and hunger

The first MDG will be assessed through two targets: (1) reducing by half the proportion of people living on less than a dollar a day; and (2) reducing by half the proportion of people who suffer from hunger. At the micro-level, NGOs can initiate a number of development interventions that will assist with the achievement of MDG1. A lack of credit is a significant cause of poverty (Remenyi and Quinones, 2000). NGOs have gained significant experience and have capacity to establish micro-finance institutions that can target the very poor and provide credit to establish micro-enterprises. At the household level, such credit schemes have been very effective in lifting people out of poverty (see Rutherford, 2000). Credit may include monetary credit but may also include breeding animals for future sale or are working farm animals that can be hired to other members of the community. Agricultural extension schemes that introduce more efficient or effective farming or animal husbandry practices is an effective way for NGOs to increase household incomes but also reduce 'food-shortage' months. In this same way, water programmes can also assist farmers increase their harvest for either sale or personal consumption. When communities are unable to provide sufficient food for themselves, NGOs may be required to implement feeding programmes, especially for children at risk of malnutrition. Advocacy activities will be largely limited to national and international campaigns to increase trade opportunities (so poor farmers have better access to international markets), debt relief (so national governments have increased resources to assist local communities) and increased international aid (so that more development interventions can be funded).

Goal 1: Case study
Makira Island is home to around 10 per cent of Solomon Island's total population. In income per capita terms, Makira is ranked seventh out of the ten provinces, thus it is one of the poorest, least developed provinces within a poor developing country. Close to all of Makira's population live rural lives, dependent upon their own labour for their food and housing. Government services are low and transport within the provinces and to other provinces are costly and unreliable. For visitors (for it is generally visitors that can afford flights to Makira's small airport), it is not uncommon for the twice weekly flights to be cancelled or delayed for a number of days at no notice.

However within this context, 18 small communities in central Makira have formed a partnership with the Solomon Islands Development Trust (SIDT) to derive income from the ngali nut. The ngali nut is native to the Solomon Islands and Papua New Guinea and grows within rainforests. It is a valuable protein source for local communities and can be eaten raw or roasted. In addition it can be processed for its oil, which has recently been recognised for its properties of pain relief. Indeed, an increasing number of medications, especially those for arthritis, are now including ngali nut oil as an active ingredient. There are in fact a number of international patents on the use of ngali nut oil for pain relief.

The SIDT provided initial training and expertise in the harvesting and processing aspects as well as assisted with locating and developing overseas markets.

This community-based enterprise distributes profits directly to the community. Income generated from this are upwards of SI$30,000 per annum. These funds are being used to directly improve the circumstances of the villagers. This money is being used to purchase health care and increase food security. People are using their proceeds to construct better housing and send their children to school. Community investment is also occurring with better roads and other infrastructure.

Not only has this community-based project assisted local people transform local natural resources into income, it has also increased their own capacity for addressing other development problems. For example, the community management committee was able to exert enough political pressure to force the exit of a large Asian logging firm from its forests – the same forest in which the ngali nut only grows. The community management committee is now addressing issues such as toxic dumping and other environmental issues faced in central Makira.

Reference

Clarke, M. (2007a), *A qualitative analysis of chronic poverty and poverty reduction strategies in Solomon Islands*, report prepared for Overseas Development Institute, London.

Goal 2: Achieving universal primary education

The second MDG will be assessed against one target: ensuring that all boys and girls complete a full course of primary schooling. NGOs can take responsibility for the provision of education services within local communities. This can include the training of teachers, building of schools, development of curriculum and in some instances the payment of teacher salaries or fees for children as well as the cost of books and uniforms. NGOs are required to undertake these interventions in certain communities, either because of a failing state being unable itself to provide these services or because the communities themselves are too marginalised from mainstream community to be able to access state-funded education. Such communities may be illegal or be ethnic minorities facing persecution or they may be living in outside mainstream society in municipal waste depots or in squatter communities. NGOs are able to access these communities where the state or market cannot due to their local links and focus on community participation. NGOs must also focus on educating parents and the wider community as to the importance of education, especially for girls. When NGOs do provide education services, they will normally increase their effectiveness by seeking community participation and ownership over activities. Advocacy occurs both at the national and international levels to increase support for universal education (see Fien and Hughes, 2007).

Such advocacy has had a long history (see Costello, 2007) that culminated in this goal being included within the MDGs.

Goal 2: Case study

Bangladesh currently has a primary school enrolment of 95 per cent. This is an increase from an enrolment rate of just over 70 per cent in 1990. Bangladesh is on track therefore to achieve universal primary education by 2015. This improvement is quite stark. In the past, 30 per cent of children left primary school before completion. The reasons for this are many, but high risk-factors include coming from a poor or disadvantaged family, being female, and having uneducated parents. Quality of education in Bangladesh has also been low. Only half of children who complete primary education have basic literacy and numeracy skills, yet nearly 90 per cent of children continue to be promoted to the next grade each year. One reason for this poor quality is the lack of resources within schools. It is not uncommon for classes to have fifty or more students and insufficient desks and textbooks for them all.

The recent improvement is a result of a number of factors. In addition to ongoing interventions undertaken by the Ministry of Education, the Primary Education Development Project (PEDP) funding improved better physical infrastructure, better teacher training, participatory approaches for community ownership and resources for basic education), NGOs have also begun to focus their efforts on education within Bangladesh. One such NGO is Plan Bangladesh. Plan Bangladesh is a non-political and non-faith-based organisation that has assumed responsibility for education delivery in parts of Bangladesh. Its strong reputation is based on innovative approaches to education provision based on community involvement.

The Community Learning Action Project (CLAP) intervention is both an education intervention and a social development strategy. At the local level, communities are engaged to directly address poor education outcomes within their own communities. In this manner their own capacity is also being built so they take responsibility for primary education services themselves. Communities themselves are involved in planning education interventions – that may include additional tuition for disadvantaged students (learning camps), improved curriculum resources, training of parents to assist in classrooms or to provide childcare to younger children within villages. These interventions involve activity building the capacity of the local communities to assume responsibility for local schools. By increasing the community control, quality outcomes are enhanced. CLAP not only seeks to improve education outcomes for students, but also seeks to affect the teaching performance of teachers, response of education authorities, and the support provided to their children by their parents and families.

Since its inception, Plan Bangladesh through CLAP has directly affected over 23,000 school children in grades 1 and 2 via primary school programmes and nearly 15,000 'slow learners' in grades 3, 4 and 5 through dedicated learning camps. Plan Bangladesh is one of a number of NGOs in Bangladesh working towards and succeeding in achieving the MDG of universal primary education.

References

Plan Bangladesh (2005), *Technical Report of the Community Learning Assistance Project (CLAP)*, Plan Bangladesh, Dhaka.

Ramsay, K. (2007), 'The Community Learning Action Project (CLAP): A Bangladeshi Model for Change' in M. Clarke and S. Feeny (eds) *Education for the End of Poverty: Implementing ALL the Millennium Development Goals*, Nova, New York.

Goal 3: Promoting gender equality and empowerment of women

The third MDG will be assessed against three targets: (1) eliminating gender disparity in enrolments in primary education; (2) eliminating gender disparity in enrolments in secondary education; and (3) eliminating gender disparity in enrolments in tertiary education. The role of NGOs in assisting to achieve this MDG is limited to some degree. While NGOs will certainly be able to assist with the elimination of gender disparity in primary education directly through their interventions to achieve universal primary education (the term 'universal' implicitly includes all girls as well as all boys), interventions to eliminate disparity at higher levels of education are more difficult. Education for girls and young women is a low priority within developing countries (Furniss, 2007). Whilst NGOs have assumed responsibility for the provision of primary education, provision of secondary education and certainly tertiary education generally remains in the provost of the state. Secondary and tertiary education opportunities often do not exist within local communities. Secondary schools are normally located within town centres and rural students must travel daily or board thus adding additional costs of education. Tertiary institutes are also limited and located within the largest urban centres requiring students from other locations to board with all the associated costs this entails. Throughout other community development interventions, NGOs will highlight the benefit of education for girls and young women, but it is then generally left to the individual families to seek out these opportunities beyond primary schools. NGOs are largely limited to providing financial assistance to those families wishing to send their children (especially girls and young women) to advanced studies.

Goal 3: Case study

World Vision Bangladesh recognised the need to provide direct financial assistance to young women to allow them to attend tertiary institutions to further their education. This scholarship scheme was limited to women from poor families. This intervention was highly unusual as it provided direct benefits to individuals rather than seeking to provide benefits to a whole community. The decision to undertake such a individual-centric programme though was primarily to increase the female participation at this level of study

Applicants had to be endorsed by their local community and demonstrate a commitment to community development and a desire to continue living and working within their community following their studies. While this was not able to be enforced, the expectation of their communities was an important factor in determining their post-study employment (at least in the first few years following graduation). Whilst studying, recipients were required to volunteer with World Vision Bangladesh within their local community.

The women selected to receive this bursary studied across a number of disciplines, ranging from law to medicine to accounting to arts to science. The bursary was sufficient to meet tuition fees and provide some assistance towards living expenses.

The direct number of beneficiaries was quite limited. However, it was intended that the flow-on effects to the young women's families and communities would be significant – both through the women's professional skills but also through their example to other young women and the wider community regarding the importance of education for all.

Reference

World Vision Bangladesh (undated), *Girl Scholarship for University*, mimeo, World Vision Bangladesh, Dhaka.

Goals 4 and 5: Reducing of child mortality and improving maternal health

The fourth MDG will be assessed against one target: reducing by two thirds the mortality rate among children under five. NGOs can be very effective in improving the health and mortality rates of young children. The greatest killers of children are preventable illness. Simple interventions can be undertaken to eradicate illness such as diarrhoea, malaria, pneumonia, measles, etc. (SCF, 2007). NGOs are well placed to work closely with communities to improve health outcomes. NGOs provide direct medical health care through the provision of health clinics and medicines. NGOs also provide training for health professionals and provide support and training for state-run public health officials. NGOs undertake these development interventions at the micro- and meso-levels. Some NGOs will provide health care to very small communities (perhaps street children in an urban centre) or entire health programmes at the provincial level (for example in PNG and Cambodia). NGOs are also able to initiate advocacy campaigns to apply political pressure on governments to increase resources available for children's health. Such campaigns are most likely limited to national borders as funding for children's health will generally be funded by the state rather than a regional body.

The fifth MDG will be assessed against one target: reducing by three-quarters the maternal mortality ratio. The ability of NGOs to achieve this MDG is very closely related to the achievement of MDG4 as the health of mothers and their children are closely linked. Therefore the grouping of health interventions to improve under-five mortality rates and maternal mortality rates within *child and maternal health* programmes is common. When NGOs implement health interventions discussed above, they simultaneously provide health care for expectant and mothers of young children. These interventions may include training for traditional birth attendants, the provision of neo-natal care, training on breastfeeding and food preparation, child spacing and other birth control, etc. Similarly, advocacy interventions aimed to increase provision of services to improve maternal mortality will be closely linked to advocacy campaigns seeking to improve child mortality outcomes and again will be largely limited to the macro-level.

Goals 4 and 5: Case study

Sayaboury Province lies in the north-west of Laos – three hours drive from Luang Probang. Over the past 15 years, under-five child mortality and maternal mortality rates have fallen by over 80 per cent, largely due to a primary health care programme established by Save the Children.

Sayaboury has an estimated population of around 330,000, of whom around 310,000 live outside of the main provincial town living as subsistence farmers in small villages. Due to its geographical isolation (separated from the rest of Laos by mountain ranges and the Mekong region) development in Sayaboury is low. Government provision for health and education services are poor and there is a low level of infrastructure (with electricity only being connected to the provincial town in 2003).

Prior to the work of Save the Children, women would normally give birth under the care of an untrained traditional birth attendant or by themselves in forests huts built especially for this purpose. Neither ante- or post-natal care existed. Often umbilical cords would be cut with sharp bamboo or a unsterilised knife resulting in high levels of neonatal tetanus and sickness to both the child and mother.

In 1990, under-five mortality rates in Sayaboury Province were 130 per 1,000 children. Following the local community-based interventions undertaken by Save the Children, under-five mortality is now 19 per 1,000 children. Maternal death rates were 530 per 100,0000 births but are now just 77 per 100,000 births.

Reducing child mortality occurred as a result of a number of different development interventions across the province undertaken over a period of years. Save the Children focus on five key interventions to reduce child mortality: 1) skilled care during childbirth which simply may be the training of traditional birth attendants and provision of a 'matchbox' delivery kit comprising a sterilised needle and thread, bandages and razor to cut the umbilical cord can reduce neonatal tetanus and improve longer-term health difficulties; 2) breastfeeding in the first six months of life reduces malnutrition and improves growth and immunity; 3) measles immunisation prevents death and also prevents a number of other disabilities including blindness, hearing loss, brain damage and pneumonia; 4) oral rehydration therapy is a simple solution to diarrhoea, itself a major killer of children under-five each year; and 5) pneumonia care including simple antibiotics also saves lives. In addition to these interventions, Save the Children established a network of health centres across the provinces focusing on maternal and child health and supported this with a mobile clinic. Village volunteers have received training in malnutrition and monitoring of children who display signs of stunted growth. While food shortages occur in Sayaboury at times, more often malnutrition is caused by the poor preparation of food or unbalanced diets. Training for families in food hygiene and dietary requirements has reduced levels of malnutrition across the province and therefore reduced associated diseases. Education across this broad spectrum of health care issues is provided in all villages using a variety of techniques, including having local women act in role plays.

Save the Children has achieved these two MDGs at the cost of US$4 million over the last 12 years. Given the population of Savaybouray, this equates to around US$1 per person per year.

References

Perks, C., Toole, M. and Phounthonsy, K. (2006), 'District Health Programs and Health-Sector Reform: Case Study in the Lao People's Democratic Republic', *Bulletin of the World Health Organisation*, Vol. 84, pp. 132–8.

Toole, M. (2004), *Evaluation of Sayaboury Primary Health Care Project, Phase IV Lao People's Democratic Republic*, mimeo, Save the Children Australia, January/ February.

Goal 6: NGOs and combating HIV/AIDS, malaria and other diseases

The fifth MDG will be assessed against two targets: (1) halting and beginning to reverse the spread of HIV/AIDS; and (2) halting and beginning to reverse the incidence of malaria and other major diseases. NGOs have played an important role throughout the world in trying to prevent the spread of human HIV/AIDS through inducing behaviour change. HIV is transmitted through the exchange of bodily fluids. This occurs generally through sexual intercourse, sharing needles containing infected blood, incorrect dressing of infected wounds and from mother to child across the placenta or whilst breast-feeding. Behaviour change can eliminate all these modes of transmission (with the exception of intra-uterine transmission which can only be lowered with appropriate ARV treatments). Underlying all NGO interventions is the premise that changing people's behaviour is the key to reducing the incidence of HIV/AIDS (see Clarke, 2002; Renzaho, 2006). NGOs have developed numerous methodologies to achieve behaviour change. NGOs have undertaken these interventions at the micro- and meso-level. However, given its pandemic status, NGO interventions must occur not only within countries, but across regions as well. For this reason NGOs are often involved in intra-national and international responses to HIV, working closely with governments to ensure that the response is effective and appropriate in terms of changing epidemiology and transmission patterns. Action by NGOs against malaria and other diseases are generally located within the micro- and meso-levels and involve education campaigns and distribution of treated malaria nets in addition to health care for those suffering malaria. NGOs also led international advocacy campaigns on behalf of those with HIV/AIDS to access ARV treatment. These campaigns have been protracted and difficult as they often involved commercial companies rather than simply national or international bodies. However, they have been successful in having low-cost generic medicines made available in developing countries (MSF, 2007a), which whilst not adding the achievement directly of halting the spread of HIV/AIDS has had a significant impact on improving the lives of those already infected with HIV/AIDS.

Goal 6: Case study

It is estimated that over 550,000 people in Thailand or 1.4 per cent of the adult population are HIV positive. In addition, a further 20,000 Thai children under fifteen years of age are also HIV positive (UNAIDS, 2006). Within Thailand, a significant focus of development interventions by both NGOs and government organisations has been on achieving behaviour change in order to halt and reverse HIV/AIDS transmission. World Vision Foundation of Thailand has undertaken a number of different behaviour change interventions (which also included the care of those already infected) since 1991. Within these interventions three generations of programming can be identified (Clarke, 2002). Each generation reflects a distinct attempt to achieve sustainable behaviour change in response to changing epidemiology, transmission patterns and lessons learned over time in effective programming interventions.

World Vision Foundation of Thailand's projects were located throughout Thailand, from the north to the south and west to east. They were located in Chiang Mai, Ranong, Mae Sai, Mae Sot, Songhkla, and Hat Yai. Due to the coordination amongst NGOs in the field, no other NGOs worked with the same communities as World Vision Foundation of Thailand. However, organisations such as the Red Cross, Population and Community Development Association and other local NGOs were working within neighbouring communities. World Vision Foundation of Thailand also collaborated with local Ministry of Public Health (MOPH) officials in these locations. As well as providing general information to the wider population, the specific target groups of these interventions also changed over time and across locations, but included commercial sex workers, their clients, adolescents, fishermen, taxi drivers, men-who-have-sex-with-men, intravenous drug users and factory workers. Underlying all generations of programming has been the premise that changing people's behaviour is the key to reducing the incidence of HIV/AIDS. The first generation of programmes focused on simple information dissemination. The second generation focused on more specific target groups and information and counselling for those with the virus. The third generation programmes focused on establishing an environment, which enabled people to change their behaviour.

The prevalence rate of HIV/AIDS in Thailand appears to have been halted in recent years. It is not possible to attribute success to a single agency or programme. Certainly though NGOs have played a role in working towards this MDG6. World Vision Foundation of Thailand's programmes occurred within a positive public policy environment throughout Thailand. The Thai government first acknowledged the existence of HIV/AIDS in 1991 and soon began implementing public communication campaigns. These campaigns focused on public education and promotion of condom use. In addition, the government began undertaking testing and surveillance in order to develop and maintain accurate records of the epidemic. Whilst World Vision Foundation of Thailand's programmes evolved significantly over the decade, public policy whilst acknowledged as world leading remained primarily anchored in public education campaigns, testing and surveillance. However, such an environment assisted the evolution of World Vision's programmes.

References

Clarke, M. (2002), 'Achieving Behaviour Change: Three Generations of HIV/AIDS Programming and Jargon in Thailand', in *Development in Practice*, Vol. 12, No. 5, pp. 625–36.
UNAIDS (2006), 2006 Report on the Global AIDS Epidemic, UNAIDS, Geneva.

Goal 7: NGOs and ensuring environmental sustainability

The seventh MDG will be assessed against three targets: (1) integrating the principles of sustainable development into country policies and programmes and reversing loss of environmental resources; (2) reducing by half the proportion of people without sustainable access to safe drinking water; and (3) achieving significant improvement in the lives of at least 100 million slum-dwellers by 2020. Achieving goal seven requires substantial financial resources and policy coordination at the macro- and supramacro-level. NGOs are able to assist communities reverse some environmental losses by building local capacity and increase knowledge and education around natural resources use. NGOs will be able to implement some activities in terms of improving access to water as this requires community participation in planning the installation of water infrastructure at the micro-level, but the actual supply of this infrastructure requires expertise and specialist skills beyond the capacity of most NGOs. NGOs do provide models of community participation that are necessary for achieving sustainable development at the macro- and supramacro-levels (Sharma, 2003). NGOs have long advocated on behalf of slum-dwellers (Placid, 2003). Certainly the difficulties slum-dwellers face, especially in relation to water and sanitation, are significant (UNDP, 2006). While NGOs do work closely with slum-dwellers at the micro-level, undertaking a wide range of interventions aimed to improve their lives, such as literacy classes, micro-credit schemes, health clinics, child shelters, legal aid, general education, etc., requires cooperation between NGOs and the state.

Case study: MDG 7

WaterAid Bangladesh has been the lead NGO in achieving improvements in water and sanitation across Bangladesh since 2000. By partnering with both government bodies and smaller NGOs, Water-Aid Bangladesh has achieved great success through a programme of Community-Led Total Sanitation (CLTS). The World Bank has estimated that Bangladesh has already achieved this MDG as a direct result of CLTS.

CLTS differs from traditional interventions in that there is no subsidy provided to install toilets and that sanitation is considered a public health issue. In this sense, CLTS is a community-wide approach to public health. Therefore, rather than focusing on individuals and seeking behaviour change at the private level, the whole community (including the most poor and vulnerable) are targeted and behaviour change is sought at the public level.

As a public health approach, the emphasis of CLTS is to break the faecal-oral chain in order to improve health outcomes. To do this, the CLTS promotes 100 per cent adherence to:

- Use of hygienic toilets (no flies, no smell, no view of faeces)
- Full maintenance of toilets
- Good personal hygiene practices
- Effective hand washing after defecation and before food handling
- Safe water use for all domestic purposes

- Proper garbage and animal excreta disposal
- Hygienic waste water disposal

The ability of CLTS to quickly change current practices is largely dependent upon the involvement and participation of the entire community. To ensure that the entire community is aware of the importance of breaking the faecal-oral chain, a number of participatory rural appraisal activities are undertaken, including, transect walks, social mapping, defecation site visits, faeces calculation and cause-effect analysis, and well-being ranking. Community committees are also established at the initiation of the CLTS intervention to ensure community ownership. Committee members receive training in project management and monitoring as well as leadership development and group management.

As the CLTS intervention is a public health intervention, there is a constant provision of training on health and hygiene for all community groups, especially mothers and children. These educational activities are also purposely participatory.

While CLTS was initiated in Bangladesh, variants of it have now been introduced to other Asian and African countries.

References

Sabur, M. (2007), 'The Total Sanitation Revolution', presented at *Water, Sanitation and Hygiene – Let's Come Clean Conference*, Deakin University, World Vision Australia and WaterAid Australia, Melbourne, 8 June.

UK House of Commons International Development Committee (2007), 'Evidence 323 From World Bank – Sanitation: from South Asia to Global Innovation', Sixth Report of Session 2006–07, Vol. II Oral and Written Evidence of April 2007, UK House of Commons, London.

Goal 8: NGOs and developing a global partnership for development

The eighth MDG will be assessed against eight different targets focusing on trade, needs of least-developed, land-locked and small island countries, debt, employment for the young, affordable medicines, and sharing new technology. Achieving these targets will depend on actions undertaken at the macro- and supramacro-levels. NGOs will seek to garner public support (especially in developed countries) to pressure all governments to achieve these targets. The most prominent activity undertaken thus far has been the *Make Poverty History* campaign – which itself evolved out of the debt relief campaign *Jubilee 2000*. Both campaigns were global in nature and sustained over a number of years. In 2005, at the summit held at Gleneagles, eight of the world's richest countries (known collectively as the G8) agreed to cancel most of the multilateral debts of some of the world's poorest countries as the latest in a series of debt reductions for these countries. Other developed countries (collectively known as the G20) have made similar pledges. To assist with the achievement of the MDGs, it will be important for donors to honour the commitments that they have made to debt relief and expand debt relief to other poor countries that have high debt burdens. A number of the G20 donors have been active in extending debt relief by offering debt for development swaps with poor countries (Feeny and Clarke, 2006). These pledges are largely due to the public pressure brought about through these long-standing MGO-led campaigns.

Goal 8: Case study

Médecins Sans Frontières (MSF) seeks to improve people's health in developing countries through both programming and advocacy actions. To achieve wide-ranging success against Goal 6, MSF has been prominent in advocating both private sector firms and national governments to increase availability of affordable essential drugs in developing countries in line with Goal 8. Seeking to gain public focused outcomes from commercially-orientated private firms is a difficult task.

In November 2006, the Thai Government announced it would issue a compulsory licence for use by the government to improve access to a key HIV/AIDS medicine, efavirenz. This licence would allow the government to both import and manufacture local generic versions of the drug. Initially, it was planned that the Thai Government would import generic efavirenz from India, before local production would begin in 2007. This would halve the costs for this drug and expand procurement options to ensure sustainable drug supply. This would allow much greater access to this drug to the almost 12,000 people requiring efavirenz. MSF was prominent amongst a number of NGOs in advocating the need for this compulsory licence.

Such use of generic medicines has been issued previously in Thailand. In 2002, the Thai Government launched a generic version of HIV/AIDS triple therapy. This resulted in a 18-fold reduction in the costs of treatment. As a direct result, over 85,000 people with HIV/AIDS are presently receiving treatment. The success of NGOs, such as MSF, advocating on behalf of the poor mean that Thailand is the only Southeast Asian country to have over half the number of people on AIDS treatment who need it.

However, it is not sufficient for MSF (and others) to simply lobby national Governments. As a result of the latest announcement, the large pharmaceutical firm Abbott, announced in 2007 that it would withdraw all applications to register drugs in Thailand, including new HIV/AIDS drugs in order to avoid having its goods being subject to compulsory licences.

MSF is now seeking to lobby Abbott to reverse its decision.

References

Médecins Sans Frontières (MSF) (2006), 'MSF Welcomes Move to Overcome Patent On Aids Drug In Thailand', media release, MSF, Geneva, 30 November.

Médecins Sans Frontières (MSF) (2007b), 'MSF: Abbott should reconsider its unacceptable decision to not sell new medicines in Thailand', media release, MSF, Geneva, 23 March.

6   Conclusion and policy recommendations

NGOs can positively impact upon the MDGs by targeting interventions explicitly to achieve various targets. NGOs predominately work at the grassroots level, focusing on community development interventions. The standard focus of NGOs on improving health, education, economic security and gender equality are all very much in accordance with the MDGs (Hunt, 2004). In many Asian and Pacific communities, NGOs, rather than government agencies are the primary institutions delivering public services. These organisations are able to work closely with very vulnerable communities and provide school and immunisation programmes, for example, which government agencies could not due to political pressures and an inability to gain trust and access to the poor. NGOs will play an increasingly important role in nations in which the government delivery of services is poor and where NGOs have themselves become the *de-facto* primary deliverer of development services and interventions. There are a number of ways NGOs could increase their impact in achieving the MDGs.

(i) Improving MDG advocacy

NGOs could increase their advocacy activities to pressure both developing country governments and international aid donors to make achievement of the MDGs their primary purpose. Long-term national development strategies are becoming the key driver of development in developing countries. These strategies outline the priorities for the country and outline how resources should be allocated in ways consistent with the achievement of these strategies. NGOs should pressure governments to incorporate the MDGs into these strategies. NGOs should see themselves playing a legitimate and useful role at the national level in designing national development strategies. If NGOs are excluded from such national councils, this should be a priority advocacy activity, coordinated from a peak body.

Further, some donor-countries are yet to explicitly link their aid programmes to the MDGs. This is very important for donors to effectively assist with MDG achievement and should be an integral part of NGO advocacy campaigns. NGOs are likely to be most effective at MDG advocacy by forming coalitions and lobbying as a group.

(ii) Monitoring progress

Monitoring progress towards the MDGs will play an important role in their achievement. NGOs should closely monitor progress (and lack of progress) towards each MDG target in order to hold governments and international aid donors accountable. Monitoring progress will also identify areas which require greater resources and can assist in identifying which interventions are working and which aren't.

(iii) Improving coordination

NGOs can often act in isolation of one another. It is not uncommon for NGOs to replicate interventions within the same communities. Indeed, some reports from the Asian Tsunami in 2005 suggest that NGOs were competing with one another over providing services to some communities (Clarke, 2008a). Greater coordination is required by NGOs to ensure that scarce resources are expended most efficiently. This does not mean that multiple NGOs cannot work with the same community, but should they do so, they coordinate with one another so that interventions compliment rather than compete. This may require establishment of peak or coordinating bodies amongst NGOs to provide a designated forum for discussing and planning interventions.

It is also important for NGOs to coordinate their activities with developing country governments and international government aid donors. Not only will this lessen the chances of duplication but will highlight areas which need greater attention.

(iv) Scaling up impact

NGOs can increase their impact by scaling up their activities. Scaling up does not necessarily increase their size, but rather refers to increasing their impact (Chambers, 1992; Edwards and Hulme, 1992). It is not necessary, nor is it necessarily desirable, that smaller NGOs increase in size.

Uvin and Miller (1994) suggest there are four ways in which NGOs can increase their impact: 1) Quantitative – this involves increasing the absolute size of the beneficiaries reached by the intervention. The number of projects must increase either through direct expansion of the NGOs own interventions or by assisting other NGOs to replicate these interventions but in new locations; 2) Functional – this involves seeking new interventions to complement pre-existing interventions. Such additions may be 'horizontal' or 'vertical'. Examples of horizontal expansion may be a HIV/AIDS education programme now offering care and medical support for those infected or a micro-credit programme now offering numeracy and literacy workshops to its members. An example of a vertical expansion may be the connection of micro-credit grocery retailers in urban centres with farmers within agricultural projects; 3) Political – this involves beginning to seek alliances with other NGOs and build a constituency beyond the immediate community with whom the NGO is directly working. Becoming political allows NGOs to begin advocating on behalf of their communities rather than simply implementing programmes to improve their circumstances. This may also involve smaller NGOs forming single larger NGOs or forming federations or networks; 4) Organsiational – this involves seeking some level of financial freedom. Many smaller NGOs rely on a single or small number of donors. This limits their ability to respond to the changing environment. It also leaves them vulnerable to financial instability. By diversifying funding streams or indeed, directly earning their own revenue independently of donors, NGOs gain greater freedom and potential leverage to undertake innovative development interventions.

(v) Improving evaluation

To effectively assist with MDG achievement NGOs must improve their knowledge of which interventions work best and what don't. NGOs have a responsibility to the communities they work with as well as those who financially support them to evaluate their intervention rigorously to determine what is effective and why. NGOs have an unenviable place within the international community surrounded by 'hype and myth created around the ability of NGOs to address a plethora of issues' (Zaidl 1999, p. 270). The pressure to meet this hype is great, but NGOs must honestly reflect on what they do and the outcomes they achieve to ensure that they (and thus their intended beneficiaries) actually improve the lives of the poor both within the framework of the MDGs, but also outside of it.

Part II

4
Achieving the MDGs in Papua New Guinea: A Focus on Governance[1]

1 Introduction

Papua New Guinea (PNG) is the largest country in the Pacific with a population of almost six million. The country gained independence from Australia in 1975 after decades of colonial rule. Despite being rich in resources, PNG has made little progress in many areas of development since its independence. Most indicators of well-being are poorer than in the country's Pacific neighbours and living conditions deteriorated for many in PNG during the 1990s. There are large disparities in well-being between (and within) PNG's 20 provinces with many in isolated rural areas lacking access to infrastructure and basic services. The country has virtually no chance of achieving the original MDGs and the government has subsequently tailored the goals in response.

Poor governance is often cited as the main factor responsible for PNG's recent poor development record. In response, international aid donors and NGOs are increasingly focusing their activities on improving governance in order to improve provision of basic services and infrastructure, improve law and order and stimulate broad-based economic growth. This is exemplified by the Enhanced Cooperation Program (ECP) which was initiated by the Australian government in 2003. The ECP resulted from concerns over deteriorating governance and the programme led to a number of Australian advisors taking up positions in the PNG public service. In 2005, PNG's Supreme Court found that aspects of the ECP contravened the country's constitution and Australian police were subsequently withdrawn from PNG. However, a number of Australian officials remain in other government departments.

---

[1] This chapter draws on Cox and Feeny (2007).

The increasing focus by the international community on improving governance applies to many developing countries in addition to PNG. Improving governance is often seen as an important means (or prerequisite) to achieving the MDGs. Governance broadly refers to the management of a country's resources. The World Bank defines governance as the traditions and institutions by which authority in a country is exercised for the common good. This includes (i) the process by which those in authority are selected, monitored and replaced, (ii) the capacity of the government to effectively manage its resources and implement sound policies, and (iii) the respect of citizens and the state for the institutions that govern economic and social interactions among them (World Bank, 2007a). The United Nations Development Programme (UNDP) defines governance as the exercise of economic, political and administrative authority to manage a country's affairs at all levels (UNDP, 1997). Governance therefore includes upholding the rule of law, promoting human rights, adopting sound economic policies and adopting transparent, participatory and accountable decision making processes (UN, 2005).

While the focus of this chapter is on the role of governance in PNG and how government donors and NGOs can improve it, the chapter also discusses other interventions which will be necessary to assist PNG with the achievement of the MDGs. In fact, the chapter argues that the focus on governance by government donors is a long-term and risky strategy with no guarantees for success. Greater resources devoted to the health, education and water and sanitation sectors directly will also be very important. In the proceeding section, this chapter examines the current level of human well-being in PNG and identifies the constraints to the country's development of which poor governance is an important component. PNG's progress towards the MDGs is also provided. The current activities of government aid donors and NGOs in PNG are examined in section 3 before a discussion of the ways which aid can improve governance is provided in section 4. Finally, section 5 concludes with some policy recommendations for PNG's aid donors.

2 Human well-being and the MDGs in PNG

Table 4.1 provides a comparison of PNG with other Pacific countries using a number of selected indicators of well-being. According to many indicators, PNG has the lowest level of well-being in the Pacific and on some indicators it is comparable to many African countries. Although a lack of reliable data makes inter-temporal comparisons very difficult, it

Table 4.1   Selected Indicators for Pacific Countries

	Poverty (Headcount index – national poverty line %)	Life expectancy at birth (2003)	Primary School enrolments (net) (2001)	Infant Mortality (per 1,000 live births) (2003)	Population without access to an improved water source (%)
PNG	54 (2003)	55.3	73	69	61
Fiji	25.5 (1990–91)	67.8	100	16	53
Solomon Islands	–	62.3	–	19	30
Vanuatu	40 (1998)	68.6	93	31	40
Samoa	20.3 (2002)	70.2	95	19	12

Source: UNDP (2005a), UN (2005), Abbott and Pollard (2004), World Bank (2004a).

is widely believed that many aspects of human well-being in PNG have deteriorated during the 1990s.

The World Bank (2004a) estimates that the proportion of the population living on less than US$1 a day in PNG has increased from 24.6 per cent in 1996 to 39.1 per cent in 2003. An alternative measure of poverty based on 2,200 calories per day and an allowance for basic non-food expenditure, the World Bank also estimated that the proportion of the population living in poverty in PNG increased from 37.5 per cent in 1996 to approximately 54 per cent in 2003. Yet, despite these high figures, PNG's customary social systems help to protect people from starvation and outright destitution. However, many people in PNG suffer what is often referred to as 'poverty of opportunity' and a lack of access to basic social services. Participants in an Asian Development Bank (ADB) Participatory Assessment of Hardship (PAH) identified the following causes of hardship: a lack of employment and cash earning opportunities; a lack of education (particularly for women and girls); a lack of basic infrastructure; poor access to basic services (including water and sanitation and education and health services); a breakdown of the family unit; poor information and communication facilities; and poor governance standards. In addition, those surveyed in urban areas identified a lack of land, unemployment, crime and drug and alcohol abuse as causes of hardship (Abbot and Pollard, 2004, also see J. Cox, 2006 for a further discussion of well-being in PNG). These causes and characteristics of poverty and hardship are closely related to the achievement of the MDGs.

Other indicators of well-being highlight the poor access to basic services in PNG. Life expectancy is the lowest in the Pacific, literacy rates and school attendance and completion rates are low and are believed to have improved only marginally in recent years. The rate of infant mortality is very high while the percentage of the population without access to an improved water source is a staggeringly high 61 per cent.[2] This latter statistic is the highest for all countries in the Asia-Pacific and

---

[2]Improved water sources include household connections, public standpipes, boreholes, protected dug wells, protected springs and rainwater collections. Unimproved water sources are unprotected wells, unprotected springs, vendor-provided water, bottled water (unless water for other uses is available from an improved source) and tanker truck-provided water (WHO, 2006). Although water from unimproved water sources might be of a good quality, these sources are susceptible to pollution implying that people are vulnerable to contamination and outbreaks of disease such as diarrhoea and typhoid.

has not changed since 1990. A lack of sanitation is also a problem in PNG. Sewerage systems that do exist mostly serve the developed sections of town. 'Many residents have a low awareness of good sanitation and hygiene and its effects on health. In many towns, inadequate sanitation is a source of major health hazards. For many poor communities living in the urban fringes, defecating in open areas is the only option. Human waste often pollutes water sources used for all purposes, while raw or poorly treated sewage flows into watercourses and pollutes beaches and coastlines' (ADB, 2004a, p.39)

Given the poor development progress made by PNG over since 1990, it is not surprising that a MDG Technical Working Group found that achieving most of the original MDGs in PNG is very unlikely by 2015 (GoPNG and UNDP, 2004a). After many years of economic stagnation, it is an unrealistic challenge for PNG to achieve the MDGs as outlined in the Millennium Declaration. Consequently, the MDG targets have been tailored by the Department of National Development and Rural Planning to reflect the realities of the country. The achievement of these adjusted targets has been incorporated into PNG's Medium Term Development Strategy (2005–2010). Some goals and targets have been tailored to become less ambitious for PNG while others have been tailored to be more appropriate for the country. For example, rather than halving the proportion of people living on less than a dollar a day, the revised target seeks to reduce the proportion by 10 per cent by 2015 and a further 10 per cent by 2020. Further, the original MDG target of halving the proportion of people who suffer from hunger has been replaced by a target for increasing agricultural production. PNG has kept the target for achieving universal primary education and has added further targets of increasing literacy and enrolments at the secondary and tertiary levels. The amended goals and targets are listed in the appendix to this chapter.

Unfortunately, with current rates of progress, PNG is still unlikely to meet many of these less ambitious targets by 2015. The proportion of the population living on less than \$1 a day in PNG has barely changed since 1990 and the primary school enrolment rate is not expected to reach 100 per cent by 2015. Large gender gaps exist in many areas of education, health and employment. It is highly unlikely that the MDG targets for child and maternal health will be achieved, and the number of people with HIV/AIDS is increasing exponentially.

These poor results are exacerbated by significant disparity between regions. PNG has one of the highest prevailing rates of income inequality in the world and inequalities in other measures of well-being are also high. There is a very large rural-urban divide with an estimated 93 per cent of the poor living in rural areas with the vast majority reliant on agriculture for a living (ADB, 2000). The World Bank (2004a) reports that despite the subsistence safety net, practically every socio-economic indicator is significantly worse in rural areas. Moreover, on indicators relating to health, the gap is widening further. This provides a strong argument for devising sub-national targets. National targets might be of little relevance and use to policy makers at the local of provincial level. For example, as the UNDP notes, a national (average) target could yield complacency for the authorities in provinces approaching that target. Conversely, in provinces far off from reaching the target, the authorities will most likely ignore the unrealistic national target (GoPNG and UNDP, 2004b).

Composite MDG Indices (CMI) based on 24 variables for each of the country's 20 provinces have been produced (GoPNG and UNDP 2004a).

Table 4.2　**The Human Poverty Index and Composite MDG Index by Province**

Region	Province	Population	CMI (rank)
Southern	Western	153,304	0.630 (9)
	Gulf	106,898	0.489 (18)
	Central	183,983	0.656 (8)
	Milne Bay	210,000	0.683 (5)
	Oro (Northern)	133,065	0.611 (10)
	National Capital District	254,158	0.773 (1)
Highlands	Eastern Highlands	432,972	0.554 (15)
	Simbu (Chimbu)	259,703	0.574 (12)
	Western Highlands	440,025	0.587 (11)
	Enga	295,031	0.514 (17)
	Southern Highlands	546,265	0.478 (19/20)
Momase	Morobe	539,725	0.570 (13)
	Madang	365,106	0.557 (14)
	East Sepik	343,180	0.551 (16)
	West Sepik (Sandaun)	185,741	0.478 (19/20)
Islands	West New Britain	184,508	0.658 (7)
	East New Britain	220,133	0.723 (3)
	New Ireland	118,350	0.715 (4)
	Manus	43,387	0.727 (2)
	Nth Solomons (Bougainville)	175,160	0.676 (6)
	NATIONAL	5,190,694	0.607

Sources: GoPNG and UNDP (2004a), NSO (2006).

The 24 variables all relate directly to MDG targets. The score and ranking of the CMI by province are provided in Table 4.2. The table demonstrates that the lowest CMIs are experienced by those living in the Highlands and Momase regions of the country, home to two-thirds of the population. International aid donors and NGOs should be focusing their activities in the provinces of these regions, in particular, West Sepik and the Southern Highlands. The National Capital District records the highest score relating to the CMI.

3   Governance in Papua New Guinea

Assessing the level of governance in developing countries is a very difficult exercise. The factors which constitute good governance are very difficult to measure. The World Bank notes that 'good governance is epitomised by predictable, open, and enlightened policy-making, a bureaucracy imbued with a professional ethos, an executive arm of government accountable for its actions, and a strong civil society participating in public affairs – all operating under the rule of law' (World Bank, 1999a, p.103). Similarly, the ADB identifies four basic elements of good governance: accountability for economic and financial performance; participation by all stakeholders; predictability of legal and regulatory frameworks; and transparency of decision-making and information-sharing (ADB, 2006a). Despite the difficulties in determining levels of governance, the World Bank has published governance rankings which are based on aspects which are broadly viewed as being important to good governance and which are also measurable (World Bank, 2007b).

Although caution must be exercised when comparing the indicators across countries, PNG ranks particularly poorly for political stability, government effectiveness and control of corruption. Its low score for controlling corruption is confirmed by data from Transparency International (2003). PNG's rankings are more favourable for voice and accountability, regulatory quality and rule of law. The main characteristics and causes of poor governance in PNG are discussed in turn.

Since independence in 1975, PNG has been characterised by political instability. Arguably, a Westminster style of democracy with a central government is not appropriate for a country like PNG. Traditionally, decisions are made by tribal chiefs in small villages and communities rather than by politicians located in grand buildings located a long distance away from the people they are meant to represent. Elections are held every five years but only recently has a government served a full-term in office. There are regular allegations of bribery and corruption among politicians and frequent changes of government have followed motions of no-confidence and political resignations. The *wantok* system (whereby loyalties go to clan members) underlies the political system and is often cited as a source of political instability. When in power, PNG's politicians face pressure from their wantoks for greater resources and access to services, often to the detriment of the national interest. However, despite experiencing periods of civil unrest and political instability, PNG has always maintained its democracy.

Until recently, elections in PNG have used the first-past-the-post system. However, a large number of politicians and political parties compete in each election which often results in candidates winning parliamentary seats despite claiming a very small proportion of the vote. Further, successful political parties often consisted of fragile coalitions with politicians frequently changing allegiances. To help reduce these sources of political instability, a Limited Preferential Vote system (LPV) was used for the first time in the 2007 elections whereby voters rank their top three candidates. Under this system, candidates with the lowest number of votes are eliminated and other preferences are reallocated until one candidate has at least 50 per cent of the vote.

Civil unrest and demands for independence from the island of Bougainville have also added to PNG's political instability. In 1988, violent protests began on Bougainville, due to islanders wanting a greater share of the financial benefits of the Panguna copper mine. Attacks on the mine and its staff led to the PNG defence force being deployed to Bougainville and the mine subsequently closed in May 1989. The Bougainville Peace Agreement was signed in 2002 and greater autonomy has since been granted to the region.

PNG has also experienced serious law and order problems which have reportedly worsened during the 1990s. Crime rates in PNG are high and in many areas they are increasing. Crime in urban areas is particularly high which is largely attributed to a lack of income earning opportunities, especially for youth. Port Moresby is now regarded as one of the most dangerous cities in the world and lawlessness is also increasing in the highland areas of the country. Crime and poor law and order are largely responsible for low levels of foreign and private sector investment in PNG. In addition to huge social costs, poor law and order has high economic costs, deterring investment and increasing the cost of doing business. This is often cited as a very large obstacle to private sector development.

Corruption is also an important element of governance in PNG. 'Corruption is endemic and it happens at all levels of government and public sector organisations..... Except for the judiciary, the media, the PNG Ombudsman Commission and civil society most government institutions are perhaps tolerant and passive towards corruption' (TI, 2003, p.5). The ADB find that 'As in many other resource-rich and capacity-poor economies, policy and institutional weaknesses have facilitated rent-seeking behaviour by public officials, led to pervasive corruption in pubic administration, and weakened confidence in government' (ADB, 2006a, p.6). Duncan (2007) notes that it is sometimes argued that the Melanesian tradition of gift giving makes corruption difficult to define in PNG. It can make any distinction between gift giving and vote buying, for example, very difficult. However, politicians are increasingly being questioned over their use of traditional practices to defend their actions.

Public sector reform has often been an important objective of World Bank and ADB programes in PNG. The country has a big public sector accounting for large proportions of employment and expenditure. A number of *ghost workers* are included on the payroll and nepotism occurs in civil service recruitment. There is little capacity for strong policy formulation and even though legislative frameworks are strong, implementation is often weak.

In combination, this corruption and weak governance, results in the poor delivery of basic social services. Certainly, poor access to such services is an important constraint on PNG achieving the country's MDGs by 2015. In particular, much of the population have poor access to health, education and water supply and sanitation. Service delivery in rural areas is poorer and has deteriorated during the 1990s. All three tiers of government in PNG, national, provincial and local governments, have responsibilities regarding service delivery, although there has always been uncertainty regarding their specific roles. The 1995 New Organic Law on Provincial and Local-Level governments sought to improve service delivery throughout the country through decentralisation. More powers were granted to provincial and local level government. Unfortunately the 1995 reforms failed to improve service delivery since there was still very little clarity over the specific roles and responsibilities of each level of government. Arguably the reforms actually led to less transparency and accountability (ADB, 2006a).

A related issue is the inadequate level of resources which have been devoted to basic infrastructure. Poor transport infrastructure in PNG also hampers the delivery of basic services as well as constraining economic growth. It prevents local produce accessing domestic and international markets, isolates rural communities and prevents social cohesion. It increases the cost and risk of travel. Poor communications infrastructure (including local newspapers and radio, government information services, telephones, and the internet) also hamper development.

Another symptom of the poor governance is economic mismanagement which has occurred at varying times in PNG over recent decades. Despite high revenues from oil and mining, the economy failed to prosper during the 1990s, recording negative economic growth in many years. Mismanagement has led to a large part of the government budget now being used to service debt and resources have been diverted away from development priorities. Economic growth which has occurred has not been broad based and has failed to provide employment opportunities for many in the country.

4   International aid to PNG

As outlined in Chapter 2, ownership is widely regarded as being crucial for foreign aid effectiveness. Government aid donors should therefore support and align their programmes with the PNG government's Medium Term Development Strategy 2005–10 (provided in the chapter's appendix). The role of the MTDS is to provide an overarching development strategy which provides the framework for prioritising expenditures and guiding donor support. At the same time, donors must be aware that development strategies and plans which lay out good intentions to reduce poverty are not always realised and living standards often fail to improve. This has been the case in PNG. Similar to the MDGs, achieving the objectives of the MTDS will depend on political will and capacity.

The MTDS 2005–10 sets out the revised goals and targets for PNG. While the revised MDGs targets are incorporated into the MTDS, the MTDS itself moves beyond simply signalling the targets and sets out the actual strategies to achieve these and others goals and development objectives. The overarching development strategy is one of export-driven economic growth, rural development and poverty reduction, through good governance and the promotion of agriculture, forestry, fisheries and tourism on a sustainable basis (GoPNG, 2004). The expenditure priorities for the MTDS are: (i) rehabilitation and maintenance of transport infrastructure; (ii) promotion of income earning opportunities; (iii) basic education; (iv) development-oriented informal adult education; (v) primary health care; (vi) HIV/AIDS prevention; and (vii) law and justice.

Australia is by far the largest donor of foreign aid to PNG providing US$234m in 2005, or 88 per cent of total foreign aid. Table 4.3 provides a breakdown of ODA disbursements to PNG from all donors, by sector, for the years 2002 to 2004. Ideally donors would report their activities against MDG criteria to assess how much is being devoted towards each MDG and to identify areas of priority. Unfortunately, this does not occur. The table indicates that most aid is provided to the social infrastructure and service sector. It also demonstrates that improving governance is now the dominant focus of aid donors to PNG. This is particularly true for Australia. In 2004–05, almost half of the Australian aid programme was directed towards this sub-sector largely under the

Table 4.3   Net ODA Disbursements by Sector to Papua New Guinea (2000–04)

Sector/Sub-sector	2002 (%)	2003 (%)	2004 (%)
I. SOCIAL INFRASTRUCTURE & SERVICES	**69.1**	**71.8**	**71.0**
I.1 Education	16.6	23.5	20.6
I.2 Health	24.0	15.4	14.8
I.3 Population Programmes	2.4	3.2	4.9
I.4 Water Supply & Sanitation	3.9	1.1	1.8
I.5 Government & Civil Society	16.3	18.2	24.5
I.6 Other Social Infrastructure & Services	6.0	10.3	4.5
II. ECONOMIC INFRASTRUCTURE	**25.3**	**19.9**	**22.6**
II.1 Transport & Storage	24.8	18.6	19.2
II.2 Communications	0.0	0.6	2.3
II.3 Energy	0.0	0.0	0.0
II.4 Banking & Financial Services	0.2	0.3	0.4
II.5 Business & Other Services	0.2	0.4	0.7
III. PRODUCTION SECTORS	**3.2**	**6.2**	**5.1**
III.1 Agriculture – Forestry – Fishing, Total	3.2	6.1	4.6
III.2 Industry and Mining	0.0	0.1	0.3
III.3 Trade Policy and Regulations	0.0	0.0	0.1
III.4 Tourism	0.0	0.0	0.0
IV. MULTISECTOR	**2.4**	**2.1**	**1.4**
V. TOTAL SECTOR ALLOCABLE (I+II+III+IV)	**100**	**100**	**100**

Source: OECD (2006).

Enhanced Cooperation Program (ECP) which is aimed at improving the performance of the PNG public sector. Large amounts of aid are also provided to improve health and education in PNG. Almost 60 per cent of total aid is directed towards these three sub-sectors. The proportion of aid directed towards water supply and sanitation is surprisingly low, accounting for less than 2 per cent of total aid in 2004. Foreign aid directed towards economic infrastructure accounted for 22.6 per cent of total aid in 2004, the vast majority of which was allocated to the transport sector. Just 5 per cent of aid was directed towards the production sectors, with most of this aid being allocated towards agriculture.

Unfortunately, an analysis of aid projects in PNG by geographical location is not possible due to a lack of publicly available data. However, an analysis of Australia's project and programme profiles in PNG reveals that the majority of projects are national in nature and many are located in the capital, Port Moresby. The political will to assist those in isolated rural areas is weak and there are also problems regarding the cost effectiveness of projects in the rural areas of the country. However, if the revised MDGs are to be achieved, rural areas, where most of the poor are located, must be targeted.

Obtaining data relating to NGO activities in PNG is very difficult. There is currently no peak body to collect and analyse such information. However, some data are available for Australian NGOs which have an

Table 4.4   **Value of Australian NGO Activities in PNG by Sector**

Sector	Value of NGO activities ($A) 2005	Share (%)
HIV/AIDS	18,999,225	33.4
Health	9,078,769	15.9
Multisector	7,270,758	12.8
Education	5,477,734	9.6
Child rights	3,730,000	6.5
Other	3,314,359	6.0
Microfinance	2,511,072	4.4
Water	2,389,146	4.2
Forestry	1,606,700	2.8
Church partnership	1,334,352	2.3
Technical Assistance	1,250,000	2.2
TOTAL	56,962,115	100.0

Source: ACFID (2006).

extensive involvement in PNG. In 2005/06, 39 members of the Australian Council for International Development (ACFID) were working with over 200 partner organisations on more than 150 programmes/projects involving over 300 staff and volunteers (ACFID, 2006). They work in a number of sectors as demonstrated by Table 4.4. The greatest focus of Australian NGOs in PNG is on health and HIV/AIDS which account for almost 50 per cent of the total value of NGO activities.

Table 4.5 below provides the level of Australian NGO expenditure per capita in PNG by province. The table also provides each province's CMI to examine whether Australian NGOs focus their activities in the

Table 4.5   Australian NGO Expenditure Per Capita in PNG and CMI by Province

Province	NGO Expenditure per capita (A$) 2005	Rank	CMI	Rank
National Capital District	13.5	5	0.773	20
Manus	25.8	2	0.727	19
East New Britain	0.3	19	0.723	18
New Ireland	0.6	17	0.715	17
Milne Bay	8.0	6	0.683	16
North Solomons (Bougainville)	40.5	1	0.676	15
West New Britain	3.0	14	0.658	14
Central	5.7	8	0.656	13
Western (Fly)	5.2	11	0.630	12
Oro (Northern)	16.6	3	0.611	11
Western Highlands	2.0	15	0.587	10
Simbu (Chimbu)	13.9	4	0.574	9
Morobe	6.2	7	0.570	8
Madang	5.5	9	0.557	7
Eastern Highlands	4.2	12	0.554	6
East Sepik	5.4	10	0.551	5
Enga	0.5	18	0.514	4
Gulf	3.5	13	0.489	3
Sandaun (West Sepik)	1.0	16	0.478	2
Southern Highlands	0.2	20	0.478	1

Source: ACFID (2006) and GoPNG and UNDP (2004a). Note: A significant proportion of NGO activities are identified as multi-province, so the actual expenditure in each province is likely to be higher. However, the distribution and ranking of NGO activities across provinces is likely to be very similar to that shown in Table 4.5. High rankings of NGO expenditure per capita indicate provinces receive greater funding while higher CMI rankings indicate lower ratings of MDG indicators.

neediest parts of the country. It is apparent from Table 4.5 that Australian NGO activity tends not to be targeted at the poorest parts of the country. It is possible to calculate a Spearman's Rank Correlation Coefficient (SRCC) to examine the relationship between the amount of aid per capita a province receives and its progress towards achieving the MDGs. If donors are allocating their aid to the provinces where least progress has been made we would expect a SRCC of -1 while if more aid was provided to those provinces making most progress towards the goals, the SRCC would take the value of 1. The correlation between the value of NGO activities in provinces and their CMI is close to zero.

The lawless environment in many rural parts of PNG explains the lack of activity in some places. The imbalance in funding by province is further exaggerated by the relatively high cost of working in poorer and more remote areas. NGOs might also choose to work in the geographic areas and sectors in which they can make a difference. However, if their role or objective is to improve well-being in the poorest parts of the country, targeting the poorest regions of PNG is, of course, necessary. A balance between undertaking projects and programmes with a likely chance of success and seeking to work in new areas to address chronic poverty is likely to be appropriate in many circumstances. The constraints to operating in the most remote or poorest areas of PNG should be tackled either directly by NGOs or indirectly through pressurising national and provincial government on issues such as rural infrastructure and law and order.

5   How can foreign aid improve governance?

Establishing democracy is often regarded as the crucial starting point for good governance. Weak governance and corruption will continue to prevail in developing countries unless their populations have the effective means to vote and remove poorly performing governments. Ensuring that countries have the ability to undertake free and fair elections is therefore often a priority of the international community. In PNG, donors have worked to improve the electoral process by assisting with the move to LPV.

Other foreign aid policies for improving governance can focus either on the supply side such as strengthening government institutions and departments or the demand side which relates to strengthening civil society. To date, a great deal of foreign aid has already been used to improve governance in PNG through the supply side. Aid projects have been devoted to public sector reform (including capacity building in a number of government ministries and departments such as the auditor general, public accounts committee and ombudsman's office), strengthening economic management, improving the legal and judicial environment, and improving the electoral process. While some of these aid interventions have had obvious success, others, in particular those devoted to civil service reform, have not yielded the desired results. A World Bank (1999a) review of its own civil service reform initiatives found that only one-third of these activities achieved satisfactory outcomes. Even when outcomes were found to be desirable, they were found not to be sustainable. An AusAID (2004) evaluation of public sector reform activities and an AusAID (1999) evaluation of institutional strengthening projects in PNG also highlighted some of the difficulties in achieving project objectives.

Poor outcomes can be explained by a lack of ownership, lack of political will and weak capacity within the public sector to implement reforms. Frequent changes of government and a high turnover of officials and staff undermine reform processes as do government officials' loyalties to their own wantok. The sustainability of these projects is often questioned. When reforms have been implemented, they have sometimes been reversed in later years. Institution strengthening projects can once again be undermined by high staff turnover and a low level of skills transfer. It is sometimes asserted that the technical assistance associated with the ECP has displaced many in PNG rather than build their capacity raising questions over its long-term effectiveness.

Smaller amounts of aid have been used to strengthen civil society, although Australia has pledged to scale up aid for this purpose. The effectiveness of aid at raising the demand side of governance in PNG remains to be seen. However, the additional resources devoted to these activities is promising given the relatively poor record of aid at improving the supply side of governance. Strengthening civil society involves equipping civil society organisations (CSOs), NGOs and other organisations with the tools to act as watchdogs and effectively monitor government activities, identify government failure, raise awareness, inform the public of its rights, and hold the government accountable. Civil society should be able to monitor the actions of a government in a transparent manner and freely act to pressure governments on shortfalls. Exposing the government to effective public scrutiny is likely to dramatically reduce corruption. Supporting media organisations is an important component of strengthening civil society. Resources and training can be provided to all types of journalists to improve both coverage and quality of their reporting.

More specifically aid donors can assist in strengthening civil society organisations through training CSOs and NGOs, providing them with financial resources and the skills to analyse government information such as national budgets, expose and publicise corruption and undertake public awareness campaigns. Making the government more accountable can be achieved through establishing and funding certain watchdogs and by undertaking government scorecards whereby surveys are undertaken relating to government effectiveness. Aid donors can also work to achieve a safe and secure environment for civil society to function effectively.

Recommendations for government donors and NGOs

Government donors to PNG need to strike a more appropriate balance between aid devoted to improving the supply side of governance versus aid devoted to improving the demand side. While aid supporting both sides of governance is important, it is argued that aid devoted to strengthening government institutions and capacity building in numerous government departments should be better balanced with more assistance provided for strengthening civil society in PNG to more effectively demand improved governance from its leaders.

Given that one of the most serious consequences of weak governance in PNG is poor delivery of social services in rural areas, donors should arguably focus on interventions to improve this. Aid focused on improving the supply of good governance must focus on strengthening provincial and local level government (in addition to national government) given their pivotal role in the delivery of social services. AusAID's Sub-National Initiative takes a promising lead which aims to strengthen financial management and service delivery of three PNG provincial governments. Addressing corruption in the delivery of basic services at both national and provincial levels should also be an important focus. It will necessarily involve assisting civil society in rural areas to effectively hold local and provincial governments accountable for their actions. Greater decentralisation in PNG should have increased accountability as greater responsibility for service provision has been transferred to local level government. However, this has not happened. Political will to assist those in rural areas is weak and this has been coupled with a concentration of donor activities in urban areas.

To effectively increase the pressure to improve governance in PNG, donors must work together and act as a group to demand and push for the same improvements in governance. They must have similar standards and definitions of good governance so that the PNG government does not receive mixed messages. At the same time, donors must be aware that improving governance is a complex process and takes a lot of time for any tangible results to be realised.

Improving governance is arguably an area which warrants more focus from NGOs. Such organisations are in a position to yield improvements from the bottom up – focusing on governance at the community level. They should focus on building the capacity of those living in PNG to hold local, provincial and national leaders accountable for their actions. Strengthening their ability to this should enhance the delivery of social services and improve standards in other areas which they are concerned about. NGOs will need to work closely with all levels of the government to achieve these outcomes.

6 Other priorities for aid donors

Arguably the greatest threat to PNG's development and progress towards the MDGs is HIV/AIDS. The incidence rate for adults currently stands at an estimated 2 per cent and annual infection rates are estimated to be between 15 and 30 per cent (UNAIDS 2006). The epidemic could have catastrophic impacts on the country if left unchecked. Donors must increase efforts on combating HIV/AIDS, examining which are the most effective interventions and scaling them up quickly. Table 4.4 indicates that combating HIV/AIDS is the priority for Australian NGOs operating in PNG. However, the percentage of bilateral and multi-lateral aid devoted to the health sector has been decreasing at a time when it should be increasing.

One particular sector which stands out as being noticeably under-funded by aid donors is water and sanitation. More than 60 per cent of the population do not have access to an improved water source and 55 per cent lack access to sanitation. Further, access to water and sanitation has not improved since 1990. As noted in a recent UNDP's (2006) Human Development Report, access to safe water and good sanitation is fundamental for development. The need for improved access to water and sanitation in PNG is increasing. The mining and forestry industries are placing increasing stress on PNG's environment and waterways. Levels of waterborne disease such as diarrhoea are already high in PNG and will continue unless access to improved water and sanitation is secured. The 2006 Human Development Report recommends that a minimum target of 1 per cent of GDP be devoted to water and sanitation spending. Analysis of the 2006 PNG Budget Papers indicates that this is more than ten times the amount spent on this sector in 2005. Increasing water access and improving sanitation will make a very effective contribution to the health sector, with important and large flow on effects to education and other areas of the economy.

Given that income poverty is increasing and the vast majority of the poor are found in rural areas, agriculture and roads are a further two sectors where greater resourcing would encourage private sector development and increase rural incomes. Aid donors are generally regarded as having been successful in implementing aid projects in these sectors. Greater amounts of foreign aid could be used for irrigation and extension facilities, high yielding crop varieties, agricultural research, and agricultural education and training. Strengthening the agricultural sector will not only lead to higher incomes in rural areas but will also assist in stemming the flow of rural-urban migration in PNG. Improving the quality and quantity of roads in PNG, particularly in rural areas, will provide better access to basic services, lower transportation costs for producers, greater export revenues, and will assist in creating greater social cohesion with the movement of people and information between communities. Increased provision of communications infrastructure such as radio, telephone, newspapers and computers is an important complement to improved transport infrastructure, to facilitate access to technical information, market reports and government information.

An important activity that government donors and NGOs can assist with is the collection of data and the monitoring of MDG related activities. It is going to be impossible to judge whether PNG has achieved many of its revised MDGs in 2015 due to a lack of relevant data. For example, monitoring of progress against poverty and hunger won't be possible unless PNG conducts another independent household income and expenditure survey. The same is true for gender, child and maternal mortality, HIV/AIDS, and there is hardly any monitoring at all of environmental degradation.

Recommending any change in the focus of NGO activities is difficult. There is however scope for a higher level of coordination, especially in an integrated, service delivery-oriented governance programme as outlined above. The establishment of an umbrella organisation to enable NGOs to work together more effectively to monitor the government would be a useful step towards increasing their effectiveness. International NGOs could assist domestic groups to monitor and assess the behaviour of politicians, push for freedom of information and ensure corruption is exposed and the justice system deals with it. Pressure for improvements in service delivery should be a priority for NGOs. Given that rural fragmentation and isolation is core to PNG's development problems, NGOs might also need to examine how they can contribute to the development of rural infrastructure such as roads, airstrips, telecommunications and electrification, even though they out of their traditional remit.

7 Conclusion

PNG is an example of a developing country facing significant development challenges. The country has had a poor development record since 1990 and the MDGs, as originally outlined in the Millennium Declaration, are simply too ambitious for a country like PNG to achieve in the short time frame. To strengthen support for the MDGs and ensure that actions are taken towards their achievement, the goals have been tailored to be more appropriate for PNG. These tailored goals are still ambitious and will require coordinated responses from all levels of government within PNG, donors, NGOs and local communities. However, according to current rates of progress, the country is off-track to achieve the tailored goals by 2015.

Weak governance in often cited as an important contributory factor to PNG's poor development record and improving governance has become the focus of international donor activities. Most efforts have been directed towards improving the supply of governance – with activities focused on strengthening institutions and the public sector. While this is important, it needs to be better balanced with interventions which increase the demand for good governance. Aid donors can assist with increasing this demand by strengthening civil society. Such initiatives are likely to complement donor efforts at strengthening institutions and reducing corruption. Donors should also focus on improving the aspects of governance which underlie poor service delivery in PNG, given that a large proportion of PNG's population lack adequate access to health, education and clean water.

Improving governance is at least implicitly regarded as the means to achieve the MDGs and help improve well-being in PNG. However, donors must also achieve an appropriate balance between improving governance and directing their resources to alternative areas which will yield improvements in development. Focusing heavily on governance is in many ways a risky strategy. The track record of aid at improving governance is mixed at best and successful interventions are likely to take many years to yield any tangible results.

Chapter 4 Appendix: The MDGs and PNG's tailored goals

GOAL 1: Eradicate extreme poverty and hunger

MDG Target 1	Proposed PNG Target 1
Halve between 1990 and 2015, the proportion of people whose incomeis less than one dollar a day	Decrease the proportion of people whose income is less than a dollar per day by 10 per cent by 2015 and by 10 per cent by 2020 (using 31 per cent as the benchmark poverty measurement figure)
MDG Target 2	Proposed PNG target 2
Halve, between 1990 and 2015, the proportion of people who suffer from hunger	By 2015 increase by 10 per cent the total amount of agriculture commercially produced and by 34 per cent the amount of subsistence agriculture production

GOAL 2: Achieve universal primary education

MDG Target 3	Proposed PNG target 3
Ensure that, by 2015, children every where, boys and girls alike, will be able to complete a full course of primary schooling	To achieve universal primary education (up to grade 8) by the year 2008 but no later than 2015
	Proposed PNG target 4
	To increase the General Literacy Rate to 70 per cent by 2010 and to at least 80 per cent by 2020
	Proposed PNG target 5
	To achieve at least a 30 per cent increase in combined enrolment in secondary and technical/vocational schooling by 2020

GOAL 3: Promote gender equality and empower women

MDG Target 4	Proposed PNG target 6
Eliminate gender disparity in primary and secondary education preferably by 2005 and to all levels of education no later than 2015	Eliminate gender disparity in primary education by 2005, in secondary education by 2015 and to all levels of education no later than 2020
	Proposed PNG target 7
	Raise the National Gender Development index Value above 0.600 by 2015
	Proposed PNG target 8
	Raise the Gender Empowerment Measure value above 0.300 by 2010 and above 0.400 by 2020

GOAL 4: Reduce child mortality

MDG Target 5	Proposed PNG target 9
Reduce by two-thirds, between 1990 and 2015, the under-five mortality rate	To reduce the child mortality rate to 18/1000 live births by 2010 and to below 15 by 2020
	Proposed PNG target 10
	To reduce the infant mortality rate to 53/1000 by 2010 and to less than 40 by 2020

GOAL 5: Improve maternal health

MDG Target 6	Proposed PNG target 11
Reduce by three-quarters, between 1990 and 2015, the maternal mortality ratio	To reduce the maternal mortality rate to 274 per 100,000 live born children by 2015

GOAL 6: COMBAT HIV/AIDS, MALARIA AND OTHER DISEASES

MDG Target 7	Proposed PNG target 12
Have halted by 2015, and begun to reverse, the spread of HIV/AIDS	Have controlled by 2015, and stabilized the spread of HIV/AIDS by 2020
MDG Target 8	Proposed PNG target 13
Have halted by 2015, and begun to reverse, the incidence of malaria and other major diseases	Have controlled by 2015, and either stabilise or reverse the incidence of pneumonia, malaria and other major diseases by 2020

GOAL 7: Ensure environmental sustainability

MDG Target 9	Proposed PNG target 14
Integrate the principles of sustainable development into country policies and programmes and reverse the loss of environmental resources	Implement the principles of sustainable development through sector specific programmes by 2010 and no later than 2015
	Proposed PNG target 15
	By 2020, increase commercial use of land and natural resources through improvements in environmentally friendly technologies and methods of production.
MDG Target 10	Proposed PNG target 16
Halve, by 2015, the proportion of people without sustainable access to safe drinking water resource	Increase to 60 per cent the number of households with access to safe water by 2010 and to at least 85 per cent by 2020 (as per definition from DOH)
	Proposed PNG target 17
	Increase to 60 per cent the number of households with access to safe water by 2010 and to at least 85 per cent by 2020 (as per definition from DOH)

GOAL 7: Ensure environmental sustainability – *continued*

MDG Target 11	Proposed PNG target 18
By 2020, to achieved a significant improvement in the lives of at least 100 million slum dwellers	By 2020, to have achieved a significant improvement in the lives of disadvantaged and vulnerable groups in urban areas
MDG Target 17	Proposed PNG target 22
In cooperation with pharmaceutical companies, provide access to affordable, essential drugs in developing countries	To increase the triple antigen immunisation rate (3rd Dose) to 70 per cent by 2010 and to 100 per cent by 2020

GOAL 8: Develop a partnership for global development

MDG Target 12	Proposed PNG target 19
• Develop further an open, rule based, predictable, non discriminatory trading and financial system • Includes a commitment to good governance, development, and poverty reduction-both nationally and internationally	Increase the proportion of ODA to basic social services (basic education, primary health care, agriculture, nutrition, safe water and sanitation)
MDG Target 15	Proposed PNG target 20
Deal comprehensively with the debt problems of developing countries through national and international measures in order to make debt sustainable in the long term	To reduce the debt to GDP ratio by 25 per cent by 2007, by 10 per cent by 2010 and by 10 per cent by 2020
MDG Target 16	Proposed PNG target 21
In cooperation with developing countries, develop and implement strategies for decent and productive work for youth	Increase the employment rate of 15–24 year olds by 5 per cent based on the 2000 benchmark by 2010 and by at least 10 per cent by 2020

GOAL 8: Develop a partnership for global development – *continued*

MDG Target 18	Proposed PNG target 23
In cooperation with the private sector, make available the benefits of new technologies especially information and communications	Increase the proportion of households with access to mass media by at least 50 per cent

Source: GoPNG and UNDP (2004a).

The Medium Term Development Strategy 2005–10: Ten Guiding Principles

1. Private Sector-led Economic Growth
Ensure the private sector becomes actively engaged in a growing economy (including those in rural communities).

2. Resource Mobilisation and Alignment
Mobilise and align land, labour and financial resources to development priorities.

3. Improvements in the Quality of Life
Ensure that economic growth translates into higher living standards for all Papua New Guineans.

4. Natural Endowments
Maximise the value of natural resources and the environment through sustainable production and processing.

5. Competitive Advantage and the Global Market
Focus interventions on goods and resources in which PNG has a competitive advantage

6. Integrating the Three Tiers of Government
Integrate national, provincial and local level governments to help implement the MTDS

7. Partnership through Strategic Alliances
Enhance strategic alliances between government, the private sector, donors, churches and community-based organisation to deliver the MTDS.

8. Least Developed Areas Intervention
Facilitate interventions in the least developed districts and provinces

9. Empowering Papua New Guineans and Improving Skills
Help Papua New Guineas help themselves through improving access to basic health and education, information, markets and appropriate technology particularly for the informal sector.

10. 'Sweat Equity' and Papua New Guinean Character
Encourage Papua New Guineans to contribute to development through sweat equity – putting in their time and effort without direct financial compensation

Source: GoPNG (2004).

5
Achieving the MDGs in Cambodia: Improving Aid Efficiency

1   Introduction

Cambodia borders Thailand, Laos and Vietnam and has a population exceeding 14 million (World Bank, 2006a). The country is still recovering from the brutal Khmer Rouge regime, which ruled the country from 1975 to 1979. During this period, an estimated two million lost their lives through execution, torture, starvation and illness. The regime implemented polices of forced labour, the closure of schools and hospitals, the confiscation of property, eradicating money and banning religion. By the time the regime was overthrown in 1979 by the Vietnamese, there was very little infrastructure and very few skilled and experienced people left in Cambodia. Rebuilding institutions, infrastructure and human capital from such a low base will take many decades. Moreover, despite reconstruction efforts commencing in 1979, political instability and civil unrest continued until 1998, hampering development progress. Similar to Papua New Guinea (PNG) and the Solomon Islands, Cambodia is often classified as a fragile state characterised by weak governance.

However, since 1998, Cambodia has experienced relative stability and has subsequently made good development progress. Economic growth in the decade up to 2004 averaged between 6 and 7 per cent per annum (World Bank, 2006a). This growth has yielded important reductions in income poverty. However, poverty has been reduced at a much slower pace in rural areas with limited access to basic services, roads and markets. This has exacerbated already high rates of inequality and limited progress towards achieving the MDGs.

In 2003, Cambodia tailored the MDGs to suit the specific circumstances of the country. While most of the goals remain the same as those devised in the original Millennium Declaration, Cambodia has included a number of additional targets to strive for by 2015. Further,

Cambodia has added a ninth MDG related to de-mining in the country. Mines and unexploded ordinance (UXO) in many parts of the country represent a significant constraint on development. Targets for this goal include eliminating civilian casualties by 2012 and clearing 100 per cent of suspected contaminated areas. A comprehensive list of the Cambodian MDGs (CMDGs) and their targets are provided in the appendix to the chapter.

International aid will play an important role in the achievement of the CMDGs. Cambodia is highly dependent on foreign aid, currently receiving over US$500 million of ODA per year (OECD, 2007b). In 2005, ODA accounted for approximately 9 per cent of the country's Gross National Income (GNI) or the equivalent of US$38 per capita (World Bank, 2006a). There are 25 aid donors to Cambodia providing relatively equal shares of support (with a few exceptions) and each supporting a wide variety of sectors (RGC, 2007). This provides a formidable aid coordination challenge for both the Cambodian government and to its development partners. The Paris Declaration (PD) in Chapter 1 highlighted the importance of development partners' coordinating activities to avoid duplication of development efforts and aligning with government priorities and procedures to reduce the administrative burden on recipient country officials. The principles of the PD are highly relevant therefore for the delivery of aid to Cambodia.

Until recently there were not any effective mechanisms in place to ensure aid was well coordinated and consistent with government priorities. As a consequence, the country has been subjected to poor aid practices with numerous donors implementing hundreds of poorly integrated projects. This imposed a huge administrative burden on Cambodian officials as they faced negotiation, management and reporting requirements not just for a large number of projects but also with a large number of donors. These projects were not always consistent with national objectives and priorities (see Acharya *et al.* (2004) for a discussion of the costs of aid proliferation). Further, technical consultants filled skill gaps in government and advice from different donors was uncoordinated and often contradictory. In response, Cambodia has established an extensive aid architecture to deal with the delivery of aid and adhere to the principles of the PD. Efforts to improve the management of aid began in earnest in 2004. This chapter examines whether this architecture is working and examines other measures which need to be taken to improve the effectiveness of aid to Cambodia. Concordance with the PD principles has recently become synonymous with aid effectiveness in Cambodia. However, the PD is a means to an end and while aid working towards the PD is very important, the effectiveness of aid should ultimately be judged according to its impact on poverty and well-being and hence the achievement of the MDGs.

The next section of this chapter examines human well-being in Cambodia and assesses the country's progress towards the MDGs. Section 3 examines the level and composition of foreign aid provided to Cambodia by government and non-government organisations (NGOs). The distribution of foreign aid by province is also examined. Section 4 provides an overview of the architecture which has recently been established in Cambodia to improve the delivery of foreign aid and thereby its effectiveness. Section 5 discusses the effectiveness of this architecture and looks at other ways in which the effectiveness of foreign aid could be improved. Finally, section 6 concludes with some policy implications.

2   Well-being and the MDGs in Cambodia

Cambodia is one of the poorest countries in Asia. Table 5.1 presents data for a number of development indicators for Cambodia and its Asian neighbours. The data indicate that Thailand has the highest development indicators followed by Vietnam. Cambodia is more comparable to Laos across the indicators although Cambodia has by far the highest rate of infant mortality.

Cambodia's relatively poor development indicators are not surprising given the country's history. However, the country's recent development record has in many respects been very impressive. The country has experienced remarkable rates of economic growth and income poverty has been reduced considerably (albeit slower in rural areas). In

Table 5.1   Development Indicators for Cambodia and Other Selected Asian Countries

Country	GDP per capita (PPP US$)	Population living on less than $1 a day	Human Development Index (HDI) (Rank)	Infant mortality rate (per 1,000 live births)
Cambodia	2,423	34.1	0.583 (129)	97
Thailand	8,090	2.0	0.784 (74)	18
Vietnam	2,745	–	0.709 (109)	17
Laos	1,954	27.0	0.553 (133)	65

Source: UNDP (2007a).

2004, an estimated 35 per cent of Cambodians lived below the national poverty line, down from an estimated 47 per cent a decade earlier (World Bank, 2006a).[1]

However, economic growth in Cambodia has been largely driven by the garment, tourism and construction industries which are mostly urban-based activities. Urban-rural linkages in Cambodia are not strong and the vast majority of the poor, located in rural areas have not therefore, benefited from the large increases in economic growth in recent years. There are large regional differences in poverty and increasing rates of inequality. The poorest provinces are located in the northeast of the country and around the Tonle Sap. The most recent UNDP Human Development Report for Cambodia emphasises the problems of widening inequality in incomes and opportunities, as well as persistent rural poverty (UNDP, 2007b).

Progress has also been made in improving democracy and governance. Since 1993 Cambodia has been regarded as a democratic society which has held free and fair elections. Despite the country having an active civil society and media there are on going questions regarding their freedom. Members of the media and NGOs, as well as members of opposition political parties have been detained for their dissenting views. Moreover, despite efforts to strengthen the public sector, capacity remains weak and corruption is widespread. There are also problems relating to the governance of land and security of land tenure (UNDP, 2007b).

Therefore, despite some progress in a number of areas, Cambodia is unlikely to achieve many of the CMDGs (RGC, 2005). Table 5.2 shows Cambodia's progress against the CMDGs and some of their targets. Progress towards eradicating extreme poverty and hunger in Cambodia has been made but this progress is heavily concentrated in urban and more accessible rural areas, exacerbating already high rates of inequality. An estimated 35 per cent of the population have an income less than the national poverty line with 20 per cent below the food poverty line (RGC, 2005). Achieving these targets is unlikely unless growth becomes more inclusive of those in the more remote parts of the country. Progress has also been towards achieving universal primary education. However, the goal is unlikely to be achieved with current

---

[1]However, it is also important to note that the 1994 and 2004 household surveys on which the reduction is based, are not directly comparable (World Bank, 2006a). This is an example of the difficulties of accessing reliable and rigorous data within the Asia-Pacific region.

Table 5.2 Progress Towards the CMDGs

CMDG 1: Eradicate Extreme Poverty and Hunger	
Target: Halve, between 1993 and 2015, the proportion of people whose consumption is less than the national poverty line	Unlikely
Halve, between 1993 and 2015, the proportion of people who suffer from hunger	Unlikely
CMDG 2: Achieve Universal nine-year basic education	
Target: Ensure all children complete primary schooling by 2010 and nine year basic schooling by 2015	Unlikely
Target: Eliminate gender disparity in nine-year basic education	Unlikely
CMDG 3: Promote Gender Equality and Empower Women	
Target: Reduce significantly gender disparities in upper secondary education and tertiary education	Possible
Target: Eliminate gender disparities in wage employment in all sectors	Likely
CMDG 4: Reduce child mortality	
Target: Reduce under five mortality rate, per 1,000 live births	Likely
CMDG 5 : Improve Maternal Health	
10. Reduce maternal mortality	–
CMDG 6: Combat HIV/AIDS, malaria and other diseases	
11. Decreasing the spread of HIV/AIDS	Likely
12. Decreasing the spread of malaria, DF and TB	Unlikely
CMDG 7 : Ensure environmental sustainability	
14. Halve by 2015 the proportion of people without sustainable access to safe drinking water	Likely
15. Halve by 2015 the proportion of people without sustainable access to improved sanitation	Possible
CMDG 9 : De-mining, UXO and Victim assistance	
Move towards zero impact from landmines and UXOs	Unlikely

Source: Adapted from RGC (2005).

rates of progress. Moreover, survival rates at all levels of education in Cambodia are low and have fallen in recent years.

With regard to gender equality, women in Cambodia have benefited from employment in the garment industry and higher enrolments rates for girls in schools have helped close literacy gaps. It is possible that Cambodia will reach some of its CMDG targets relating to gender. Yet these positive gains are offset by high levels of domestic violence.

The goal of reducing child mortality by half by 2015 is likely to be achieved if progress continues at the same rate. However, levels of child mortality remain very high in comparison to other countries in the region. Data to track progress towards reducing maternal mortality is unavailable but achieving this goal is believed to be a considerable challenge. Maternal mortality rates in Cambodia are among the highest in the region. Cambodia has started to reverse rates of HIV infection, malaria and Tuberculosis. However, HIV prevalence rates are still the highest in the region and rural infection rates are slowly increasing (RGC, 2005).

With regard to ensuring environmental sustainability, there are grave concerns over the issue of deforestation. Access to safe water and sanitation have been improved considerably. In 2004, the proportion of people getting potable drinking water was approximately 40 per cent but just 4 per cent among the lowest-income one-fifth of the population (UNDP, 2007b). The target of halving the proportion of people without access to safe water is likely to be achieved but more progress needs to be made to improving access to sanitation in urban areas. The target of zero impact from landmines and UXOs by 2012 is unlikely to be achieved according to current progress. However progress has been made and the completion year has been re-set to 2015. The number of civilian deaths from landmines and unexploded ordnance was nearly 800 in 2005 (RGC, 2005).

3   Foreign aid to Cambodia

As noted earlier, Cambodia is highly dependent on aid which is provided by a large number of international donors. Foreign aid is clearly a critical input to the attainment of the CMDGs. Total ODA to Cambodia amounted to US$538 million in 2005 (OECD, 2007b). The largest donors included the Asian Development Bank, the World Bank, the US and Japan. The RGC (2007) finds that the annual funding levels for 2005 and 2006 are broadly in line with the targets outlined by Cambodia's medium term development strategy known as the National Strategic Development Plan (NSDP) 2006–10. However, the World Bank and the Asian Development Bank have adopted a policy of performance based allocations and have reduced their levels of aid to Cambodia in recent years due to perceived deteriorating governance. The achievement of the NSDP might be jeopardised if this trend continues.

The RGC (2007) also finds that the aid environment in Cambodia is one of the most deconcentrated in the world. Concentration reflects both the number of donors providing aid to Cambodia as well as their relative shares. The RGC finds that while a country such as Afghanistan has just one donor which provides more that half of the country's total aid, Cambodia has about 25 donors which (with a few exceptions) provide relatively equal shares of support. Moreover, the aid environment has become even more deconcentrated in recent years. In such an environment, donors are likely to compete for influence in forums and policy-making decisions which can raise the transaction costs associated with foreign aid. There is also a danger that donors focus on their own results and lose sight of national priorities.

The number of projects being implemented in Cambodia has also risen in recent years. In 1997 there were an estimated 257 aid projects being implemented in Cambodia while in 2005, this number had increased to 532. This high degree of aid fragmentation applies in particular to the health, education and governance sectors (RGC, 2007). High levels of fragmentation can lead to a weakening of local capacity since donors will compete to achieve results which might result in abandoning the use of recipient country staff.

Table 5.3 provides a breakdown of ODA from all donors to Cambodia since 1995. The table indicates that foreign aid is fairly widely spread across a number of different sectors. Approximately 60 per cent of aid is provided to five sectors: transportation, rural development and land management, governance and administration, education and health. It is difficult to assert whether some sectors are under or over funded since this depends upon the resources required as set out by the NSDP, RGC contributions to the sector and to how much donors and the RGC agree upon appropriate levels of funding. The RGC (2007) finds

Table 5.3   Distribution of ODA by Sector (1995 to 2007)

Sector	Per cent of total
Agriculture	6.5
Community and Social Welfare Services	5.5
Education	12.1
Environment and Conservation	2.5
Governance & Administration	12.3
HIV/AIDS	3.6
Health	10.3
Power & Electricity	9.5
Rural Development & Land Management	13.7
Transportation	13.9
Water and Sanitation (excluding Agriculture)	3.2
Other	3.6
Not Specified	3.3
Total	100.0

Source: CDC (2007).

that at a broad sector level, health, governance, mining and trade were overfunded (relative to NSDP requirements) while transportation, agriculture and water and sanitation were underfunded (RGC, 2007). Over the period 2001 to 2005, approximately 30 per cent of aid has been provided in the form of aid loans and 30 per cent as technical cooperation (OECD, 2007b).

Table 5.4 provides a breakdown of ODA per capita by province. The Table also compares the rank of provinces by ODA per capita with their ranking of the Cambodia Millennium Development Goals Index (CMDGI). The CMDGI is a composite index based on the relative performance of provinces across a number of CMDG indicators. Equal weights are given to each indicator. The index can take values between zero and one, with higher values indicating greater progress across a number of CMDG indicators. Similar to the analysis carried out in Chapter 4, it is possible to calculate a Spearman's Rank Correlation

Table 5.4   Distribution of ODA by Province (1995 to 2007)

Province	ODA per capita	Rank	CMDGI	Rank
Banteay Meanchey	185	13	0.55	13
Battambang	171	16	0.52	16
Kampong Cham	56	24	0.58	8
Kampong Chhnang	126	20	0.55	12
Kampong Speu	137	18	0.55	14
Kampong Thom	250	10	0.56	11
Kampot	313	5	0.61	6
Kandal	103	22	0.65	2
Koh Kong	128	19	0.55	15
Kracheh	177	14	0.59	7
Krong Kep	254	9	0.62	5
Krong Pailin	212	11	0.52	17
Krong Preah Sihanouk	1229	1	0.62	4
Mondul Kiri	366	4	0.40	23
Otdar Meanchey	988	2	0.41	22
Phnom Penh	293	6	0.87	1
Preah Vihear	171	15	0.52	18
Prey Veng	99	23	0.57	9
Pursat	196	12	0.51	20
Ratanak Kiri	265	7	0.35	24
Siem Reap	262	8	0.43	21
Stung Treng	808	3	0.51	19
Svay Rieng	168	17	0.63	3
Takeo	122	21	0.56	10

Source: CDC (2007).

Coefficient (SRCC) to examine the relationship between the amount of aid per capita a province receives and its progress towards achieving the CMDGs. If donors are allocating their aid to the provinces where least progress has been made we would expect a SRCC of –1 while if more aid was provided to those provinces making most progress towards the goals, the SRCC would take the value of 1. In fact, the actual value of the SRCC is –0.28 indicating that there is only a weak negative relationship between the two. This provides strong evidence that aid donors are failing to prioritise those provinces in greatest need from an MDG perspective.

NGOs have played a very important role in Cambodia's development to date, particularly in the post Khmer Rouge era. NGOs will continue to provide a crucial role in assisting the country achieve the CMDGs through capacity building, strengthening civil society and equipping the country with skilled health and education professionals.

There are very large numbers of NGOs operating in Cambodia. In 2005, there were almost 800 registered Cambodian NGOs and over 300 international NGOs operating in the country. Indeed, the total number of NGOS has increased steadily from just 180 in 1994 to over 1,100 in 2005 with a total contribution exceeding US$120 million (NGO Forum, 2006). As indicated by Table 5.5, NGO activities are focused in the health, human rights and social development sectors. Agriculture and environment and education and training also receive large shares of NGO disbursements. Having so many NGOs operating in a relatively small country implies that NGOs are likely to face similar problems of coordination that government aid donors face.

Data relating to the value of NGO activities by province are not available. However, some data are available on the number of NGO

Table 5.5   Total NGO Aid by Sector (2000–2002)

Sector	%
Agriculture & Environment	11
Education and Training	13
Health	22
Human Rights	20
Humanitarian and Relief	2
Organisational Development	6
Rural Development	9
Social Development	17
Total	100.0

Source: NGO Forum (2006).

projects by province from the Cambodia NGO Forum (2002). The data indicate that there were over 40 NGO projects being undertaken in each of three provinces: Battambang, Phnom Penh and Kandal while far fewer NGO projects are undertaken in the poorer northern provinces of the country. Data suggest that less than ten projects are carried out in the provinces of Preah Vihear, Stung Treng, and Ratanakiri and Mondulkiri. This suggests that NGOs could also do far more to target the poorer areas of Cambodian to assist with the achievement of the CMDGs.

4   The aid architecture in Cambodia

To improve the management and delivery of aid and adhere to the PD Principles, a number of organisations and mechanisms have been established in Cambodia. The aid effectiveness pyramid displayed in Figure 5.1 provides the framework for the architecture. The pyramid covers three broad areas: ownership by recipient countries of the development process; alignment of development assistance with Cambodia's development priorities; and harmonisation of donor practices to rationalise their policies, and procedures. The most important elements of Cambodia's system of aid management and delivery are discussed in turn, followed by an examination of how the system assists with improvements on PD principles.

Figure 5.1   The Aid Effectiveness Pyramid

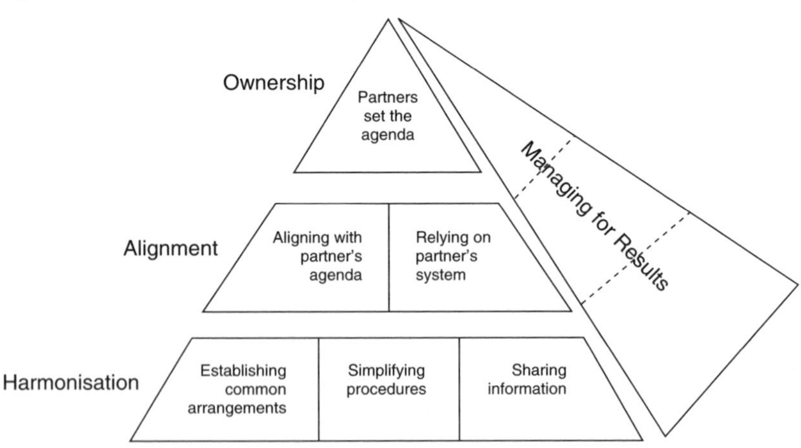

Source: OECD (2004).

Table 5.6   Cambodia's Aid Architecture

Organisation	Role
The Cambodia Development Cooperation Forum (CDCF) formerly the Consultative Group Meeting	An annual event with representatives from government, donors countries and NGOs. It is held to discuss a range of development issues and challenges and to assess the country's future financing needs. It is chaired by the RGC.
The Cambodian Rehabilitation and Development Board of the Council for the Development of Cambodia (CRDB/CDC)	Established in 2005 the CRDB/CDC acts as the main focal point for the RGC, donors and NGOs to improve foreign aid effectiveness. The CRDB/CDC helps to mobilise and allocate foreign aid and assists government ministries and donors formulate and implement development policies and plans.
Joint Technical Working Groups (TWGs)	Consist of government and development partner representatives and established at the sector or thematic level. Their role is to improve cooperation and collaboration between government and donors. There are currently 18 TWGs which are chaired by the RGC and each with one or more lead donor facilitators.
The Harmonisation Alignment andResults Action Plan (HAR/AP) 2006–10	Outlines actions needed to achieve the PD indicators and monitors progress towards their achievement. A TWG on Partnership and Harmonisation has the role of implementing and reporting on progress of the HAR/AP.
Government Donor Coordination Committee (GDCC)	Established to oversee and coordinate the work of the TWGs, implement the HAR/AP and to monitor progress on particular issues.
Strategic Framework for DevelopmentCooperation Management	Established in 2006 and developed in consultation with aid donors. The framework outlines the roles and responsibilities for both government ministries and aid donors while reaffirming the RGC's ownership and leadership of the development process.
National Operational Guidelines (NOG)	Outline the policies and operational procedures for the planning, management and implementation of development cooperation activities. The guidelines form an important element of the HAR/AP.

As demonstrated by Table 5.6, Cambodia has developed an extensive aid architecture, with a number of organisations and frameworks recently established to help improve aid effectiveness.

Cambodia is also a member of the OECD-DAC Working Party of Aid Effectiveness which was established in 2003 and has the role of monitoring progress towards the PD principles. In 2007 the OECD released results from its first (2006) survey on monitoring the PD in which Cambodia took part. Since it is the first survey, its primary role is to provide baseline data. However, the survey is useful in providing an indication of the challenge of aid management and delivery in Cambodia and whether the country's aid architecture is assisting with progress towards the PD. In summary, the survey found that levels of ownership, managing for results and mutual accountability were moderate but that levels of alignment and harmonisation were low. Each principle of the PD is discussed in turn.

Ownership

Ownership relates to the ability of a country to exercise effective leadership over its development policies and strategies and is widely believed to be crucial to aid effectiveness (OECD, 2007c). An important indicator of ownership is whether a country has an operational development strategy with which donors can align their support. The overarching development strategy in Cambodia is the RGC's Rectangular Strategy for Growth, Employment, Equity and Efficiency, adopted in 2004. The strategy covers (i) the enhancement of the agricultural sector, (ii) rehabilitation and construction of physical infrastructure, (iii) private sector growth and employment, and (iv) capacity building and human resource development.

The rectangular strategy is currently being operationalised by the National Strategic Development Plan 2006–10. The plan adopts targets from a number of (previous) national strategies such as the second Social Economic Development Plan 2001–05 (SEDPII), the 2003 National Poverty Reduction Strategy (NPRS) (known as Cambodia's PRSP) and the Cambodian Millennium Development Goal Report 2003. Importantly, achieving the CMDGs is the highest priority of the NSDP. The NSDP is also supplemented with a number of plans at the sectoral level and provinces are expected to tailor relevant goals to their circumstances.

The TWGs (led by government) and the Strategic Framework for Development Cooperation Management were both established to enhance government ownership of the development process. However, having this framework in place does not guarantee ownership. For effective ownership, the government must also have the capacity to implement its development strategies. This is an area in which Cambodia has experienced difficulties. The World Bank asserts that aligning Cambodia's annual budget, Public Investment Program and Medium-Term Expenditure Framework with the country's medium term strategic priorities remains a key implementation challenge (World Bank, 2006a). Most pertinently is that the budget does not fully align resources with national priorities identified by the NSDP. Further, true ownership of the development process entails the participation of national stakeholders in the formulation and implementation of policy. While the formulation of the NSDP did consult a range of stakeholders, the involvement of civil society and the private sector was limited (OECD, 2007c).

Alignment

Alignment refers to donors matching their aid programmes to the development strategies and priorities of recipient governments. Alignment can also include ensuring that aid projects and programmes use existing government systems rather than bypassing them. RGC (2007) concludes that 'development assistance, in the main, is relatively well aligned to national priorities, although alignment must take place at more than an aggregate priority level if a real impact is to be assured toward meeting the Cambodia Millennium Development Goals (CMDGs), in particular on maternal mortality' (RGC, 2007, p.25).

Programme-Based Approaches (PBAs), discussed in Chapter 2, can greatly assist with alignment. PBAs include aid provided in the form of direct budget support and Sector Wide Approaches (SWAps). However, many donors view PBAs as very risky and open to corruption and financial mismanagement. They have concerns over the efficiency of public sector procedures and mechanisms in Cambodia and as a consequence, many donors have established and use Project Implementation Units (PIUs). These units provide donors with far greater transparency over their aid flows and ensures they have close control over their disbursement. The OECD (2007b) found that there are an estimated 59 PIUs in Cambodia although the RGC (2007) estimates the number as 152. To improve aid effectiveness, donors should abandon these units as Cambodia's public sector procedures are strengthened. Integrating PIUs into government structures and moving to PBAs of aid delivery will also reduce this large number of PIUs.

Some but not all donors have ceased their own Country Assistance Strategies (CAS) and fully aligned with the NSDP. A joint country assistance strategy has been devised between the World Bank, Asian Development Bank (ADB) the UK's Department for International Development (DfID) and UN agencies which supports the NSDP and is aligned to the Rectangular Strategy. Other donor agencies should do the same to ensure their assistance is aligned with the developmental priorities of Cambodia.

The alignment of donor support to national systems is far weaker than for national priorities. Currently only 10 per cent of aid to Cambodia makes use of the country's systems (OECD, 2007c). The implementation of a Public Financial Management reform programme is expected to improve this percentage since donors will have greater confidence in Cambodia's capacity to manage aid flows effectively. Eventually all aid should flow through the budget since this strengthens existing systems and procedures and will also provide the RGC with a better idea of the extent of service delivery and how much it costs. Moves towards PBAs can strengthen existing capacity within government.

The PD also calls for more predictable aid so that recipient governments can improve planning and make more effective use of aid. Figures indicate that there are large discrepancies between the amount of aid committed by donors and the actual amount disbursed and this is another area in which donors need to improve.

Harmonisation

Harmonisation relates to improved coordination among aid donors. This can involve common management systems or joint programmes to streamline and rationalise procedures and share information on conditionalities, evaluations and planned aid flows.

Pooled funding can be one way to improve efficiency in the delivery of aid. Many donors have started forging such partnerships whereby aid from multiple donors channel their aid through a single donor. Some donors are also turning to PBAs and Sector Wide Approaches (SWAps) to improve harmonisation. Such moves will strengthen ownership and the management capacity of recipients, provide greater predictability of flows, lower the administrative burden and transfer acceptance of responsibility for ongoing maintenance of the funded activity. Currently 24 per cent of aid to Cambodia makes use of PBAs (OECD, 2007c). SWAps have been implemented for education, health, decentralisation, public financial management and private-sector development. Such arrangements require government and donors to collaboration funding and methods of aid delivery.

Another way of improving harmonisation is through reducing the number of missions undertaken by donor or by undertaking joint missions. Donor missions are typically visits by donor aid agencies to their development partners to discuss the progress of their aid projects and programmes and discuss any problems or issues which have been identified. The OECD (2007c) estimates that just 26 per cent of 568 donor missions to Cambodia were coordinated imposing a very high transaction cost on Cambodian public sector officials. More positively, the OECD estimates that 60 per cent of country analysis was coordinated.

Managing for results

Managing for Results relates to governments and donors working together to use information to improve decision making. It can be measured by examining the quality of development information, stakeholder access to information and the extent of coordinated country level monitoring and evaluation. The quality of development information is improving in Cambodia through the strengthening of the National Institute of Statistics. The objectives include conducting regular surveys and provision of better quality and timeliness of statistics. Statistics are increasingly becoming available to the public, largely through government websites and the NSDP has been translated in Khmer. Information on aid management and disbursement data is made available on the CRDB/CDC website.

There is a fairly high level of coordinated country level monitoring and evaluation in Cambodia. The GDCC has taken responsibility for a framework to monitor the NSDP and the country's numerous TWGs assist with ensuring progress towards the plans and goals (which include the CMDGs). Joint Monitoring Indicators (JMIs) are agreed upon at the annual CDCF meeting and are devised to assist with progress in implementing the NSDP. These issues are discussed at the annual CDCF.

Mutual accountability

The PD principle of mutual accountability calls for donors and partner countries to work together and be accountable to each other. Progress towards mutually agreed indicators should be undertaken jointly. Progress towards Mutual accountability in Cambodia is being achieved through TWGs, the Harmonisation Alignment and Results Action Plan (HAR/AP) 2006-10 and through its JMIs. The ODA database administered by the CRDB/CDC assists with the joint monitoring of aid flows and also includes data relating to PD indicators. The website also provides access to a range of documents, regulations and statistics relevant to the management and delivery of aid in Cambodia.

4 Improving aid effectiveness in Cambodia

There is little doubt that the aid architecture recently established in Cambodia is leading to some progress towards the PD principles and improving the effectiveness of foreign aid. Donor funded programmes to combat HIV/AIDS are an example of how adherence to PD principles can lead to success. Cambodia is one of just a few countries to successfully reduce infection rates. The factors contributing to the success include commitment from government, community involvement, good donor coordination, and a sustained education campaign. Conversely, the water and sanitation sector provides an example of the consequences of poor coordination among donors. A number of donors have built water wells throughout Cambodia which have recently needed to be examined due to the discovery of naturally occurring arsenic in many parts of the country. However, since donors often provided or built wells in isolation from one another it has been very difficult identifying their location.

Despite the establishment of a comprehensive architecture to deal with aid management and delivery, tangible improvements are likely to take time. A 2006 GDCC review of the TWGs found mixed results with some TWGs functioning very well while others clearly needing to improve their efficiency and effectiveness. About a third of the 18 TWGs are perceived to be working very well; a third are just beginning to make progress; and a third are still quite some distance away from establishing themselves as effective bodies (RGC, 2007). It can often be very hard to obtain a consensus within TWGs given the multiple stakeholders and there is sometimes a culture clash between donors. Effective leadership and partnership were shown to be crucial ingredients for successful TWGs.

There is also evidence that a great deal of time is being spent on working towards the PD principles sometimes at the expense of other aid activities such as project design and implementation. A 2005 survey of donors found that the majority feel that too much time is spent on aid coordination activities (Blunt and Samneang, 2005). Many donors officials report that they spend as much as 20 to 30 per cent of their time on aid coordination (M. Cox, 2006). This is a pertinent issue given that the PD principles are meant to reduce transaction costs rather than increase them. While some of the costs associated with the PD will be transitional and short term in nature, there will also be some permanent costs associated with changing the way aid is delivered in Cambodia.

There is no consensus among donors whether they should increase the proportion of aid provided through PBAs rather than using projects. PBAs require strong leadership and accountable systems. Some donors believe a balance should be maintained between project aid and PBAs arguing that in some sectors they will not work due to a lack of political will, leadership and commitment. The PFM works because the Ministry of Finance is the champion of reform. However, attempts at legal and judiciary reform have largely failed due to a lack of government commitment.

There are also concerns regarding the effectiveness of aid provided to Cambodia in the form of technical assistance. It is often argued that technical consultants have led to capacity substitution rather than to capacity building. Chief technical advisors see themselves as managers rather than as facilitators, trainers or communicators (Godfrey *et al.*, 2000). Advisors are often involved in overlapping and uncoordinated projects and sometimes conflicting advice has been provided. Aid projects involving large amounts of technical assistance are more supply driven and there is little ownership on the recipient side. This problem is exacerbated when most aid projects do not use existing government channels. Technical assistance must focus on building capacity and should slowly be phased out and be replaced by skilled and trained Cambodians. An important and related issue is the large number of skilled Cambodian nationals who are drawn to work for donor agencies and international NGOs. Skilled nationals are one of Cambodia's scarcest resources and the practice raises the price of skilled labour (Mysliwiec, 2004).

While improving the management and delivery of aid is of great importance to Cambodia, aid effectiveness is ultimately concerned with impact on poverty reduction. While following the PD principles, there are still other measures that donors could take to increase the impact of their aid.

Arguably, agriculture needs greater attention from aid donors. Agriculture accounts for about 40 per cent of GDP and is the main source of income for the majority of the population. It holds great potential for poverty reduction (IMF, 2006). In recent years the agricultural sector has not performed particularly well. Part of the explanation is that there is inadequate supporting infrastructure. Cambodia has a very limited railway system and roads in rural areas are sparse and are often in very poor condition. Another part of the explanation is the lack of irrigation in rural areas, implying that many farmers rely on rainfall and agricultural productivity is low. Landlessness and insecure property rights also impact on the agricultural sector. The World Bank (2006a) estimates that in 2004, 20 per cent of rural households lacked land for cultivation. Further, as much as 80 per cent of rural households that owned land were without land titles in 2004.

While donors can certainly improve the effectiveness of their aid by adhering to the PD principles, the full potential of aid will only be reached when donors are aligned to a transparent and accountable government with poverty reduction as its main objective (World Bank, 2004b). Similar to Papua New Guinea discussed in chapter four, donors need to ensure their aid to effectively tackle elements of governance in Cambodia. Concerns regarding governance often focus on corruption in Cambodia. Corruption is systemic with World Bank survey reporting that 82 per cent of firms in the country pay bribes to public officials (World Bank, 2004b). Civil service salaries are very low and are sometimes cited as a reason for corruption.

Cambodia also suffers from weak public sector management since many members of key institutions do not have the experience, skills and resources to carry out their jobs. Institutions are still being established and reformed in the post-conflict era. As an example, judges fled or were killed in the Khmer Rouge era. Although the situation has been improved, the majority in the current legal profession do not have law degrees. A strong legal and judicial environment underpins good governance and is crucial to attract foreign investment. Progress in legal and judiciary reform has been slow hampering efforts to improve the overall level of governance in Cambodia (IMF, 2006). Similar to the recommendations outlined in Chapter 4, donors could increase efforts to strengthen the demand side of good governance by strengthening civil society and the private sector.

The enforcement of property rights needs improvement in Cambodia. Property rights were effectively abolished under the Khmer Rouge regime. Without strong enforcement Cambodia's resources will continue to be exploited and this can have important impacts on MDG achievement, given the strong link between poverty and access to natural resources in Cambodia. In particular the poor are reliant on forestry and fishing resources, often termed Common Property Resources (CPR). The rural poor rely greatly on access to natural resources and that improved management of such resources is required to preserve access to and sustain the natural resource base (CDRI, 2006).

While the PD was devised for the delivery of government donors the importance of coordination among donors applies equally to NGOs in Cambodia. There are over 1,000 NGOs operating in the country and although coordination occurs to some extent this needs to be improved. They should ensure that development efforts are not being duplicated and that they don't end up competing with each other. However, rather than align with the governments priorities, NGOs in Cambodia should identify and operate in sectors where there is less government commitment and address issues which are not covered by the MDGs.

6   Conclusion and policy recommendations

This chapter has highlighted the importance of aid to Cambodia and the need to improve its effectiveness. Cambodia has made important progress towards some of the goals in recent years but the country's future is uncertain. Cambodia has very large reserves of oil and gas and is receiving increasingly large grants and loans from China. How Cambodia manages these revenues will largely dictate the country's future. These revenues could lead to increased corruption and rent-seeking activity by Cambodia's leaders leading to a situation commonly referred to as the resource curse. These revenues do not have any conditions attached which imply that donors will have less leverage with the RGC in the future. At the same time, donors have built good relationships with the RGC over time and the recent mechanisms to improve the management and delivery of aid could lead to far greater effectiveness in the future.

One issue which is arguably still hampering aid effectiveness in Cambodia relates to the number of donors. There are still numerous donors operating in many different sectors in Cambodia and donors might need to consider withdrawing from the country and challenging their aid through fewer agencies. Practically, of course, it will be difficult for some donors to relinquish ownership over their aid programmes. Alternatively donors should seek to streamline their activities, focusing on the aid activities in which they have comparative advantage. A greater division of labour could be a further way of improving aid effectiveness.

While aligning to the NSDP and the achievement of the MDGs, donors need to respond quickly to areas which are not progressing as well as planned. At the moment this includes maternal mortality since women still suffer from long journeys to health centres due to a lack of roads and transport. Further, the centres are also ill equipped with poor staffing levels.

Recent increases in economic growth have been focused in just a few sectors and for growth to become more pro-poor the agricultural sector must become a far greater priority. Increasing agricultural productivity and incomes will have a large impact on poverty reduction in Cambodia (World Bank, 2006a). It will also help reduce inequality in the country. In terms of the promotion of agriculture, CDRI (2006) recommends government, the private sector and aid donors support small farmers through: (1) promoting secure land tenure and access to natural resources, (2) providing more effective water management, (3) removing barriers to efficient marketing, (4) making affordable credit more available and (5) establishing better extensions services for both crop intensification and diversification, as well as for livestock production. Agricultural productivity is low compared to other countries in the region (World Bank, 2006a). This is particularly true for rice, which has great importance for the livelihoods of rural households. Improvements in agricultural yield rates can make an important contribution to poverty alleviation (UNDP, 2007b).

Much of the recent growth in the numbers of NGOs in Cambodia has been driven by donor funding and NGO effectiveness might be improved if they were able to develop and become less dependent on donor support. However, increasing private funding is likely to remain very difficult. Relationships between NGOs and the RGC are often strained which makes the important tasks of strengthening human rights and improving governance also difficult but efforts must continue.

It is important that NGOs operating in Cambodia improve coordination. While the Cooperation Committee for Cambodia (CCC) has played a role in strengthening cooperation between NGOs in Cambodia there must be greater information sharing regarding the location and type of projects to avoid duplication of development efforts. By increasing their collaboration and effectiveness, NGOs should be able to yield greater influence in forums with the RGC and with donors and to continue shaping policy for the needs of the poor.

Chapter 5 Appendix: The Cambodian Millennium Development Goals (CMDGs)

The Cambodian Millennium Development Goals (CMDGs) include 9 goals, 25 overall targets, and 106 specific targets.

CMDG 1: Eradicate extreme poverty and hunger

Overall target 1: Halve, between 1993 and 2015, the proportion of people whose income is less than the national poverty line

Target 1.1: Decreasing the proportion of people whose income is less than the national poverty line from 39 per cent in 1993 to 19.5 per cent in 2015

Target 1.2: Increasing the share of poorest quintile in national consumption from 7.4 per cent in 1993 to 11 per cent in 2015

Target 1.3: Decreasing the proportion of working children aged between 5–17 years old from 16.5 per cent in 1999 to 8 per cent in 2015

Overall target 2: Halve, between 1993 and 2015, the proportion of people who suffer from hunger

Target 1.4: Decreasing the prevalence of underweight (weight for age <2 SD) children under-five years of age from 45.2 per cent in 2000 to 22 per cent in 2015

Target 1.5: Decreasing the proportion of population below the food poverty line from 20 per cent in 1993 to 10 per cent in 2015

Target 1.6: Decreasing the prevalence of stunted (height for age <2 SD) children under five years of age from 44.6 per cent in 2000 to 22 per cent in 2015

Target 1.7: Decreasing the prevalence of wasted (weight for height <2 SD) children under five years of age from 15 per cent in 2000 to 9 per cent in 2015

Target 1.8: Increasing the proportion of households using iodised salt from 14 per cent in 2000 to 90 per cent in 2015

CMDG 2: Achieve universal nine year basic education

Overall target 3: Ensure all children complete primary schooling by 2010 and nine-year basic schooling by 2015

Target 2.1: Improving net admission rate from 81 per cent in 2001 to 100 per cent in 2010

Target 2.2: Improving net enrolment ratio in primary education from 87 per cent in 2001 to 100 per cent in 2010

Target 2.3: Improving net enrolment ratio in lower-secondary education from 19 per cent in 2001 to 100 per cent in 2015

Target 2.4: Reducing the proportion of 6–14 years old out of school from 35 per cent in 1999 to 0 per cent 2015

Target 2.5: Increasing the survival rate from grade 1 to 5 from 58 per cent in 2001 to 100 per cent in 2010

Target 2.6: Increasing the survival rate from grade 1 to 6 (last grade of primary cycle) from 51 per cent in 2001 to 100 per cent in 2010

Target 2.7: Increasing the survival rate from grade 1 to 9 (last grade of basic cycle) from 33 per cent in 2001 to 100 per cent in 2015

Target 2.8: Increasing the literacy rate of 15–24 years old from 82 per cent in 1999 to 100 per cent in 2015

Overall target 4: Eliminate gender disparity in nine-year basic education by 2010

Target 2.9: Improving the ratio of girls to boys in primary education from 87 per cent in 2001 to 100 per cent in 2010

Target 2.10: Improving the ratio of girls to boys in lower-secondary education from 63 per cent in 2001 to 100 per cent in 2010

CMDG 3: Promote gender equality and women's empowerment

Overall target 5: Reduce significantly gender disparities in upper secondary education and tertiary education

Target 3.1: Improving the ratio of girls to boys in upper secondary education from 48 per cent in 2001 to 100 per cent in 2015

Target 3.2: Improving the ratio of girls to boys in tertiary education from 38 per cent in 2001 to 85 per cent in 2015

Target 3.3: Improving the ratio of literate females to males 15–24 years old from 87 per cent in 1998 to 100 per cent in 2010

Target 3.4: Improving the ratio of literate females to males 25–44 years old from 78 per cent in 1998 to 100 per cent in 2010

Overall target 6: Eliminate gender disparities in wage employment in all economic sectors

Target 3.5: Increasing the female share in wage employment in agriculture (primary sector) from 35 per cent in 1998 to 50 per cent in 2005

Target 3.6: Increasing female share in wage employment in industry (secondary sector) from 44 per cent in 1998 to 50 per cent in 2005

Target 3.7: Increasing the female share in wage employment in services (tertiary sector) from 21 per cent in 1998 to 50 per cent in 2015

Overall target 7: Eliminate gender disparities in public institutions

Target 3.8: Increasing the proportion of seats held by women in the National Assembly from 12 per cent in 2003 to 30 per cent by 2015

Target 3.9: Increasing the proportion of seats held by women in the Senate from 13 per cent in 2003 to 30 per cent by 2015

Target 3.10: Increasing the proportion of female ministers from 8 per cent in 2003 to 15 per cent by 2015

Target 3.11: Increasing the proportion of female secretaries of state from 6 per cent in 2003 to 18 per cent by 2015

Target 3.12: Increasing the proportion of female under secretaries of state from 5 per cent in 2003 to 20 per cent by 2015

Target 3.13: Increasing the proportion of female provincial governors from 0 per cent in 2003 to 10 per cent by 2015

Target 3.14: Increasing the proportion of female deputy provincial governors from 1 per cent in 2003 to 15 per cent by 2015

Target 3.15: Increasing the proportion of seats held by women in commune councils from 8 per cent in 2003 to 25 per cent by 2015

Overall target 8: Reduce significantly all forms of violence against women and children

Target 3.16: Increasing the proportion of cases of domestic violence counselled by qualified personnel to 100 by 2015

Target 3.17: Increasing the percentage of awareness that violence against women is wrongful behaviour and a criminal act to 100 by 2015

Target 3.18: Developing and implementing laws against all forms of violence against women and children according to international requirements and standards by 2005

Target 3.19: Collecting annual statistics to monitor violence against women by 2005

Target 3.20: Developing and Implementing a Prevention Plan by 2005

CMDG 4: Reduce child mortality

Overall target 9: Reduce the under-five mortality rate

Target 4.1: Reducing the under-five mortality rate from 124 in 1998 to 65 per 1,000 live births by 2015

Target 4.2: Reducing infant mortality rate from 95 in 1998 to 50 per 1,000 live births by 2015

Target 4.3: Increasing the proportion of children under 1 year immunised against measles from 41.4 per cent in 2000 to 90 per cent by 2015

Target 4.4: Increasing the proportion of children aged 6–59 months receiving Vitamin A capsules from 28 per cent in 2000 to 90 per cent by 2015

Target 4.5: Increasing the proportion of children under 1 year immunised against DPT3 from 43 per cent in 2000 to 90 per cent by 2015

Target 4.6: Increasing the proportion of infants exclusively breastfed up to 6 months of age from 11.4 per cent in 2000 to 49 per cent in 2015

Target 4.7: Increasing the proportion of mothers who start breast-feeding newborn child within 1 hour of birth from 11 per cent in 2000 to 62 per cent in 2015

CMDG 5: Improve maternal health

Overall target 10: Reduce the maternal mortality ratio

Target 5.1: Reducing the maternal mortality ratio from 437 in 1997 to 140 per 100,000 live births in 2015

Target 5.2: Reducing the total fertility rate from 4 in 1998 to 3 in 2015

Target 5.3: Increasing the proportion of births attended by skilled health personnel from 32 per cent in 2000 to 80 per cent in 2015

Target 5.4: Increasing the proportion of married women using modern birth spacing methods from 18.5 per cent in 2000 to 60 per cent by 2015

Target 5.5: Increasing the percentage of pregnant women with 2 or more ANC consultations from skilled health personnel from 30.5 per cent in 2000 to 90 per cent in 2015

Target 5.6: Reducing the proportion of pregnant women with Iron Deficiency Anaemia from 66 per cent in 2000 to 33 per cent in 2015

Target 5.7: Decreasing the proportion of women aged 15–49 with BMI<18.5Kg/Sq. meter from 21 per cent in 2000 to 8 per cent in 2015

Target 5.8: Decreasing the proportion of women aged 15–49 with Iron Deficiency Anaemia from 58 per cent in 2000 to 19 per cent in 2015

Target 5.9: Increasing the proportion of pregnant women who delivered by Caesarean Section from 0.8 per cent in 2000 to 4 per cent in 2015

CMDG 6: Combat HIV/AIDS, malaria and other diseases

Overall target 11: Decreasing the spread of HIV/AIDS

Target 6.1: Reducing HIV prevalence rate among adults aged 15–49 from 2.6 per cent in 2002 to 1.8 per cent in 2015

Target 6.2: Reducing the HIV prevalence rate among pregnant women aged 15–24 visiting ANC from 2.7 per cent in 2002 to 1.5 per cent in 2015

Target 6.3: Increasing the condom use rate among commercial sex workers during last commercial sexual intercourse from 91 per cent in 2002 to 98 per cent in 2005

Target 6.4: Increasing the percentage of young people aged 15–24 reporting the use of a condom during sexual intercourse with a non-regular sexual partner from 82 per cent in 2002 to 95 per cent in 2015

Target 6.5: Increasing the proportion of condom use reported by married women who identified themselves at risk from 1 per cent in 2000 to 10 per cent in 2015

Target 6.6: Increasing the percentage of HIV infected pregnant women attending ANC receiving a complete course of antiretroviral prophylaxis to reduce the risk of MTCT from 2.7 per cent in 2002 to 50 per cent in 2015

Target 6.7: Increasing the percentage of people with advanced HIV infection receiving antiretroviral combination therapy from 3 per cent in 2002 to 75 per cent in 2015

Overall target 12: Decreasing the spread of malaria, DF and TB

Target 6.8: Decreasing the malaria case fatality rate reported by public health sector from 0.4 per cent in 2000 to 0.1 per cent in 2015

Target 6.9: Increasing the proportion of population at high risk who slept under insecticide-treated bed nets during the previous night from 57 per cent in 2002 to 98 per cent in 2015

Target 6.10: Decreasing the number of malaria cases treated in the public health sector per 1000 population from 11.4 in 2000 to 4.0 in 2015

Target 6.11: Increasing the proportion of public health facilities able to confirm malaria diagnosis according to national guidelines with 95 per cent accuracy from 60 per cent in 2002 to 95 per cent in 2015

Target 6.12: Decreasing the number of dengue cases treated in the public health sector per 1000 population from 1 in 2001 to 0.4 in 2015

Target 6.13: Decreasing the dengue case fatality rate reported by public health facilities from 1.5 per cent in 2003 to 0.3 per cent in 2015

Target 6.14: Decreasing the prevalence of smear-positive TB per 100,000 population from 428 in 1997 to 135 in 2015

Target 6.15: Decreasing the TB death rate per 100,000 population from 90 in 1997 to 32 in 2015

Target 6.16: Increasing the proportion of all estimated new smear-positive TB cases detected under DOTS from 57 per cent in 2002 to more than 70 per cent in 2010 and 2015

Target 6.17: Maintaining the proportion of registered smear-positive TB cases successfully treated under DOTS above 85 per cent through 2005

CMDG 7: Ensure environmental sustainability

Overall target 13: Integrate the principles of sustainable development into country policies and programmes and reverse the loss of environmental resources

Target 7.1: Maintaining forest coverage at the 2000 level of 60 per cent of total land area through 2015

Target 7.2: Maintaining the surface of 23 protected areas at the 1993 level of 3.3 million ha through 2015

Target 7.3: Maintaining the surface of 6 new forest-protected area at the present level of 1.35 million ha through 2015

Target 7.4: Increasing the number of rangers in protected areas from 600 in 2001 to 1,200 by 2015

Target 7.5: Maintaining the number of rangers in forest protected areas at the level of 500 through 2015

Target 7.6: Increasing the proportion of fishing lots released to local communities from 56 per cent in 1998 to 60 per cent in 2015

Target 7.7: Increasing the number of community-based fisheries from 264 in 2000 to 589 in 2015

Target 7.8: Increasing the surface of fish sanctuaries from 264,500 ha in 2000 to 580,800 ha in 2015

Target 7.9: Reducing the fuel wood dependency from 92 per cent of households in 1993 to 52 per cent in 2015

Overall target 14: Halve by 2015 the proportion of people without sustainable access to safe drinking water

Target 7.10: Increasing the proportion of rural population with access to safe water source from 24 per cent in 1998 to 50 per cent in 2015

Target 7.11: Increasing the proportion of urban population with access to safe water source from 60 per cent in 1998 to 80 per cent in 2015

Overall target 15: Halve by 2015 the proportion of people without sustainable access to improved sanitation

Target 7.12: Increasing the proportion of rural population with access to improved sanitation from 8.6 per cent in 1996 to 30 per cent in 2015

Target 7.13: Increasing the proportion of urban population with access to improved sanitation from 49 per cent in 1998 to 74 per cent in 2015

Overall target 16: Increase the proportion of the population in both urban and rural areas with access to land security by 2015

Target 7.14: Increase the percentage of land parcels having titles in both urban and rural areas from 15 per cent in 2000 to 65 per cent in 2015

CMDG 8: Forge a global partnership for development

Overall target 17: Develop further an open, rule-based, predictable, non-discriminatory trading and financial system

Indicator 8.1: Net ODA as percentage of DAC donors' GNI [targets of 0.7 per cent in total and 0.15 per cent for LDCs]

Indicator 8.2: Proportion of ODA to basic social services (basic education, primary health care, nutrition, safe water and sanitation)

Overall target 18: Address the Special Needs of the Least Developed Countries

Indicator 8.3: Proportion of ODA that is untied

Indicator 8.4: Proportion of ODA for environment in small island developing states

Indicator 8.5: Proportion of ODA for transport sector in land-locked countries

Indicator 8.6: Proportion of exports (by value and excluding arms) admitted free of duties and quotas

Indicator 8.7: Average tariffs and quotas on agricultural products and textiles and clothing

Overall target 19: Address the Special Needs of landlocked countries and small island developing states

Indicator 8.8: Domestic and export agricultural subsidies in OECD countries

Indicator 8.9: Proportion of ODA provided to help build trade capacity

Overall target 20: Deal comprehensively with the debt problems of developing countries through national and international measures in order to make debt sustainable in the long term

Indicator 8.10: Proportion of official bilateral HIPC debt cancelled

Indicator 8.11: Debt service as a percentage of exports of goods and services

Indicator 8.12: Proportion of ODA provided as debt relief

Indicator 8.13: Number of countries reaching HIPC decision and completion points

Overall target 21: In cooperation with developing countries, develop and implement strategies for decent and productive work for youth

Indicator 8.14: Unemployment rate of 15–24 year old

Overall target 22: In cooperation with pharmaceutical companies, provide access to affordable, essential drugs in developing countries

Indicator 8.15: Proportion of population with access to affordable essential drugs on a sustainable basis

Overall target 23: In cooperation with the private sector, make available the benefits of new technologies, especially information and communications

Indicator 8.16: Telephone lines per 1000 people

Indicator 8.17: Personal computers per 1000 people

Cambodia MDG9: De-mining, UXO and Victim Assistance

Overall target 24: Moving towards zero impact from landmines and UXOs by 2012

Target 9.1: Reduce the annual number of civilian casualties recorded to 0 by 2012

Target 9.2: Clear completely all high/medium/low suspected contaminated areas by 2012

Overall target 25: Eliminate the negative humanitarian and socio-economic impacts of landmines and UXOs by 2025

Target 9.3: Develop a comprehensive victim assistance framework by 2005 and fully implement it.

Target 9.4: Increase the numbers of Landmine/UXO victims receiving an assistance package and integrated into the society (to be set).

Source: (UNDP, 2007b).

6
Achieving the MDGs in Solomon Islands: Development Goals in a Post-Conflict Environment

1   Introduction

The Solomon Islands is located in the Pacific Ocean and comprises approximately 1,000 islands. Whilst 300 of these islands are populated, 80 percent of the country's 533,000 people live on a small number of larger islands (including Guadalcanal, Choiseul, Santa Isabel, Malaita, San Cristobal and New Georgia). These larger islands are mountainous, and thickly forested, occasionally skirted by thin coastal plains that provide fertile but limited agricultural land (less than one percent of land is presently under cultivation). The total land area is 28,370 km^2 whereas the total sea area of Solomon Islands is 1.35 million km^2. The Solomon Islands is the third largest archipelago in the South Pacific. The vast majority of the population are Melanesian who settled the islands over 3,000 years ago, but over 100 languages are spoken throughout the country. English is the official language, however most people use Pidgin to communicate with those from other language groups.

Progress in Solomon Islands has stalled in recent years due to recent civil unrest. This civil strife, roughly drawn along ethnic lines, has disrupted the achievement of the MDGs quite considerably with the government being unable to function in an effective manner during this time, thereby disrupting the provision of education, health and other social services throughout the country. Non-governmental organisations (NGOs) in Solomon Islands have played an important role as alternative providers of social services in the absence of a functioning public sector. Regional mediation (led by Australia and New Zealand) has recently brought some stability to Solomon Islands and provided substantial aid cooperation in the form of the Regional Assistance

Mission to Solomon Islands (RAMSI). However, the purpose of this large-scale intervention has been the achievement of improved governance and peace rather than the achievement of the MDGs.

Progress towards the achievement of the MDGs in Solomon Islands is difficult to assess. Apart from the general lack of data available on overall development indicators within Solomon Islands, there is a distinct lack of data that can be utilised to assess the extent of progress towards the achievement of the MDGs. This data constraint is recognised within official documents – see SIG, 2005b; ADB, 2005b; IMF, 2005. For example, no national accounts have been produced since 1994. Data on income, education, health, water and sanitation and other targets are, by and large, outdated, incomplete or insufficiently disaggregated for any proper analysis. What is known though is that the majority of Solomon Islanders live in rural areas, with very limited access to education, health or other social services, are serviced by poor or non-existent transport infrastructure, and live subsistence lifestyles. According to the UNDP (2006), the Solomon Islands is one of the least developed countries within the Pacific. Further, given the contracting economy, low school enrolment rates, poor gender equality and poor environmental indicators, it is reasonable to assume that it is unlikely that the Solomon Islands will achieve its MDG targets. So 'although data are insufficient to update ...(the) MDG indicators, social conditions have almost certainly worsened over the period of ethnic tension and conflict, and disparities between Honiara and the provinces are wide' (UNDP, 2006, p.1). The recent civil strife has further diminished what little government services existed.

Recent governments have initiated development plans that seek to revive the economic and social development of Solomon Islands. This paper will review how these policies address the MDGs and whether it is likely if these policies (if implemented) will positively impact on achievement of the MDG targets throughout the islands.

This chapter is set out as follows: Section 2 briefly describes the current political and economic situation in the Solomon Islands with an emphasis on the recent period of civil strife and the response to that civil strife in the form of RAMSI – an understanding of both is central to understanding development in Solomon Islands. Section 3 focuses specifically on describing the state of progress and the achievement of the MDGs. This is made difficult because of significant data constraints. A description of how the MDGs can be incorporated into poverty reduction strategies is undertaken in section 4. Section 5 describes the role that aid and NGOs can have in assisting in the achievement the MDGs in Solomon Islands, before the chapter concludes with section 6 which includes some policy recommendations addressing how the MDGs might be modified and contextualised for post-conflict environments.

2   Overview of Solomon Islands

Great Britain granted independence to Solomon Islands in 1978. Since that time, the Solomon Islands has been negatively affected by political instability and more recently civil unrest, with sixteen different governments (including nine different Prime Ministers). For example, in April 2006, Mr Snyder Rini was elected Prime Minister, only to be replaced by Mr Manasseh Sogavare in May, 2006. In December 2007, a new Prime Minister was elected – Mr Derek Sikua. Throughout this period, successive governments have been accused of corruption and the misuse of public office (UN, 2002). As a result, there has been low levels of public confidence in all government institutions since their inception around thirty years ago (Roughan, 2004). Resentment towards successive governments is also linked to the perceived hoarding of power and influence to the capital city of Honiara, located in Guadalcanal Province. Public sentiment holds that resources are being removed from all other provinces and being invested in infrastructure and facilities in Honiara rather then being redistributed amongst the poor provinces. Successive governments have also been accused of fiscal irresponsibility through the inefficient monitoring of log exports resulting in the failure to capture potential revenue via duties and other taxes and the provision of tax exemptions and duty remissions to various individuals and firms (UN, 2002; ADB, 2004b; Allen, 2005).

So whilst the Solomon Islands has been a nation for 30 years, these continuing political failings have exacerbated a lack of nationalism that itself fuelled the recent civil unrest. Nationalism within Solomon Islands is limited as 'most people carry with them competing clan, island, province and nation identities – in that order' (UN, 2002, p.x). Basic allegiances remain to the family and clan, not to the nation (Mamaloni, 1985; Jourdan, 1995; Moore, 2004; Kabutaulaka, 2005).

Political instability and perceived corruption in conjunction with this lack of a strong unifying sense of nationhood led to long-held ethnic-based rivalries and tensions to transform into bloody civil strife that lasted between 1999 and 2003 but continues to simmer to the present day. Understanding Solomon Islands' progress (or lack thereof) to the MDGs can only be properly understood in the light of this period of civil strife.

The civil strife

The direct impact on achieving the MDGs of the civil strife was the immediate disintegration of law and order and the near cessation of the provision of government services that followed. Thus, the period between 1999 and 2003, although relatively short, should not be understated when discussing the current social and economic circumstances of the Solomon Islands and its present development plans. While the immediate events leading to the period of civil strife are clearly identified, it must be understood that they were just symptoms of underlying causes that have a longer history (see Bennett, 2002; Moore, 2004; Kabutaulaka, 2001, 2002 and Dinnen, 2003 for additional analysis of the civil strife). Central to both the longer smouldering of tension and then incendiary of violence is that of resource ownership and resource use. 'The underlying causes derive from a linkage between poverty, resources, and governance. A poverty of resources caused some to seek opportunities elsewhere. The host landowners became resentful at the numbers of settler relatives who followed and were also upset at the failure of Government to channel to them a fair share of the benefits accruing from large-scale developments on their islands' (UN, 2002, p.xii).

The formal economy is largely centred in the capital city of Honiara (located in Guadalcanal Island) in which around only 10 per cent of the total population resides. There has been a migration from other provinces to Guadalcanal over time as Solomon Islanders seek to participate in the formal economy. Following this relocation of many non-Guadalcanlians from neighbouring provinces (particularly Malaitans), pressure on land resources occasionally resulted in violence. This pressure came to a head in mid-1998 when the provincial Premier of Guadalcanal demanded government compensation for the deaths of 25 Guadalcanal people murdered over the previous 20 years by various Malaitans. Prime Minister Bartholomew Ulufa'alu, himself a Malaitan, paid the compensation (but withheld a corresponding amount from grants paid to the Guadalcanal Province). Almost immediately, Guadalcanal youth took up arms and began harassing, raping and assaulting Malaitans killing at least 28 people by 1999.

Two opposing forces were formed along ethnic lines: the Isatabu Freedom Movement (IFM) made up of Guadalcanalians and the Malaitian Eagle Force (MEF). The violence between both sides (including the involvement of innocent bystanders) was severe and included arson, pack-rapes, and beheadings (Moore, 2004). Over 20,000 people fled the violence in Honiara to their home provinces, including many educated and senior bureaucrats (again adding to the disintegration of government services). Following a number of failed attempts of mediation, the MEF marched on Parliament in November 1999 demanding compensation for the damages suffered by Malaitans. This claim was denied and violence escalated. Violence continued until October 2000 when a peace agreement was reached in Townsville, Australia. Whilst peace was reached formally between the IFM and MEF, there was little disarmament and harassment and violence continued – often in more rural areas (Moore, 2004; Kabutaulaka, 2005). The civil strife had serious consequences for the country as a whole. 'It was a situation in which state structures never completely collapsed but were subverted and utilised to serve the interest of a self-defined and privileged few. Some people in the government, the police and the public service in general increasingly cultivated cliental relationships, used state institutions to serve their interest, and extorted money from the state coffers' (Kabutaulaka, 2005, p.292). While the civil strife and violence was centred in Honiara, a general breakdown of law and order occurred in other provinces and rural areas as well. Not unsurprisingly, economic growth was negative during this time, with the economy contracting by 14 per cent in 2000 and another ten per cent in 2001. This state of decay and collapse continued until the Australian-led Regional Assistance Mission to the Solomon Islands (RAMSI) was implemented in July 2003.

The RAMSI intervention was seen as a pivotal point in re-establishing opportunities for economic development in the Solomon Islands. Also, 'without restoring law and order and re-establishing a secure and safe environment for people in the country, it would be difficult for progress to be made in other aspects of development' (SIG, 2005b, p.64). Fearful that the Solomon Islands may become a failed state, the initial purpose of the RAMSI intervention was to restore and strengthen (but not replace) existing government institutions (Moore, 2004; Kabutaulaka, 2005). Australia, New Zealand and other Pacific countries initially deployed over 2,000 public servants and armed police and defence force personnel with the express purpose of restoring law and order. Almost immediately, 2,500 weapons and 300,000 rounds of ammunition were either voluntarily handed-in or confiscated. This immediate success quickly resulted in the reduction of armed personnel being replaced by a police presence. However, this did not fundamentally change the focus of RAMSI away from restoring and maintaining law and order. As such, the Solomon Islands' largest aid intervention remains only indirectly related to the achievement of the MDGs. There has also been assessment of RAMSI to coincide with the fifth anniversary of its inception with some critics suggesting that despite its success in re-establishing security and improving macroeconomic stability, it has failed to materially improve living standards for the rural population (which accounts for 80 per cent of the total population) (Sodhi, 2008).

The economy

Solomon Islands' economy faces several constraints that impact on the achievement of the MDGs. These constraints include it's: 1) remoteness; 2) susceptibility to natural disasters; 3) low institutional capacity; 4) limited diversification of economic activity; and 5) poor access to capital and investment (ADB, 2005b). Solomon Islands' economy primarily consists of three productive sectors: forestry, fishing and agriculture. The forestry sector accounts for roughly 7 per cent of GDP, but relies on unsustainable harvesting. Current harvesting is five times the sustainable yield of about 200,000 m^3 (SIG 2005b) and it is estimated that current logging rates will exhaust natural forests by 2015 (IMF, 2005). Much of this natural resource has now been destroyed and future income from this sector is unlikely (see PDP Australia, 1991 for an early warning of this expectant resource loss). The fisheries sector though is more sustainable. It presently accounts for nearly ten per cent of GDP and nearly twenty per cent of total exports. However, non-Solomon Island fishers catch the vast majority of fish caught within the Solomon Islands. Indeed, Solomon Islanders land just over ten per cent of fish caught each year (UN, 2002). The agricultural sector accounts for around 5 per cent of GDP but its economic and social significance is far greater as more than 80 per cent of the population relies on subsistence agriculture for its livelihoods.

There has been long held pessimism about how Solomon Islands might develop and secure its economic development which is necessary in underwriting interventions required to achieve the MDGs. Consider for example these two pessimistic assessments made over 25 years ago: 'Taken together, and on the basis of present knowledge and available technology, the size and locational disadvantages of the smaller Pacific developing countries place them in a position where those with a mainly agricultural base appear to have no hope of achieving independence of aid at a level of incomes commensurate with the aspirations of their peoples' (Fisk, 1982, p.33) and 'given the severe physical and human resource constraints..., and the problems created by dispersion and small size, it is doubtful whether [continued real income growth] is a realistic objective, except in conditions of increasing dependence on foreign aid, not simply for capital investment, but also for direct support of higher consumption levels of both private and government provided goods and services' (Castle, 1980, p.135). Skills shortages have negatively impacted upon Solomon Islands' growth as has inflationary pressures brought about by past governments fiscal imbalances.

To overcome these structural issues and constraints, the Solomon Islands must:

- Establish stability in the political security and law and order spheres;
- Seek to secure stable aid flows in a volatile aid environment to assist with continuing investment;
- Establish land tenure;
- Promote export diversification; and
- Enhance educational attainment and skill of labour (Gounder and Xayavong, 2001, p.16).

It is difficult to predict short-term economic growth levels in the Solomon Islands. There are two major forces that are simultaneously driving and inhibiting economic growth. The introduction and implementation of new legislation to reduce logging rates to sustainable levels will contract economic growth. Much of Solomon Islands' economic activity to date has resulted from this unsustainable activity and therefore any reduction in logging will be seen in reduced economic growth rates (IMF, 2005). However, this contraction may be compensated from gains in economic activity associated with the general benefits associated with improved law and order, ongoing structural reforms, and restarting of economic activities disrupted by the civil-strife, all made possible through RAMSI and normalisation of societal relations (ADB, 2005a). If economic growth does not continue at levels greater than the population rate (presently around 3 per cent per annum), then living standards will stagnate or fall. Given that much of this economic growth (and its associated benefits) are centred on a narrow population base within urban centres, those on the rural areas remain at risk of becoming entrenched within (chronic) poverty.

3   MDGs and Progress: Limited Indicators (tell a limited story)

The headline goal of the MDGs is eradicating extreme poverty and hunger. Yet, it is very difficult to clearly identify the poor because, like many Pacific nations, data constraints hinder accurate assessment of poverty eradication within the Solomon Islands (Feeny and Clarke,

2008; Moore, 2004; ADB, 2005b). The recent civil strife has exacerbated this data constraint. Solomon Islanders have undeniably poor well-being, ranking near the lowest in the Human Development Index (HDI) amongst all Pacific nations. Indeed, its HDI ranking has fallen in recent years and it is now ranked 129 (out of 177 nations). While Solomon Islands as a whole is considered to be a country of high need, there is a striking difference in circumstances between provinces, but also within provinces (ADB, 2005b). Considerable inequality exists within the Solomon Islands, with a clear demarcation between the livelihoods experienced in the urban areas compared to those in rural areas (SIG, 2005b). Research in the early 1990s indicated that urban households had incomes almost four times as high as rural households. More recent household income and expenditure surveys indicate per capita expenditure is more than 3.5 times greater in the capital city of Honiara than in some rural provinces (SISO, 2006a, 2006b). 'As with every aspect of the country's development there has been a focus on the capital and lesser urban areas to the detriment of the wider rural community' (UN 2002, p.xii).

The Solomon Islands Development Trust (Roughan, 2004) has more recently, reported that despite improvements in law and order (which are significant), the living standards of the rural poor have not improved since the arrival of RAMSI. For example, the Central Hospital in Honiara receives just under one-third of the country's health budget, and services just 15% of the country's population. 'For the 85 per cent of the population living in villages, hardship appears to have increased as cash income generation has been outpaced by rising costs of basic goods and services such as salt, rice, soap, kerosene, school fees, and ship transport (ADB, 2005a, p.218). Thus, it is arguable that the economic benefits emanating from the recent economic growth have yet to benefit the majority of Solomon Islanders and the majority of non-urban population are chronically poor. Yet, having noted this, unlike many other Pacific countries, the Solomon Islands is well endowed with natural resources (PDP Australia, 1991) and thus some hope must be held that it is possible to address and overcome this situation. Of course, by what criteria the effectiveness of RAMSI should be judged is contentious (see ADB, 2005b; Sodhi, 2008 and Oxfam, 2006a for alternative views).

The MDGs and Social Development

It is likely that Solomon Islands will not achieve the MDGs (ADB, 2003) (see Table 6.1). As discussed, in terms of the first goal – Eradicate

Extreme Poverty and Hunger – there are no official data on poverty within Solomon Islands. There are also no data on the proportion of the population below US$1 per day (PPP values in %), poverty gap ratio, or share of the poorest quintile in national consumption. The prevalence of child malnutrition has halved, from 23.0 per cent to 11.0 per cent from 1989 to 2000, suggesting that the second target of the first

Table 6.1   Solomon Islands Progress Toward the Millennium Development Goals and Targets

	1990	2000	2002–03	Target for 2015
Goal 1: Eradicate Extreme Poverty and Hunger				
Prevalence of child malnutrition (per cent of children under five)	23	21	...	11
Goal 2: Achieve Universal Primary Education				
Net enrolment ratio in primary education	39	74	79	100
Goal 3: Promote Gender Equality				
Ratio of girls to boys in primary education (per cent)	81	86	...	100
Ratio of girls to boys in secondary education (per cent)	58	70	...	100
Proportion of seats held by women in national parliament (per cent)	...	2	0	...
Goal 4: Reduce Child Mortality				
Under five mortality rate (per 1,000)	36	30	22	12
Infant mortality rate (per 1,000 live births)	76	68	19	29
Goal 5: Improve Maternal Health				
Maternal mortality ratio (per 100,000 live births)	...	130	...	...
Births attended by skilled health staff (per cent of total)	...	...	87	...
Goal 6: Combat HIV/AIDS, Malaria and Other Diseases				
Incidence of tuberculosis (per 100,000 people)	392	89	60	...
Incidence of malaria (per 100,000 people)	45,000	15,172	19,600	Less than 8,000

Table 6.1   Solomon Islands Progress Toward the Millennium Development Goals and Targets – *continued*

	1990	2000	2002–03	Target for 2015
Goal 7: Ensure Environmental Sustainability				
Forest area (per cent of total land area)	92	90.6	87	…
Nationally protected areas (per cent of total land area)	…	0	1.3	…
CO2 emissions (metric tons per capita)	0.5	0.4	…	…
Access to an improved water source (per cent of population)	…	71	70	100
Access to improved sanitation (per cent of population)	…	30	…	…
Goal 8: Develop a Global Partnership for Development				
Fixed line and mobile telephones (per 1,000 people)	16	…	19	…
Personal computers (per 1,000 people)	…	25	44	…

Source: ADB 2005b.

goal will be achieved. However, it appears very unlikely that the second goal of attaining universal primary education will be achieved with net enrolments actually falling from 83.3 per cent in 1990 to 66.0 per cent in 2001. Goal three – promoting gender equality – also seems unlikely to be achieved. Whilst there has been some improvement in the ratio of boys to girls in primary education, improvements in secondary enrolments are marginal, literacy data is unavailable and there are no female members in the national Parliament. MDGs 4 and 5 (child mortality and maternal health) are more likely to be achieved with strong improvements in under-five mortality and maternal mortality ratios. Data for HIV/AIDS and other infectious diseases – for goal 6 – are limited, as are data for goal 7 around environmental sustainability.

Despite increases in government spending on health (from 3.8 per cent of GDP in 1994 to 5.9 per cent in 2001), the ratio of population to doctors has worsened, increasing about one-third from 6,355 to 9,513 (in 1999). However, life expectancy has increased just over ten years, from 54.6 years in 1986 to 65.4 years in 2002 (female life expectancy is greater than male life expectancy – 67.4 years compared to 63.6 years).

Data on education are not available beyond 1999. Yet, notwithstanding this constraint, significant improvements in both male and female literacy were achieved over the period 1991 to 1999. Total adult literacy increased from 22 per cent to 76.6 per cent, with female literacy increasing from 17.0 to 69.0 per cent and male literacy increasing from 27 per cent to 83.7 per cent. However, as previously noted, primary enrolments have recently decreased. Urbanisation has increased from 13.0 per cent of the population in 1986 to 20.8 per cent in 2002. Access to electricity is less than ten per cent in rural areas and access to telecommunications (mobile and fixed line) and internet services are also low in absolute terms.

However, some consideration needs also to be given to the relevance of all the MDGs to Solomon Islands. It may be that the first (and headline) indicator – poverty eradication – is not entirely relevant. Many Pacific countries, including Solomon Islands, prefer the term 'hardship' to poverty. Social networks often prevent hunger and outright destitution (World Bank, 1991; IMF, 2005). 'There is a social understanding in this community: nobody goes short of food; there's always somewhere to stay; the old and young are looked after; and the mentally ill, the disabled and the chronically sick are looked after' (Webber, 1985, p.45). Thus, the nature of poverty often relates to a lack of access to basic services and a lack of income earning opportunities. The ADB has recently sponsored Participatory Assessments of Hardship (PAH) among communities in a number of Pacific countries. Results from these assessments indicate that poverty and hardship in Pacific countries are defined as 'inadequate levels of sustainable human development through access to essential public goods and services and access to income opportunities' (Abbot and Pollard, 2004, p.xi). Within Solomon Islands specifically, poverty is considered a lack of land and sea resources.

Access to basic services, such as clean water, education, health and shelter dissipates as one moves away from the urban or semi-urban settlements. For example, more than 85 per cent of housing in urban areas is permanent, but only around one-fifth of housing is permanent in rural areas. Likewise, access to education and health services, employment opportunities, and peace-building campaigns are all biased towards the urban areas, particularly Honiara (SIG, 2005b; UN, 2002).

Provincial comparisons

Following the cessation of hostilities, a household income and expenditure survey was conducted in 2005 across all Provinces (SISO, 2006a, 2006b). Whilst limited, it does allow some disaggregated analysis of the standard of development experienced between regions but not on specific MDG achievement.

Achievement of the MDGs is complicated by the high population growth across all of Solomon Islands, which has averaged around 4 per cent per annum over the past 15 years. Total population has increased from 315,000 in 1990 to an estimated 533,000 in 2005, however the reliability of this data is questionable as the last census was taken in 1999 and the next planned census will be 2009. These intermediate projections are based on household income and expenditure survey undertaken in 2005/6 (SISO, 2006a and 2006b). Some provinces, notably Rennell-Bellona, Malatia and Choisel had even greater levels of growth (see Table 6.2). Malaita, Guadalcanal and Western provinces have the largest populations – 26, 15 and 15 per cent of the total respectively whilst Rennell-Bellona is the smallest with less than one per cent of the total population. The township of Honiara is itself considered a province (it is located on Guadalcanal Island) and has 13 per cent of the total population. Perhaps more notably, over 80 per cent of Solomon's Islands urban population reside in Honiara. Thus, there are only very small urban populations spread throughout the remaining nine provinces. Household size has remained relatively unchanged of between six to seven people per dwelling since the mid-1980s. Population density has increased in recent years and is around 20 people per km^2.

Honiara has the highest average per capita expenditure amongst all provinces of US$1,200 which is more than 3.5 times the lowest average

Table 6.2   Solomon Islands Estimated Population and Population Growth by Province, 1999–2005

	Population in 2005	Per cent of total	Population in 1999	Annual growth % (1999–2005)
Choiseul	31,329	5.86	20,008	7.4
Western	81,852	15.34	62,739	4.4
Isabel	23,638	4.43	20,421	2.4
Central	24,491	4.59	21,577	2.1
Rennell-Bellona	4,409	0.83	2,377	10.3
Guadalcanal	84,438	15.82	60,275	5.6
Malatia	140,569	26.34	122,620	2.3
Makira	50,026	9.37	31,006	8.0
Temoto	23,800	4.46	18,912	3.8
Honiara	69,189	12.96	49,107	5.7
Total	533,672	100.00	409,042	4.4

Source: SISO (2006a, 2006b).

per capita expenditure of US$320 in Temotu. Isabel has the lowest estimated inequality based on household expenditure with a Gini co-efficient of 0.260 compared to the most unequal province of Rennell-Bellona with a Gini co-efficient of 0.463.

Considering non-income indicators of development, 90 per cent of homes in Temotu have used traditional (thatched) materials for housing construction compared to just 11 per cent in Rennell-Bellona. While 43 per cent of households in Honiara use open fires as their main source of energy for cooking, the range for the rest of the Solomon Islands is between 98 per cent in Temotu and Choiseul to 83 per cent in Western. While 63 per cent of households in Honiara use electricity as their main energy source for lighting, Western is the only other province that has reasonable access (21 per cent) to this energy source. The main alternative energy source for lighting is kerosene which 92 per cent of households in Central use. Seventy per cent of house-holds in Honiara can access private piped water for cooking and drink-ing, but this compares to Rennell-Bellona which has no piped water at all and in which 81 per cent of households rely on rainwater tanks. In terms of sanitation, 58 per cent and 22 per cent of households in Honiara and Western respectively have access to private flush septic tank toilets, whereas less than one per cent of the population in Choiseul have such access with nearly 90 per cent using the sea or other water bodies for their sanitation.

Using SIG and UNDP (2002), some limited intra-spatial analysis using the HDI measure of development is possible (see Table 6.3). It should be noted that the data constraints have resulted in GDP per capita being held constant across all provinces. This means that the scores for the poor provinces are higher than they should be and the scores for richer provinces are lower than they should be, minimising the differences between provinces. Malaita, Guadalcanal, Temotu and Central provinces each had lower scores than the national average, whereas, Honiara Central and Western, Choiseul, Makira, Rennell-Bellona and Isabel provinces each had scores higher than the national average. The SIG and UNDP (2002) report also calculates a number of variations of the HDI, including the Human Poverty Index, and Gender-related Development Index all of which roughly rank Malaita and Guadalcanal as the least performing provinces and Honiara Central and Western and Choiseul provinces as the better performing areas". The absolute poverty of data is no more evident than in this situation. No more recent disaggregated HDI data for Solomon Islands is available than from 1999. Interestingly though, the Gender Empowerment Meas-ure, which includes the percentage share of women in parliament,

Table 6.3 Human Development Index for Solomon Islands Provinces – 1999

	Life Expect. at birth	Adult Literacy	Enrolment aged 5–19	GDP pc 1999 prices	GDP Index	HDI
National, 1999	**61.1**	**76.6**	**56.3**	**863**	**0.360**	**0.553**
National, 1986	**54.6**	**48.8**	**34.8**	**701**	**0.325**	**0.420**
Honiara	62.8	90.5	67.6	863	0.360	0.606
Western	61.6	94.0	65.4	863	0.360	0.605
Choiseul	61.6	92.2	63.4	863	0.360	0.599
Makira	61.9	81.0	65.2	863	0.360	0.577
Rennell Bellona	62.1	73.9	72.4	863	0.360	0.571
Isabel	60.4	75.2	66.2	863	0.360	0.557
Central	62.1	72.0	56.6	863	0.360	0.549
Temotu	62.6	60.6	61.5	863	0.360	0.532
Guadalcanal	60.7	73.1	41.1	863	0.360	0.526
Malaita	61.1	61.4	49.1	863	0.360	0.511

Source: SIG and UNDP (2002).

administrative and managerial employment, professional and technical employment and those women who are economically active, ranks Guadalcanal and Malaita provinces higher than in the other indices and Choiseul Province lower. Honiara Central is the best performing location for this measure.

It is certainly not possible to assess achievement of the MDGs either spatially or inter-temporally with any certainty using this data. Additional resources must be made available to collect data that can be used to properly assess progress within Solomon Islands across time and regions. Without this proper analysis, policies designed to improve the circumstances of these poor are in grave danger of failing.

4   Improving MDG outcomes

Progress towards the achievement of MDG in Solomon Islands can only be understood in the light of the recent period of civil unrest. Within this context, the MDGs as they currently stand may have less relevance for a country operating within a post-conflict environment. Indeed, given this post-conflict environment, it is perhaps understandable that Solomon Islands have not explicitly focussed on achieving the MDGs within their development plans. However, SIG has established a *poverty partnership* with the ADB. The focus of this poverty partnership is to increase economic growth, improve governance, increase public sector performance, enhance private sector development, reverse environmental degradation, increase gender equity and reduce vulnerability to external economic shocks and natural disasters (ADB, 1999, 2000). Solomon Island's recent conflict, ethnic tension, internal displacement, unstable government, financial crisis, high population growth and economic contraction has only served to hamper efforts to improve the lives of the poor.

Successive Solomon Island governments have released a number of development plans since its independence. The first National Development Plan for 1975–1978 stated its goals as 'changing fundamentally the aims and content of education, increasing attention to production and marketing of foodstuffs, progressively reducing foreign aid, introducing local currency with banking and currency controls, developing alternative energy sources, and broadening and strengthening the export trade base' (cited in Rofeta, 1985, p.95). More recently there has been a rush of development plans, including the *National Economic Recovery, Reform and Development Plan*, the *Vision 2020: A Brighter Future for Solomon Islands Statement*, and the *Grand Coalition for Change Policy Document Framework*. Within this fragile post-civil strife environment, it appears easier for governments to announce policies rather than implement them. However, as these various plans are not widely dissimilar they can be analysed as a suite of common poverty reduction strategies. In fact, the National Economic Recovery, Reform and Development Plan (NERRDP) for 2003–2006 can be considered the origin of these recent poverty strategies. The 'preparation of NERRDP involved extensive consultations within the government, with provincial governments, development partners, non-government organisations, the private sector and National Parliamentarians and Ministers and Premiers of the provinces' (SIG, 2006b, p.44). The ADB's Country Strategy and Program (CSP) incorporated the NERRDP into its planning and so all present and future ADB assistance to the Solomon Islands are guided by the principals set out in it. There is therefore close symmetry between these documents and the ADB CSP (ADB, 2004b; ADB, 2006b). The 'overall objective of national policies and plans is to improve living standards and quality of life (SIG, 2005b, p.4). The NERRDP has five specific goals, including: 1) normalizing law and order; 2) strengthening democracy and good governance; 3) restoring fiscal and financial stability and reforming public service; 4) revitalising productive sector and rebuilding infrastructure; and 5) restoring basic social services and fostering social development (SIG, 2005b). The enlarged brief given to RAMSI after it had secured improved law and order and normalisation of government functions are in line with these goals. RAMSI's role now includes focussing on: 1) ending corruption within the public sector, including the police force; 2) restoring collapsed infrastructure in both urban and rural areas; 3) capacity building within the public sector; 4) privatisation of State Owned Enterprises (SOEs); 5) land tenure reforms; 6) increasing private investment; and 7) economic rehabilitation (Moore, 2004).

The recommended reforms that result from these poverty reduction strategies all centre around three core themes: (i) improving productivity in various sectors; (ii) improving infrastructure; and (iii) improving the management of service delivery to communities. These are discussed in turn.

Improving productivity in various sectors

Enhancing the business environment in the Solomon Islands is vital as the private sector will be central in achieving economic growth in the future. Such a focus on the private sector has been central to previous Development Plans, see for example SIG (1989). Poor governance combined with the civil strife has resulted in a very constrained business environment and a withdrawal of private investment. 'Key strategies for overcoming the constraints on the business environment include regulatory reforms, development of transport infrastructure and utilities, SOE reform, financial sector reforms, provision of policy and governance advice to provincial governments, development of statistics to inform policy formulation, monitoring and evaluation, and formulation of sectoral policies to promote investment and growth' (ADB, 2004b, p.7). However, given that the private sector is 'essentially dysfunctional' (ADB, 2005b, p.98), it may be too optimistic to expect that this will be possible.

There are a number of sectors that can be reformed to improve the circumstances of both the urban and rural poor. Around 80 per cent of Solomon Islanders live in rural areas and rely on subsistence farming for their livelihood. If agricultural reform is to aid development outcomes, it must be directed at both commercial and non-commercial levels (ADB, 2005b). Fisheries are also a very significant sector in terms of food security and livelihoods. As with agriculture, there are both commercial (i.e. tuna industry) and non-commercial interests that must be considered in sector reform. The forests of the Solomon Islands have been harvested for sometime and provided significant income for both owners and the SIG. However, present harvesting levels are unsustainable. The SIG have recognised that 'care must be exercised to ensure that the future generation will still have the opportunity to use this resource to enjoy and enrich their livelihood through the use of the forestry resources. Since most of these resources are tribally owned, efforts must be made to ensure that resource owners benefit maximally from the use of these resources' (SIG, 2005a, p.7). This may include re-planting programmes and other land care projects.

Nearly ninety per cent of land within the Solomon Islands is held under customary and tribal ownership. Given the heavy reliance on subsistence farming by the bulk of the population, land ownership is very important. Secure land ownership, the rule of law and property rights are necessary if land is to be used in increasingly productive ways. This is particularly relevant for large-scale investment in the mining sector. Presently, commercial gold mines (such as Gold Ridge) have ceased operations due to the insecurity brought about by the civil-strife. General investment confidence was also negatively affected by the civil-strife in the commercial and trade sectors. The SIG are seeking to revitalise this sector, but also encourage investment outside of the main urban centres such as Honiara and emphasise 'regional industrial development to diversify the economic base of the country' (SIG, 2005a, p.8). The final sector that provides potential to improve the circumstances of the poor in the Solomon Islands is tourism. Not only are their direct benefits to the providers of accommodation, but there are ancillary benefits to those involved in transport, food industries and other hospitality services. The SIG have determined that tourism would be best developed at the community level rather than by pri-vate investment and should promote the Islands' diverse cultures and environments.

By enhancing the business environment, it is expected that forestry (even though this has exceeded sustainable levels), fisheries, cocoa and copra production will become the main drivers of economic growth. Whilst gold mining and oil palm production have the capacity to also enhance economic growth, the period of conflict resulted in foreign investment withdrawing from these activities and operations ceasing. Despite the proposal reforms, operations are unlikely to restart in the foreseeable future. If improvements in land tenure, employers labour- hiring rights and inter-island transport were made, it is possible that operations may begin more quickly.

Improving infrastructure

In line with the ADB's CSP, the successive SIG poverty reduction documents have identified the need for improved infrastructure to enhance prospects for economic development within the Solomon Islands. Given that only 40 kilometres (of the country's total of 1,500 kilometres) of roads are paved, improvement of transport infrastructure and services is important as 'reliable access to domestic and international markets for rural produce will be a key strategy to restart rural economies, reduce the demand for migration to the capital in search of employment, reduce conflict between groups competing for limited opportunities, and address the challenges of restoring basic social services in rural areas' (ADB, 2004c, pp.1–2). While transport infrastructure in and around Honiara are reasonable, transport infrastructure and services outside of the capital are limited. All-weather roads are either non-existent or in disrepair, and shipping and air services are unreliable and expensive. These constraints 'pose considerable barriers to market access and impede the growth of rural production' (ADB, 2004c, p.5). In response, the ADB is supporting the rehabilitation and maintenance of physical infrastructure through the provision of technical assistance within the Ministry of Infrastructure Development (MID). The technical assistance 'will support the preparation of a national transport plan to guide development, create a Transport Policy and Planning Unit to ensure implementation, establish a Transport Trust Fund (TDTF) to provide necessary finance, increase MID's capacity in project management and contract administration, and promote private sector involvement in infrastructure development' (ADB, 2004c, p.6).

The ADB also plans to provide technical assistance to improve both inter-island shipping and aviation. 'In shipping, technical assistance will be provided to work closely with a European Union initiative to ensure a minimum level of service on uneconomic routes and ensure its sustainability through the TDTF. In aviation, technical assistance will be provided to determine the current operational and financial situation of the airline, assess models for private sector participation, identify constraints to reform, recommend institutional mechanisms for implementation, and prepare an action plan for eventual restructuring' (ADB, 2004c, p.6). It is not just transport infrastructure that is limited. Less than 20 per cent of the population have access to electricity. And whilst telecommunications infrastructure is more advanced, its cost is prohibitive to most Solomon Islanders (ADB, 2005b, 2005c).

Improving the management of service delivery to communities

There are various areas that the SIG have identified as requiring reform to improve the delivery of services to all Solomon Islands communities.

Following the period of civil-strife, the SIG have nominated law and order sector reform as vital. This includes improving policing and national security to restore the 'integrity, capability, confidence, efficiency and effectiveness of the Royal Solomon Islands Police, community participation in policy and presence of policing service in every community throughout the country' (SIG, 2005a, p.10). In addition to improving general levels of legal services across the country, the SIG have resolved to maintain the independence of the judiciary. Embedded in these legal reforms is the acknowledgement of the importance of a prevailing peace throughout the country and recognition that these reforms will also bolster and support reconciliation and other peace-building processes. Improved governance will also be an important determinant of future economic development. The SIG have recognised the importance of ensuring that all Solomon Islanders have equal representation in both provincial and national governments and that representation be based on historical and social groupings to improve national cohesion (also see UN, 2002). Health, education and other social services will be delivered more effectively and efficiently if these other reforms are fully implemented.

5   Aid policies and NGO assistance required to achieve the MDGs

Upwards of 80 per cent of Solomon Islanders live in rural areas and few of these participate in any significant way within the cash economy. The subsistence lifestyle means that while most Islanders have sufficient access to local produce, they do not have access to money to pay for certain food items, such as rice and salt, nor services such as education, health care or intra-island transport (ADB, 2005a). Economic progress that has occurred is primarily located in the few urban areas (but predominately Honiara) and thus disconnected from the majority of the population. However, 'if growth can be widespread, geographically, its benefits will contribute to poverty reduction over a wider area' (ADB, 2005b, p.44). This has been recognised by civil society advocates who argue there 'is a pressing need to develop alternatives to current economic reform policies and to create initiatives that are more targeted towards reducing poverty, inequality and potential conflict and improving the quality of life for all citizens of Solomon Islands' (Oxfam, 2006a, p.8). Such alternatives involve a decentralising of economic activities, and concentration on rural livelihoods, food security and the non-formal economy. It does not mean however that the existing foci of securing law and order, improving the public sector or infrastructure should be abandoned (ADB, 2005b). It does require however additional interventions to ensure that the circumstances of the most poor are more directly addressed.

The formal economy of Solomon Islands has a very narrow base, with the majority of exports coming from just three sectors: forestry, fishing and agriculture. Yet, as noted, only around one-quarter of the population are engaged in the formal economy and thus directly exposed to the benefits derived from any productivity increases. Again, given that the rest of the population are located outside the urban centres and maintain a subsistence lifestyle, there is also few opportunities for the benefits from this narrowly-based economy to trickle-down to this population cohort in any substantive manner. Thus, policies that directly address the circumstances of the poor in Solomon Islands must occur largely outside the formal economy. As yet, only pilot schemes to 'diversify and increase rural income generation opportunities as the basis for stronger and more inclusive growth' (IMF, 2005, p.41) have been discussed but not implemented. In this post-conflict environment the aid received by Solomon Islands and the NGO sector must play prominent roles in the achievement of the MDGs.

Aid and MDGs

As has been previously discussed, the largest aid intervention in Solomon Islands in recent times has been RAMSI. Australia's total aid to Solomon Islands since 2003 is approximately US$1 billion. The bulk of this programme has been focussed on the restoration of law and order and normalising government functions so as to prevent the country from becoming a 'failed state' (Bately, 2005). This has been relatively successful, however many effects of the civil-strife remain: 'public service delivery is generally poor; property rights and the legal system are weak; the financial sector is not functioning effectively; physical infrastructure is underdeveloped; the quality and reliability of water, electricity and communications services are poor; and the costs of establishing, running and closing a business are high by regional standards' (ADB, 2005a, p.220).

As the country's largest aid intervention, it is now necessary for RAMSI to change focus and incorporate a greater focus on the achievement of the MDGs. This would not require a complete revision of RAMSI as some aspects that focus on community-building currently exist. A small component of RAMSI is the Community Peace and Restoration Fund. This Fund, which is primarily funded by the Australian Government, began in November 2000. Thus far, it has provided finance to over 500 small-scale development projects throughout all provinces of Solomon Islands to the total of AU$21 million. Greater emphasis in RAMSI on these development-type interventions is required.

The purpose of this Fund is to provide flexible and rapid responses to humanitarian needs brought about by the civil conflict. By being intentionally small, these projects can be managed by local communities with minimal external oversight. Local Provincial Coordinators (Islanders themselves) assist communities to identify and implement these development activities. This results in projects being funded that are effectively *owned* by the communities involved rather than being imposed upon them by *technical experts*. The underlying philosophy remains though that these projects should bring communities together in practical ways in order to promote peace.

One of these projects for example involved a number of neighbouring communities partnering with the Ministry of Works to repair and maintain the connecting roads. Prior to this project, the Ministry of Works was unable to maintain these roads due to its own low budget and broken machinery. This project assisted the Ministry of Works to train the local communities to repair and maintain the roads and supplied them with the basic tools to do so. The result has been a road that allows these neighbouring communities to access markets, health care and education. Perhaps more importantly, the project allowed ex-militants to be re-integrated into the communities by working as labourers on the project.

Another project involved the building of a kindergarten in an outlying community on Vanikolo Island in Temotu Province. This remote community had not received financial aid previously. The building of the community allowed an opportunity for parties of different sides of the civil strife to work cooperatively together for the common good of the community.

Projects have been funded in all MDG sectors, including health, education, adult training, gender, water and sanitation and agriculture.

NGOs and MDGs

Given the rural dispersion of 80 per cent of Solomon Islanders, attention to the rural economy is paramount. Present capacity to improve local economies is low and so NGOs have an important role to play in this void throughout all islands in all provinces (Oxfam, 2006b, 2006c). It is equally important that the focus of these interventions should be at the family level. The basic economic unit within the Solomon Islands is the family. While the family unit may extend beyond a single household, it does not extend to cover the full *wontok*. While assistance will always be extended to the wider *wontok*, the primary economic unit is more limited. Thus activities to ensure that food security and rural livelihoods are properly addressed, such as micro-finance, water and sanitation, and agricultural training and extension need to be implemented at this micro-level.

Estimates of active NGOs is Solomon Islands are difficult to make with any certainly. Prior to the civil strife there were over 100 NGOs registered with the peak NGO-body – the Development Services Exchange (DSE). Civil unrest resulted in membership of this body falling to just two financial members during this time. Presently there are more than 40 NGOs associated with the DSE (Upton, 2006). Many smaller NGOs do not register themselves as NGOs as the registration process is onerous and only grants limited benefits – such as owning property.

NGOs can be particularly effective in assisting Solomon Islanders trans-form natural resources into cash wealth that can be used to improve their material circumstances. Many opportunities exist in this regard. For example, on Simbo Island, local communities are harvesting eggs of the local megapode bird. This island lacks any commercial centre and nearly its entire population rely on subsistence farming for their livelihoods. There are limited health and education services and trans-port to other islands is expensive and dependent upon weather.

One of the local fauna on Simbo Island is the megapode bird. The megapode bird is small and roughly resembles a pigeon, though with longer legs. Communities of Simbo Island (where the megapode bird is locally known as the *lape bird*) are now harvesting the eggs for com-mercial gain. Unlike many birds, the megapode does not incubate its eggs by itself sitting on them. Rather, it allows the natural heat of the environment (temperatures range from 30–34 degrees Celsius on the island all year round) to incubate the eggs. Thus once the eggs are laid, the megpode bird is free to leave the nest in search of food. Using local knowledge, the communities of Simbo Islands, collect a sustainable number of eggs for sale. This collection is based on managing the bird population to ensure a sustainable harvest of eggs into the future. The key to the long-term success of this project is that it is community-owned. Rather than facing a potential 'tragedy of the commons' sce-nario, this development activity is a community owned enterprise. Given the size of Simbo Island and the nature of communal living, it is not possible for individuals to collect and sell eggs without the know-ledge of the wider community. This prevents over harvesting for short-term private gain.

While the community of Simbo Island have long known about the incubation of the megapode bird and known the local value of the eggs as a food source, they were not aware of any commercial potential. In conjunction with World Wide Fund for Nature Solomon Islands, a local organising committee – Simbo Megapode Management Committee – was established to coordinate the harvesting, marketing and distribution of profits through the community. Not only did WWF provide assistance with marketing of the eggs, it provided technical skills, techniques and information to ensure that the harvesting was sustainable. This project has allowed the communities on Simbo Island to convert a natural resource into a sustainable stream of income through community cooperation and participation with a NGO with specialist technical skills.

The income earned through this activity is only one part of the total development project being undertaken by this partnership of NGOs. It also includes biological research and monitoring to increase the knowledge base of the megapode bird, including its breeding and habitat requirements.

NGOs, such as these examples discussed, are seeking to work with a dispersed and diverse population to improve their circumstances. Whilst these NGOs often do not use the rhetoric of the MDGs in justifying their interventions, the direct result of this work may have this impact. NGOs have effectively work with local communities and enhance local capacity so that communities can become engaged within 'harvesting tree wealth, making fibre paper, pressing ngali oil, planting coral and seaweed... (allowing) cash starved villagers to increase their earning capacity without destroying the very basis of these new industries' (Roughan, 2002, p.86). Within a post-conflict environment and subsequent ineffective government, it is incumbent on NGOs to work with communities to improve their circumstances and in turn progress towards achieving the MDGs.

6   Conclusion and policy recommendations

Serious data constraints hamper any reasonable efforts to determine Solomon Islands' progress towards achieving the MDGs. However, it is possible to suggest that given the recent civil strife that resulted in the effective shut-down of all government services, including the provision of health, education and other social services that progress towards the MDGs has stopped and possibly reversed. Even the recent post-conflict experience of economic growth is limited to a narrow formal economy of which the majority of Solomon Islands do not participate and to whom material benefits do not flow. The focus of Solomon Island's largest aid intervention – RAMSI – remains securing law and order and improving governance. Whilst this may enhance some delivery aspects of development interventions, it in and of itself will not achieve the MDGs.

Having said that though, it may be necessary to re-configure the MDGs to more specifically address the needs existing within a post-conflict environment such as that found in Solomon Islands. This would require:

- Adding specific MDG targets addressing reconciliation between opposing communities. Many models now exist around the world for Truth and Reconciliation tribunals and involvement in such forums allows conflicting communities to move beyond past grievances.
- Adding specific MDG targets for improving general law and order throughout the country. Crimes against the person and property unrelated to any ethnic disputes often increase during periods of civil unrest. Protection under the rule of law facilitates economic and social relationships and this is necessary not only for economic growth but also for accessing basic health and education services.
- Adding specific MDG targets for the destruction of weapons throughout the country. High levels of weapons, including traditional and modern weapons, to again facilitate a sense of safety and ease of movement to participate in local economies and access basic services.
- Adding specific MDGs targets for different ethnic minorities or regions to purposely address impoverishment of certain groups that underpinned the civil unrest. Civil unrest occurs because of grievances and often these grievances are predicated on a perceived inequality between ethnic or regional groups. Addressing imbalances and inequality assist in reconciling and overcoming civil unrest.

Each of these post-conflict specific MDGs would also bolster and support the achievement of the original MDGs. Therefore, it is not necessary for countries within post-conflict environments to eschew the MDGs for an alternative set of targets. Rather, by adding additional targets that focus on reconciliation, law and order and inequalities, achievement of the original MDGs will be more likely.

The ADB's current poverty reduction strategy (in conjunction successive Solomon Island governments' statements on poverty reduction) is proceeding in the shadow of a period of civil strife that severely affected both the social and economic circumstances of the poor. Given the violence that has continued to occur spasmodically since the official cessation of hostility in 2003 – for example, in April 2006, much of Chinatown was razed to the ground following the election of a (short-lived) Government led by Mr Synder Rini. This violence was apportioned to perceptions of political interference from the business community associated with Chinese-ethnicity – much of the immediate focus of non-RAMSI development interventions within the post-civil strife period has focussed on relief and rehabil-it-ation (including for the tsunami that affected the island of Gizo within Western Province in April, 2007). 'The key challenges for the Government and the aid community are (i) to shift the focus from the short-term stabilisation process towards a medium and long-term programme for equitable growth and development; (ii) to deliver programmes and visible results in a timely and effective manner, despite extreme capacity weakness; and (iii) at the same time, to rebuild the key institutions of government' (ADB, 2004a, p.8). While important, these poverty reduction strategies are likely to 'miss' those who suffer chronic poverty by seeking to grow the formal economy. A review of poverty reduction strategies that also seeks to decentralise economic activities, and a concentration on rural livelihoods, food security and the non-formal economy is now necessary.

The outlook for Solomon Islands is not necessarily bleak. Unlike some of its neighbouring Pacific countries, it has the benefit of abundant natural resources. Community ownership of these resources combined with cohesive communities – no longer destabilised by conflict – will provide opportunities for all to benefit from the long-term harvesting of these natural resources – both on land and within the ocean, which will aid the achievement of the MDGs in all parts of Solomon Islands.

Having achieved a level of peace, the Government of Solomon Island, its donors, the NGO sector and the community itself must now work to achieve the MDGs in the coming years. Given the impact of the civil strife, it is unlikely that Solomon Islands will achieve the MDGs in this post-conflict environment. However it is important that the focus now turn towards ensuring that the benefits of this recent peace and economic growth reach the majority of

Solomon Island's population who reside in rural areas. Alternative policies that directly address the MDGs must now be implemented throughout the country if progress towards the achievement of the MDGs is to occur in any significant way in addition to policies that support reconciliation, law and order and addressing inequality between regional populations.

7
Achieving the MDGs in Thailand: What Role for Donors in a High Achieving Middle-Income Country?

1 Introduction

Thailand has a population of approximately 65 million and borders Myanmar, Laos, Cambodia and Malaysia. As with the three previous case studies, the experience of Thailand in responding to the MDGs is unique. Thailand has its own distinct history shaped by its specific geography, political experiences, and social interactions. The fact that Thailand was never colonised, is a Buddhist country, has low levels of urbanisation, and possesses an abundance of land has impacted on its development path and its approach to the achievement of the original MDGs. Yet, despite this distinctiveness, Thailand can be considered representative of many middle-income countries in that it has a dualistic economy, significant rural-urban migration, a large income gap between the rich and poor, and political instability. So whilst its history is unique, Thailand is a member of a large group of middle-income countries, all of which are seeking to increase their national income in order to reduce the incidence of poverty and increase living standards. In this regard, understanding how Thailand has engaged with the MDGs is valuable.

Thailand's recent economic experience is widely judged as successful, having regularly outperformed many developing (and developed) countries in terms of its annual growth in real GDP (World Bank, 2006b). Indeed, some observers have argued that Thailand is a potential role model for much of the Third World (Watkins, 1998; World Bank, 1999b; Vines and Warr, 2000). Consideration therefore of the role MDGs has in middle-income countries is of interest. This is particularly so if the approach to the MDGs within Thailand is considered. The Thai government adopted an *aggressive* whole-of-government approach to the MDGs from their inception by setting itself more ambitious MDG targets than those contained in the original schedule. Thailand's *MDG Plus* approach either shortens the time frame in which the original targets are to be achieved or increases those targets to be achieved across the range of Goals. Given its economic strength, Thailand would have achieved the original MDGs by adopting a business-as-usual approach. However, Thailand has instead seized the international community's commitment to improve the lives of the poor throughout the world and set itself even higher targets to ensure that the impact of the MDGs in Thailand is even greater than it might be. Even though Thailand is a middle-income country with strong economic growth, the increased targets associated with its MDG Plus will require ongoing national and international assistance.

This chapter is structured as follows. Firstly, the general features of the Thai economy are outlined along with some of Thailand's recent economic developments. Secondly, the achievement of the MDGs in Thailand are then discussed as are the framework and targets of the MDG-Plus approach. Section 4 considers the role of international finance in the Thai context, whilst section 5 considers the role NGOs have played in both the achievement of the original NGO as well as within the MDG-Plus framework. Section 6 considers lessons learned from the Thai experience before the chapter concludes with section 7.

2   The Thai economy

While the benchmark for MDGs targets is 1990, it is Thailand's economic strength that is facilitating its ability to adapt these targets to more ambitious levels and this strength can be traced back well beyond 1990. Indeed, Thailand has experienced strong economic growth for more than three decades. During the 1970s, the Thai economy was transformed from an agricultural to a primarily industrial economy, at least in terms of the composition of Thailand's real GDP. Growth in per capita GDP in this period averaged 7 percent per annum. Given the 1973 and 1979 oil price shocks, the consequent slowdown of the world economy, the withdrawal of the US military from Southeast Asia, and the considerable domestic political instability in Thailand, 'the growth of the Thai economy during the period 1971 to 1978 was remarkable' (Dixon, 1999, p.108). Yet, interestingly, this transformation occurred despite, rather than because of, explicit government policies and interventions. High levels of protection for domestic industries in the form or tariffs and fuel subsidies, together with protracted and violent political upheaval, did little to boost investor confidence. Meanwhile, Thailand's current account deficit was uncomfortably large and mounting, inflation was high, and rising government expenditure was resulting in a growing fiscal deficit. Furthermore, overseas debt (whilst comparatively low) also increased substantially during the 1970s (Dixon, 1996). It is not too unfair to characterise Thailand as being literally in the right place at the right time. Throughout the 1970s, Japan and other newly industrialising countries (NICs), such as Singapore and South Korea, began to shed their low level manufacturing operations in response to rising domestic labour costs. Thailand was well positioned to assume these industries given its relatively low labour costs, its well educated workforce, and the fact that the labour movement, though once strong, was being liberalised and losing support from the national Government.

A global slowdown in the early 1980s, saw Thailand's annual rate of growth in real GDP fall to just over 3 per cent. However, this growth was still quite strong when compared to most of the countries in the Asia-Pacific region that were experiencing a recession during this time. As the global economy strengthened in the late 1980s, so to did the Thai economy. As the Asia-Pacific region and world economy emerged from the early 1980s recession, Thailand continued to attract the industries that, because of relatively higher labour costs, the NICs were still shedding (Dixon, 1999). Continuing strong growth in the manufacturing sector was underpinned by an expansion in primary exports, a rapidly growing tourism sector, and labour migration (with the subsequent repatriation of income). But, again, Thailand's economic expansion appeared not to be the result of carefully developed economic policy. As Dixon (1999, p.128) explains:

> ...[T]here is in all of this a clustering of favourable global, regional, and national circumstances that Thailand was able to take advantage of, rather than any particular policies or strategies that could be isolated and applied elsewhere.

Indeed, Thailand experienced what may be termed a *golden age* with real GDP resurging to levels up to 11 per cent per annum (achieved in 1987). Thailand's economy doubled between 1982 and 1993, making the Thai economy one of the fastest growing in the world during this period (Jansen, 1997; Vines and Warr, 2000).

By the mid-1990s, the so-called golden age had ended. In 1996, the Thai economy was characterised by the zero growth in export earnings, an increasing balance of payments deficit, rising private sector debt levels, and, most critically, an expansion in short-term speculative capital movements that was accompanied by an over-heating of the property and financial markets. The 1997 financial crisis that struck down many Asian economies brought Thailand's decade of rapid growth in real GDP to an abrupt halt (Dixon, 1999). Fortunately, the Thai economy quickly recovered from the financial crisis and again recorded high GDP growth rates in the range of 5 per cent per annum between 1999 and 2004.

In view of the recent free trade agreements that Thailand has signed or negotiated with its large trading partners, it is likely that Thailand's real GDP will continue to grow for some time to come. Even the 2006 political coup appears not to have altered the view that Thailand is a relatively safe country for foreign investors to operate within.

Over the past three decades, economic growth (as conventionally indicated by the growth in real GDP) has been the explicitly stated priority of the Thai government (NESDB, 1996 and 2000). Indeed, as Phongpaichit and Baker (1995) have highlighted, it would seem that the government effectively abandoned a number of policies in the early 1990s in order to focus its entire attention on planning the direction and outcome of economic growth. The direct impact of this has been the dramatic reduction improvement in a range of development indicators (see Table 7.1). While other countries within the Greater Mekong region have recorded increases in per capita income, they have done so from a low base. Whereas, Thailand almost doubled its GNI per capita from a level in 1990, that not even its neighbours have yet to achieve. In non-economic terms, life expectancy in Thailand has increased since 1990 whilst under-five mortality has fallen.

However, whilst the higher tax revenue generated by the growth in Thailand's real GDP has permitted large increases in government expenditure in basic health, education and other social services, it may be that the additional government spending has not been effective in all regions of Thailand. Certainly poverty levels in Northeast Thailand have been at levels similar to those recorded in sub-Saharan countries in Africa (Watkins, 1998; Kakwani and Krongkaew, 1997).

At the same time, a number of environmental concerns have also been inadequately dealt with. Between 1985 and 2002, per capita carbon dioxide emissions in Thailand increased dramatically from 0.88 tonnes to 3.25 tonnes per person while, more alarmingly, Thailand's ecological footprint grew beyond its biocapacity (WRI, 2005). As at 2003, Thailand's ecological footprint stood at 1.4 hectares per person compared to its biocapacity of 1.0 hectare per person (Global Footprint Network, 2006). Having previously enjoyed an ecological surplus, Thailand now

Table 7.1　Key Development Indices for Mekong Region Countries

	Cambodia		Myanmar		Laos		Thailand		Vietnam	
	1990	2006	1990	2006	1990	2006	1990	2006	1990	2006
Population (million)	9.7	14.1	40.1	48.3	4.1	5.8	54.3	63.4	66.2	84.1
GNI per capita (current US $)	..	490	..	..	200	500	1550	3050	130	700
GDP composition by sector (%)										
Agriculture	..	30	57	..	61	42	12	11	39	20
Manufacturing	..	26	11	..	15	32	37	45	23	42
Services	..	44	32	..	24	26	50	45	39	38
Life Expectancy (years)	55	59	59	62	55	64	67	70	65	71
Under-five mortality (per 1,000 live births)	116	82	130	104	163	75	31	8	53	17
Official Development Assistance (current US$ million)	41.3	529	160.7	146.6	149.1	364.2	795.6	–215.6	180.5	1846.4
Girls in primary and second school (ratio of girls to boys)	..	89	..	101	..	85	..	104	..	97

Source: World Development Indictors (2008).

suffers from an ecological deficit of –0.4 hectares per person. The disconcerting aspect of this statistic is that an ecological deficit is widely regarded as an indication that a nation's natural capital is being eroded. In Thailand's case, this is no better exemplified than the evidence revealing widespread land degradation and the continuing decline in Thailand's forest stocks. It is unlikely that this environmental degradation will directly impact the short-term improvement of development indicators within Thailand leading up to 2015. However, in the medium to longer term, such environmental pressure will certainly undermine sustainable improvements in the lives of the poor unless alternative and remedial action is undertaken within the economic, social and environmental spheres (see Clarke and Shaw, 2008; Lawn and Clarke, 2008).

3   Thailand's MDG progress

Thailand can be rightly considered a MDG success story having already achieved the majority of the MDG targets as they were originally devised. Thailand has already surpassed the targets for: 1) halving the proportion of people living in extreme poverty; 2) halving the proportion of people who suffer from hunger; 3) eliminating gender disparity in primary and secondary education; 4) halting and reversing the spread of HIV/AIDS, malaria, TB and other major diseases; and 5) halving the proportion of people without sustainable access to safe drinking water and basic sanitation. Moreover Thailand is highly likely to ensure universal primary education by 2015 and likely to have achieved a significant improvement in the lives of slum dwellers by 2020. Thailand will potentially also achieve the goal of reversing environmental resources (though it is at risk of failing to achieve this goal if current pursuit of economic growth follows historical policies – see Clarke and Shaw, 2008). As Thailand already has under-five and maternal morality rates comparable to OECD levels, it is not appropriate to assess success against the targets of reducing these rates by two-thirds and three-quarters respectively. It would be misleading to suggest though that there are no remnants remaining of Thailand's past poverty. There are certain groups within Thai society that have not benefited as greatly as others. For example, small farmers in the northeast, far north and far south remain at risk. Muslim communities in the South have higher levels of maternal mortality than the country average and child malnutrition is higher in northern hill tribes (UNDP, 2005b). In addition, there are around one million illegal migrants (predominately from Burma) living in semi-permanent settlements at various crossing points along the Thai-Burma border, but also with large in-land Thai cities who have also been excluded from the benefits of recent economic development.

While Thailand's economic strength as a middle-income country is undoubtedly a key factor in the country's success in achieving the MDGs, it is not solely responsible. A range of other factors were of equal (and arguably higher) importance.

> Thailand's success can be attributed to a powerful mix of national harmony, astute policy making, stronger democratic governance, the industriousness of Thai people, public investment in social services, advantageous historic and geopolitical circumstances, and, not least, economic growth fuelled by high exports, diversified manufacturing, agriculture, mining and foreign direct investment. In general, Thailand has proven to be resilient in weathering storms and adept at repositioning itself in a fast-changing, global context. Thus, the financial crisis in the late 1990s eroded, but did not overturn prior human development progress. Since then, assiduous macroeconomic and domestic reforms have poised Thailand for impressive growth (UNDP, 2005b, p.5).

It is perhaps the coordination at the national level and the commitment of the Thai Government to the achievement of the MDGs that sets Thailand apart from other regional neighbours. The Thai Government, and more specifically the National Economic and Social Development Board (NESDB), incorporated the MDGs into their national planning almost from the inception of the MDGs internationally. In 2002, the NESDB assessed Thailand's current status against the 48 MDG indicators through a series of working papers, data surveys and focus groups. Having identified the pre-existing MDG-focussed programmes and policies, and the weaknesses and gaps of the current approaches, six *MDG Cluster Groups* were established to 'review data and the application of the MDG framework to the Thai context, including that adaptation of the MDG targets, and to suggest development strategies to achieve the MDGs' (UNDP, 2005b, p.7). The six cluster groups were: 1) poverty and hunger (covering MDG 1); 2) education (covering MDG 2); 3) gender equality (covering MDG 3); 4) health (covering MDGs 4, 5 and 6); 5) environment (covering MDG 7); and 6) global partnership for development (covering MDG 8).

These groups comprised members from Government ministries, NGOs, UN bodies and academics and meet regularly every two months. In addition, the NESDB assigned *champion's* for six different MDG cluster groups from different line ministries and from civil society to lead these different cluster groups. By selecting leaders in their respective fields and those with political influence the use of cluster champions ensured that the MDGs were given prominence at the national level.

For example, the MDG goal of halting and then reversing HIV/AIDS was prioritised in Thailand despite the country's very strong past record in addressing HIV/AIDS. In 1991, new annual infections of HIV were 140,000, but new annual infections fell in 2003 to just 20,000 as a result of government and civil society interventions and behaviour change campaigns financially supported in part by international assistance. However, such was the commitment of the Cluster Champion and Cluster Group to ensuring that HIV/AIDS infection rates be continuously reduced that the Thai Government committed itself publicly days prior to the International AIDS Conference in Bangkok in 2004 to the following actions:

- Implementing as nation-wide harm reduction programme targeting injecting drug users;
- Distribution of condoms in Thai prisons;
- Including AIDS eduction in the national school curriculum;
- Scholarships for HIV/AIDS orphans;
- Income-generating schemes for people affected by HIV/AIDS throughout the country;
- Universal and free access to anti-retroviral drugs to those with HIV;
- Protection of generic anti-retroviral drug production (including new generation drugs) in Thailand;
- Provision of anti-retroviral drugs to neighbouring countries (including Cambodia, Laos and Myanmar); and
- international assistance to the value of US$5 million to the Global Fund on AIDS, TB and Malaria.

As will be discussed later, a number of these initiatives have long been implemented by NGOs within Thailand. For example, NGOs have been very active in establishing income-generating programmes, including artificial flower-making, chicken-farming, and even manufacturing of herbal medicines dating back to the early and mid 1990s in places such as Chiang Mai and Chiang Rai (Clarke, 2002).

Whilst the importance of Thailand achieving the majority of the MDGs is significant, of greater significance has been the approach taken by the Thai Government to extend the targets of the MDGs. Rather than being a benchmark, the MDGs have become a foundation upon which to aspire to even greater development targets. These higher targets have been called *MDG-Plus*. Whilst the global MDG target for poverty reduction is to halve the proportion of people living in poverty in 1990 by 2015, Thailand has already reduced this proportion by two-thirds. Therefore, the MDG-Plus target has been set at reducing the proportion of people living in poverty to just 4 per cent by 2009. Not only is this revised target more difficult to attain, the timeline in which to attain it has been shortened as well. MDG-Plus targets have been set for all other areas as well (see Appendix 7.1).

It is important to recognise that in setting these MDG-Plus targets, the Thai Government has set ambitious challenges. Successful achievement of these revised targets will not occur through business-as-usual policies and interventions. Thailand will only achieve these MDG-Plus targets by a continual and concerted effort, which in turn will require cooperation and support of NGOs and international assistance.

4   Role of international assistance

In line with Thailand's economic growth and increase in national income per capita, official development assistance to Thailand has fallen steadily over the past decade (see Figure 7.1). During this period though, whilst

Figure 7.1   ODA Flows to Thailand, 1990 to 2006 (US$ 2005, millions)

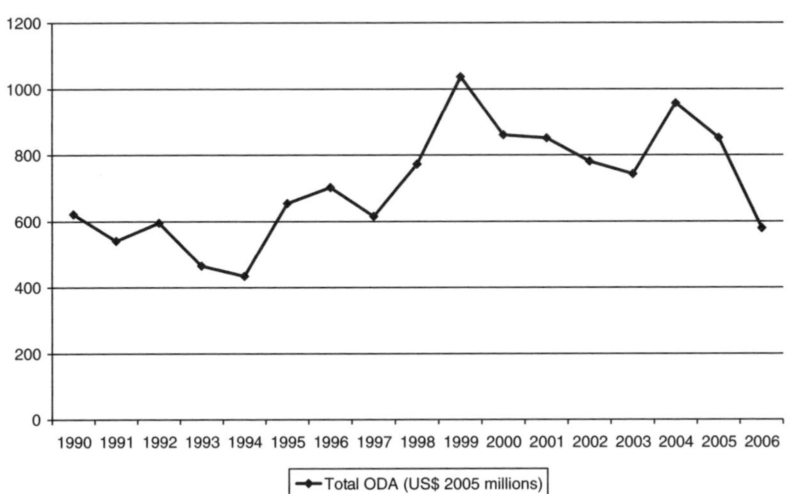

Source: OECD, 2008b.

the general trend was downward, aid to Thailand was characterised by volatility with large year-on-year fluctuations. Aid volatility for recipient countries has a negative impact on aid effectiveness. Since the announcement of the MDGs, ODA to Thailand has continued to be volatile. As Clarke *et al.* (2007) note 'the conclusions of the aid volatility literature are relatively clear and robust – large year-on-year changes in aid flows have deleterious effects on economic growth and poverty alleviation' (p.21). This deleterious effect can be partially explained by recipient governments being largely unable to optimally plan and expend aid flows. For example, using a dataset of 75 developing countries, Lensink and Morrissey (2001) examined the instability and uncertainty of aid and the impact that these have on economic growth. They argued that it is the stable, and predictable, aid flows that promote economic growth and not the level of aid *per se*, and found the externalities associated with uncertainty to be higher than those associated with overall instability of aid. Their results imply that highly volatile aid, rather than achieving the intended effect of encouraging economic growth, actually impedes it by making it harder 'for recipients to predict future aid inflows that may permit more investment and better fiscal plan-

Table 7.2   ODA Receipts for Thailand, 1990–2006 (2000 US$)

	Total ODA (million US$ 2005)		ODA per capita (US$ 2005)
	multilateral	bilateral	
1990	621.81		10.8
1991	541.01		9.4
1992	595.91		10.3
1993	465.11		8.1
1994	434.16		7.5
1995	654.60		11.4
1996	702.40		12.1
1997	615.50		10.5
1998	772.97		13.0
1999	1037.26		17.3
2000	859.98	0.95	14.2
2001	848.53	2.79	13.9
2002	779.18	1.57	12.6
2003	729.09	13.80	11.9
2004	925.29	31.59	15.3
2005	821.32	30.57	13.5
2006	516.20	63.16	9.1

Source: OECD (2008b).

ning' (p.16). Other studies report similar findings (see Gemmell and McGillivray, 1998; Bulir and Hanaan, 2001, 2003; Levin and Dollar, 2005; Fielding and Mavrotas, 2005).

However, given that per capita aid levels to Thailand are quite low (see Table 7.2), the overall impact of ODA on economic growth would be minor relative to Thailand's overall record of economic growth. Indeed, in more recent years, Thailand has actually become an aid donor and itself providing ODA to its regional neighbours.

5 Role of NGOs

It is not possible to estimate with any accuracy the number of NGOs working in Thailand. While international organisations are required to formally register with the Thai government, local community based organisations or self-help groups are both established and cease operations with little regulation, often responding to sole issues at the neighbourhood or village level. Local and international NGOs operating within Thailand have long focussed on the general sectors targeted by the MDGs – health, education, economic security, gender, environment, etc. These organisations have worked closely with the Thai government in some instances (including national commission on HIV/AIDS) but also worked independently of the government (including working with commercial sex workers and injecting drug consumers).

5.1 NGOs working closely with Government

HIV/AIDS is an interesting case study of the effectiveness of NGOs working in collaboration with the Thai Government. Whilst strong economic growth was reducing poverty levels throughout the 1980s and 1990s, the gravest development issue in Thailand was the HIV epidemic. Indeed, it was estimated that close to 10 per cent of GDP was lost due to the epidemic during the 1990s (Baker, 1997). Prevalence rates increased quickly following the first reported case in 1984. Transmitted primarily through heterosexual intercourse (again primarily within the commercial sex industry, but soon becoming more widely prevalent within the general population as clients of commercial sex workers infected their own wives and partners) prevalence rates reach 3.5 per cent of army recruits and up to 20 per cent of the Chiang Mai population in 1992 (WHO, 1995). Government funded, but often NGO implemented, education campaigns and condom distribution activities were effective in reducing the prevalence rates throughout the 1990s.

Clarke (2002) identified three distinct phases or generations of NGO activities seeking to achieve behaviour change during this time. 'The first generation of programmes focussed on simple information dissemination. The second generation focussed on more specific target groups and information and counselling for those with the virus. The third generation programmes focussed on establishing an environment, which enabled people to change their behaviour' (Clarke, 2002, p.626). Throughout this time, NGOs were financially supported by both international donors, multilateral agencies and also the Thai Government. By the mid-1990s, Thai Government funding was US$80 million per annum.

However, Government funding was dramatically curtailed following the 1997 financial crisis so that government funding fell to just one quarter of its previous amounts by 2000. The direct result of this was that many Thai Government funded projects ceased to operate. Of greatest significance was the condom distribution programme. 'This program aimed to enforce consistent condom use in all commercial sex establishments. Condoms were distributed free to brothels and massage parlours, and sex workers and their clients were required to use them. Brothels that failed to comply could be closed' (Avert, 2008, p.1). NGOs were left to fill this void and continue with this programme. Through social marketing, distribution, education programmes and counseling, NGOs throughout Thailand were able to continue this Thai Government initiated programme with limited Thai Government financial support. It has been estimated that without this campaign, infection rates in Thailand would be ten times higher than they are currently (UNAIDS, 2006).

Whilst many NGOs were involved in addressing HIV/AIDS through Thailand, perhaps the most prominent is Population and Community Development (known as PDA). Since 1974, PDA has been working in a range of fields that have impacted on the achievement of the MDGs. PDA activities include those addressing water, sanitation, the environment, micro-credit and income generation (see Melnick, 2007). Initially focussing on reproductive health, PDA is now perhaps most well known for its work on HIV/AIDS. Within Thailand, PDA has been at the fore of local efforts to raise awareness about the transmission of HIV and its prevention. So successful has the PDA been in this field that it has been credited by the World Bank with saving seven million Thais from HIV infection through their community education programmes (PDA, 2008). The PDA was instrumental in forming the Thai National AIDS Committee, of which the then Prime Minister of Thailand became Chairman.

This Government auspiced agency worked in close partnership with PDA and other NGOs in raising public awareness of HIV/AIDS, prevention of transmission and care of those affected. The PDA concentrated its efforts at the village level utilising its pre-existing networks of village reproductive health agents to inform and educate. However, the PDA also targeted those in the commercial sex industry that the Government was unable to reach through the illegal status attached to this sector. The PDA distributed condoms to both commercial sex workers and also their clientele. Workshops were held with brothel owners and education campaigns were undertaken with associated sectors including motor-cycle taxi drivers, hairdressers and beauticians. The approach of PDA was to effect behaviour change as the only effective way of preventing HIV transmission. PDA also worked with community leaders, including religious leaders, government officials, and private companies to raise awareness of the epidemic.

5.2   NGOs working independently of Thai Government

Unlike in other developing countries throughout the Asia-Pacific region, NGOs in Thailand have not been the main service delivery vehicles for the provision of basic health and education services. The Thai Government has a very effective national health service (35 THB insurance) and education system. Through various levels of government (from national to provincial to village level) access to basic services is possible for mainstream groups. However, those that are outside of the mainstream Thai population are not serviced well by the Thai Government. It is providing services to these groups – whether they are religious minorities in the south or ethnic minorities in the north – that the importance of NGOs is noticed.

This is even more evident in the MDG-Plus targets. Providing services to the chronically poor in the north and north east and the southern provinces as well as around one million illegal migrants will be difficult for Thai government agencies without NGO support. These communities have not directly benefited in Thailand's recent economic expansion and now require more specific attention. NGOs are well placed to link these communities and populations to Thai Government services as they have worked with them in the past.

NGOs can also continue to advocate on behalf of groups – such as illegal Burmese migrants, or commercial sex workers and injecting drug users – who continue to be excluded under the MDG-Plus framework. Estimates of the number of migrants within Thailand vary between 800,000 to 1.5 million (AMC, 2002) but it is commonly thought that they number no less than one million people (Thailand's population is approximately 65 million). Estimates are difficult to make as different authorities use different data on which they base their estimates. For example, estimates of migrants can differ by a factor of four between the Labour Ministry (based on registrations and employer surveys) and the Health Ministry (based on hospital treatments) (Urbano, 2006). The status of Burmese workers in Thailand is also fluid which further complicates estimates of migrants. Policies towards migrants have changed over time and enforcement of the law is largely dependent on local authorities. 'The Thai Government's treatment of migrant workers, particularly Burmese, has fluctuated with economic and political agendas. After the Asian Financial Crisis in 1997, the government cracked down on illegal migrants and expelled thousands of unregistered workers' (Urbano, 2006, p.29). More recently, the Thai Government reviewed the status of migrant workers with a 2003 Memorandum of Understanding with the Burmese Government, in which migrant workers were to be protected by certain conditions including minimum wages, eight-hour working shifts and national holidays (Belton, 2005). This is reviewed annually through Cabinet Resolutions. Whilst still considered 'illegal', registered workers are permitted to work. Whilst risky and illegal, many Burmese have sought to relocate to Thailand (either temporarily or permanently) in order to escape the turmoil occurring in their own country and take advantage of the relative prosperity available in Thailand. Certainly economic reasons underpinned migrants decisions to travel to Thailand, with migrants most commonly citing the poor employment opportunities and poverty in Burma compared to the situation in Thailand.

In terms of HIV/AIDS, simply being an illegal migrant is a significant risk factor. Illegal migrants are generally within the reproductive age and are usually single (though there are some migrant cohorts, such as construction workers who are more likely to live with their families). This often results in increased risk behaviours. For example:

- condom use is low because of negative attitudes to their use
- general knowledge on HIV, TB, sexually transmitted infections, reproductive health, etc. is low
- there exists a 'machismo' culture which includes decoration of the penis (injection of either marbles or hair oil for example), alcohol use and frequenting sex establishments
- there are few alternative forms of recreations besides drinking, etc.
- living conditions and health are poor

- payment is made in lump sums and there is difficulty accessing financial services to facilitate savings
- there is a general lawlessness.

All of which increase the likelihood of these migrants practising high risk behaviours. For example, one of the direct consequences of the growth of single male migrants within the fishing industry has been the resultant growth in the commercial sex industry servicing these men.

> Sex business exists in a variety of forms ranging from karaoke to street based freelance sex workers. Two studies that World Vision Foundation of Thailand undertook in 2000 and 2002 and the Seafarer Study initiated by UNICEF in 1999 also highlighted that the majority of fishermen were Burmese and had several sexual networks covering Thai Sex Workers, Thai Service Girls, Burmese Sex Workers, Burmese Service Girls, girlfriends, wives, and Men who have Sex with Men. Existence of these diverse sexual network patterns in combination with a highly mobile nature of fishermen greatly facilitates a rapid, massive spread of Sexually Transmitted Infections including HIV along the migration route, affecting not only fishermen but also sexual partners and host and migrant communities (WVFT, 2003, pp.5–6).

In 2002, 9.33 per cent of fishermen (90 per cent whom are Burmese) and 9.25 per cent of Thai Sex Workers servicing these fishermen in Phuket were HIV positive. In Ranong, 10 per cent of Burmese fishermen, 36.2 per cent of Burmese CSWs and 1.7 per cent of pregnant Burmese women were all HIV+. All these incidences rates are higher than those found in the Thai counterpart cohorts. Tuberculosis is also becoming increasingly prevalent amongst these migrant communities mirroring the rise of HIV infections, crowded living conditions and lack of basic health care (WVFT, 2003).

A number of difficulties can be identified that distinguish working with Burmese migrants compared to working with Thai communities. Firstly, all Burmese migrants are illegal whether they are registered to work or not. Those unregistered to work have no formal protection under law, lack access to education and health services and are regularly exploited by employers and landlords. They can also be arrested and deported without any recourse at any time. Secondly, given this precarious existence, mobility amongst these communities is also very high. It is estimated by WVFT staff (in Mae Sot) that 50 per cent of migrants move each year to avoid debt, police harassment or to seek improved employment opportunities. Working with such mobile communities is difficult. Current project interventions are largely based on training local communities in various health issues (HIV/AIDS, RH, etc.) to achieve sustainable behaviour change. However as individuals move in and out of these communities it is difficult to provide sufficient support and information to achieve this behaviour change. Likewise, project associates, such as community health volunteers, frontline social networkers, etc are similarly likely to move and thus these resources are not maintained within the community. Thirdly, not all Burmese migrants are Burmese. Numerous ethnic minorities from Burma exist within these communities. Thus, even though the IEC and BCC materials prepared are done so in Burmese, there is a proportion of the target group unable to read these materials. It is also difficult to find suitable staff with the requisite language skills to be able to training and work with this different language groups. Fourthly, cooperation from local Thai authorities is required for organisations working with Burmese migrants. This tacit approval is necessary as working with those outside of the law, necessarily places WVFT outside of the law as well. Without the support (or at least knowledge) of the Thai authorities, WVFT would be unable to work effectively. This requires strong relationships and maintaining those relationships over time. Whilst some Burmese target groups live on-site at factories, etc, many live in nominally Thai communities. As with the Thai authorities, support is also required from the local Thai community leaders as they are also wary of activities being implemented within their communities which might attract police raids, etc. Finally, unlike development interventions aimed at improving the circumstances of the Thai population, there are few (if any) institutional linkages that can expand the benefits of these projects. As migrants cannot access health and education services, projects must therefore be self-sufficient, as they cannot leverage additional goods and services from various Thai ministries.

NGOs have also been very innovative in their response to development needs across Thailand. For many years they worked closely with local communities to devise new and unexpected responses to working with difficult to reach communities. Such innovations have included income-generation activities for those affected by AIDS. These activities have often been undertaken communally rather than individually recognising that the health of those affected can be precarious and therefore put at risk on-going entrepreneurial activities. Therefore, artificial flower-making, packaging of herbal medicines, production of shopping bags and other activities occur on the premises of NGOs on a regular basis. This also has the advantage of those affected by HIV to receive regular health check-ups but also support and understanding as stigmatisation within Thai communities around HIV/AIDS can still be problematic (see Clarke, 2002). It is important to note that many of these innovative community development strategies have been implicitly adopted within the MDG-Plus framework. So whilst regular clubs for those with HIV/AIDS have been occurring since the mid 1990s, they are now being incorporated into the MDG-Plus framework.

7   Lessons learned from Thailand and MDGs-Plus

The United Nations Development Programme have identified a number of lessons from the experience of Thailand's successful engagement with the MDGs (UNDP, 2005b):

- The MDGs are an appropriate framework for which middle-income countries can concentrate their efforts and development focus, especially targeting vulnerable or chronically poor regions or population groups. Without such a framework, many groups consistently are overlooked or excluded from mainstream interventions and programming. This may be a result of political opportunism or cultural factors.
- Strong leadership at the national level provides impetus for change and allows the leverage of other governmental programmes to support MDG achievement. Improving the lives of the poor requires inventive and concentrated approaches and thinking. By widening the resources available and those able to utilise these resources, hereunto small activities or interventions that have been effective can be scaled up to impact great numbers of the population.
- Identifying natural leaders in each MDG focus area assists in mobilising key stakeholders, participation and impact of interventions. Not all leaders must be politicians and can include civil society leaders, academics, business people or civil servants. What is important is their authority in their field and ability to motivate and mobilise other decision-makers.
- Networks of interested organisations and parties enhance the opportunities for MDG targets to be achieved and interventions to reach all aspects of society. By including bodies other than government departments greater resources are garnered and increased coordination

and purpose of programmes and interventions ensures optimal outcomes and impact.

- The MDGs cannot be considered separate to the core business of governments. Thailand was successful in moving beyond the MDG targets as it incorporated achievement of the MDGs into its mainstream social and economic activities. This requires national and provincial support and understanding of the importance of the MDGs at the highest level. It also means that a wider range of interventions than might normally be considered 'developmental' can be utilised to assist in the achieving of the MDG targets.

- Global partnership for development requires both north-south cooperation, but also south-south cooperation, investment, trade and regional initiatives. As a vanguard of early success and as regional economy of strength, Thailand has shown its willingness to assist with neighbouring countries (and as far afield as Africa) in also achieving the MDGs. A strong regional economy simply reinforces and multiplies the opportunities for future development for each of the constituent countries.

- Technical expertise and assistance from multilateral and NGOs is vital to achieve the MDGs. Within Thailand, various UN organisations (particularly the UNDP) and the World Bank worked closely with the Thai Government to support the achievement of the MDGs and then assist with planning and working towards the achievement of the MDG-Plus targets.

- Focusing on a single MDG (both in programming and advocacy) can bring to great attention overlooked or forgotten development needs. Whilst Thailand had a strong history of innovative public HIV/AIDS interventions, complacency did occur around the turn of the century. Prioritising the goal of halting and reversing HIV/AIDS within the MDG-Plus strategy allowed a re-ignition of enthusiasm. It also provided a platform to successfully launch public awareness of the remaining MDG-Plus targets across the country.

As a middle-income country, the ability of the Thai government to address the development issues addressed in the MDGs was not in question. However, the political will demonstrated by the Thai Government in not only accepting the challenges offered by the MDGs but actually embracing them with a whole-of-government approach and setting additional MDG-Plus targets presents a model for other mid-income countries. But the Thai Government did not act alone. They were supported in the conceptualising the MDG-Plus framework by various multilateral bodies, and they were also supported by NGOs in implementing and reaching certain communities that had been excluded previously by mainstream development interventions. Indeed, the role of the NGOs was also one of inspiration in that many of the MDG-Plus interventions and programmes were inspired by previous community-based NGO activities. Thus the Thai Government actively sought out and learned from the past activities of NGOs when setting its more comprehensive development agenda. Throughout, the international community continued to support Thailand's efforts and did not withdraw its international assistance simply because Thailand was moving beyond MDG expectations.

8   Conclusion

Thailand must be considered a success story in terms of achieving the MDGs. Unlike many countries in the Asia-Pacific region, Thailand is a middle-income country with a strong and growing economy (notwithstanding the negative growth experienced after the 1997 Financial Crisis). Largely based on its own resources, the majority of MDG targets had been achieved in Thailand soon after the Millennium Summit was held in 2000. Rather than simply reporting its success and rest on its laurels, the Thai Government seized the rhetoric of the MDGs and challenged itself to move beyond them. The result was the MDG-Plus framework.

Working closely with a functioning government – noting the recent military intervention but relatively resumption of normal Thai democratic principles and legitimacy of government – the international community has supported the development of the MDG-Plus framework whilst the NGO community will become increasingly engaged as much of the focus of the MDG-Plus targets will be the natural constituency of NGOs, ie. those that have been previously excluded from mainstream government-run development interventions.

The lessons of the Thai MDG experience is that a post-MDG period may be possible to ensure that those not immediately impacted upon by MDG-inspired development (the other half of the proportion not lifted out of poverty or hunger and the other third and quarter respectively of child and maternal deaths not reduced) will be done so after 2015 when the MDGs are ceased. Thailand has shown that such a post-MDG agenda is possible and that it is not even necessary to wait for other countries working towards the 2015 timeline. The Thai Government, in partnership with the international community and the NGO sector provide a worthy case study of success and hope for other countries aspiring to improve the lives of the poor.

Chapter 7 Appendix: Comparison of MDG and MDG-Plus Targets

Goal	Original MDG and Indicators	MDG-Plus and Indicators
Poverty	Halve the proportion of people living in extreme poverty between 1990 and 2015 • Proportion o people below national poverty line • Poverty gap ratio • Share of poorest quintile in individual household income	Reduce poverty to less than 4 per cent • Poverty incidence in the Northeast and three southern-most provinces • Poverty severity
Hunger	Halve the proportion of people who suffer from hunger between 1990 and 2015 • Prevalence of underweight children (under five years of age) • Proportion of population below food poverty line	Unchanged goal • Prevalence of underweight highland children • Prevalence of micro-nutrient deficiency among school aged children • Proportion of population aged over 20 below minimum level of dietary energy consumption
Education	Ensure that by 2015, boys and girls alike, will be able to complete a full course of primary schooling • Net and gross enrolment ratio in primary education • Proportion of pupils starting grade 1 who reach grade 6 • Literacy rates of 15-year-olds	Universal lower secondary education by 2006 and universal upper secondary education by 2015 • Net and gross enrolment ratio in lower and upper secondary education • Retention rate in lower and upper secondary education • National test scores of primary, lower and upper secondary students • IT literacy of 15 to 24 year-olds

Chapter 7 Appendix: Comparison of MDG and MDG-Plus Targets – *continued*

Goal	Original MDG and Indicators	MDG-Plus and Indicators
Gender	Eliminate gender disparity in primary and secondary education, preferably by 2005, and in all levels of education no later than 2015 • Ratio of girls to boys in primary, secondary and tertiary education • Ratio of literate women to men of 15 to 24 years of age • Share of women in waged employment in non-agricultural sector • Proportion of seats held by women in national Parliament	Double the proportion of women in the national parliament, Tambon Administrative Organizations, and executive positions in the civil service • Ratio of girls to boys in selected fields intertiary education • Ratio of literate women to men over 40 years of age • Proportion of women's income in waged employment in non-agricultural sector • Proportion of women in Tambon Administration Organizations and executive positions in the civil sector
Child Health	Reduce by two-thirds between 1990 and 2015, the under-five mortality rates Under five mortality rate • Infant mortality rate • Proportion of one-year old children immunised against measles	Reduce infant mortality rate to 15 per 1,000 live births and reduce by half the under-five mortality rate in highland areas, selected northern provinces and three southern-most provinces • Infant mortality rate in highland areas, northern provinces and three southern-most provinces • Under-five mortality rate in highland areas, selected northern provinces and three southern-most provinces
Maternal Health	Reduce by three-quarters, between 1990 and 2015, the maternal mortality ratio • Maternal mortality ratio • Proportion of births attended by skilled health personnel	Reduce maternal mortality ratio to 18 per 100,000 live births and reduce by half maternal mortality ratio in highland areas, selected northern provinces and three southern-most provinces • Maternal mortality ratio in highland areas, northern provinces and three southern-most provinces

Chapter 7 Appendix: Comparison of MDG and MDG-Plus Targets – *continued*

Goal	Original MDG and Indicators	MDG-Plus and Indicators
HIV/AIDS	Have halted by 2015 and begun to reverse the spread of HIV/AIDS • HIV prevalence among pregnant women • Rates of constant condom use of secondary school male students • Number of children orphaned by AIDS	Reduce HIV prevalence among reproductive adults to 1 per cent • HIV prevalence among reproductive adults • HIV prevalence among injecting drug users
Malaria, TB and other diseases	Have halted by 2015 and begun to reverse the incidence of malaria and other major diseases • Incidence and death rates associated with malaria • Prevalence and death rates associated with TB • Proportion of TB cases cured under DOTS	Reduce malaria incidences in 30 border provinces to less than 1.4 per 1000 • Malaria incidence in 30 border provinces • Prevalence and death rates associated with heart diseases
Sustainable Development	Integrate the principles of sustainable development into country policies and programmes and reverse the losses of environmental resources • Proportion of land area covered by forest • Ratio of area protected to maintain biological diversity to surface area • Energy use per 1000 THB of GDP • Carbon dioxide emission and consumption of ozone-depleting CFCs • Proportion of population using solid fuel	Increase the share of renewable energy to 8 per cent of commercial primary energy use and increase the share of municipal waste recycled by 30 per cent • Mangrove forest area • Share of renewable energy in commercial primary energy use • Proportion of major rivers that do not meet DO, BOD and TCB standards • Proportion of municipal waste recycled

Chapter 7 Appendix: Comparison of MDG and MDG-Plus Targets – *continued*

Goal	Original MDG and Indicators	MDG-Plus and Indicators
Safe drinking water and sanitation	Halve by 2015 the proportion of people without sustainable access to safe drinking water and basic sanitation • Proportion of urban and rural population with sustainable access to an improved water source • Proportion of urban and rural population with access to improved sanitation	Unchanged goal and indicators
Secure tenure	By 2020 to have achieved a significant improvement in the lives of slum dwellers • Proportion of households with access to secure tenure (owned or rented)	Unchanged goal and indicators

Source: Adapted from UNDP (2005a).

Part III

8
Conclusion and the Way Forward

1 Introduction

The signing of the Millennium Declaration in 2000, represented a landmark agreement between the 191 members of the United Nations. Based on a number of international conferences carried out during the 1990s, the declaration set out the MDGs: a comprehensive list of time bound development targets. At a subsequent UN conference on Financing for Development held in Monterrey in 2002, the international community reaffirmed their commitment to achieving the MDGs, noting the important roles that both developing and developed countries have to play for the goals to be achieved by 2015. While the goals have not been met with universal enthusiasm, they have gained wide support from governments, international aid donors, NGOs and civil societies throughout the world.

At a global level, the world is on track to halve income poverty. There are still about one billion people living in extreme poverty but according to the World Bank, the figure fell by 260 million between 1990 and 2004. This is a remarkable achievement and if this progress continues, the proportion of the world's population living in extreme poverty will have halved by 2015. However, this achievement will be largely due to incredible progress made by just two countries: China and India. Unfortunately, the proportion of people living in extreme poverty in some countries in the Asia-Pacific has hardly changed over the past 15 years. Pacific countries in particular are likely to miss out on the achievement of many of the goals.

This last chapter considers the lessons that must be learned by international aid agencies and NGOs as we now pass the half-way point in terms of the MDG timeline of 2015. Section 2 considers the importance of tailoring the MDGs to country specific contexts and how different circumstances in different countries must be taken into account by the international community, national governments and civil society. Section 3 further highlights the role that international aid and NGOs play in assisting developing countries achieve the MDGs before the chapter is concluded in section 4.

2   Re-imagining the MDGs in a changing world

So what is going to happen in 2015? While there will certainly be successes, unless progress is sped up dramatically, most countries will not achieve all of the MDGs (as originally conceived). This will lead to a broad debate on the reasons why they did not. On one side, foreign aid donors are likely to be blamed for not honouring their commitments to increase the level and quality of foreign aid, relieve debt and provide greater access to their markets. Conversely, developing country governments are likely to be blamed for their high levels of corruption, poor policies and lack of genuine commitment to poverty reduction. There is likely to be truth in both of these arguments and extensive analysis should be undertaken to determine the causes of failure on a country by country basis. Lessons learnt from failures should feed into policies to achieve the next round of goals.

However, to prevent unnecessary blame it is crucial that the goals are tailored to become more realistic in some countries. This is a central theme of the book. Conflict-affected poor countries, with few natural resources and which are vulnerable to natural disasters have no chance of reaching the goals by 2015 – even with large increases in foreign aid, improvements in governance and effective NGO interventions. The goals, as they were originally devised, are inappropriate in these countries and the commitment to achieve them is weak. Tailoring the goals for some countries could lead to far greater action to achieve them.

In tailoring the goals, it is important that they remain ambitious but at the same time are achievable. If they are not ambitious, they are unlikely to lead to any significant change from business as usual. However, if they are overly ambitious, they are unlikely to gain domestic and international support. As demonstrated by this book, a few countries have taken this lead with United Nations backing. In the Asia-Pacific region, Papua New Guinea has tailored the goals, making them less ambitious but more realistic for the country to achieve by 2015. Conversely Thailand is expected to achieve all of the Goals before 2015 and has tailored them to be more ambitious. Additional goals and targets might also need to be added as demonstrated by Cambodia which has included a goal for zero impact from landmines. Other countries, such as the Solomon Islands, have yet to fully engage with the MDGs, partly explained by their recent experience of conflict. Despite the MDGs often being applied at a global level, they should be devised at a national level and are likely to differ remarkably across countries. A rapidly industrialising country with expected high levels of sustained economic growth should have very different development goals and targets than a conflict affected, landlocked poor country, vulnerable to natural disasters.

Responsibility for the achievement of the MDGs rests largely with the governments of developing countries. It is their actions, policies and commitments which will largely determine success. However, the book has indentified important roles that international donors can play. While foreign aid has its critics, it is clear that it has a crucial role in assisting with MDG achievement. Foreign aid will be a crucial source of finance for many of the interventions required for MDG achievement. International donors need to finance country-owned development plans which effectively incorporate the MDGs. Their assistance should be long term and predictable and flow to countries who need it most as well as those that can use it best. A major challenge for donors is to ensure their efforts are effective in countries or environments where the capacity or will to achieve the goals is weak. International donors must also work together to improve the delivery of their aid and minimise the administrative burden imposed on recipients.

A smaller amount of resources will be available from NGOs. However, NGOs will play an important role in MDG achievement through their programming and advocacy work. Their programming work is likely to be more effective at a micro level, ensuring basic services reach those in need while their advocacy activities will be important at all levels, to raise public awareness of the goals, monitor progress towards their achievement and hold governments and donors accountable for their actions. NGOs will play a particularly important role in countries where a government's will or capacity to achieve the goals is lacking. In some countries, NGOs must also improve the coordination of their efforts to avoid duplication of development efforts.

While these are the broad ways in which the international community can assist with the goals, the book emphasises the need for a country specific approach by donors. Different country contexts require both different MDG targets and different responses from international donors and NGOs. Four case studies are provided of countries in the Asia-Pacific to demonstrate the roles of international aid donors and NGOs in assisting with the achievement of the MDGs. Each case study represents a particular issue or theme that donors face in assisting other countries throughout the world: improving governance in Papua New Guinea (PNG); increasing the efficiency of aid in Cambodia; dealing with a post-conflict environment in the case of the Solomon Islands; and helping a well performing middle-income country in the case of Thailand.

Many view poor governance as the main factor responsible for PNG's recent poor development record and an increasing focus by the international community on improving governance applies to many other developing countries. This book argues that a focus on governance by government donors is a long term and risky strategy with no guarantees for success. It argues that efforts directed towards improving the supply of governance (such as strengthening the public sector) should be better balanced with efforts to increase the demand for good governance, by strengthening civil society.

Cambodia is an excellent example of a country in which the quality of aid must improve. There are numerous donors providing aid to Cambodia many with equal shares of support and each supporting a wide variety of sectors. This provides a formidable aid coordination challenge for both the Cambodian government and to its development partners. Unless donors embrace the Paris Declaration and improve the delivery of their aid in this country, scaling up aid further is unlikely to effectively assist with MDG achievement.

Progress towards the MDGs in the Solomon Islands was thrown off course due to civil conflict during the late 1990s. For a period, the government was unable to function in an effective manner, seriously disrupting the provision of education, health and other social services throughout the country. NGOs in the Solomon Islands have played an important role as alternative delivers of social services in the absence of the functioning public sector. A Regional Assistance Mission to Solomon Islands (RAMSI) (led by Australia) has recently brought some stability to the country. However, the purpose of the intervention has been the achievement of stability and peace rather than the achievement of the MDGs and more appropriate development targets need to be devised.

While PNG, Cambodia and the Solomon Islands differ in many respects, there are some lessons for donors which apply to all of these country contexts. All three countries have the majority of their populations living in rural areas which have not reaped the benefits of economic growth. This has led to increasing levels of inequality between urban and rural areas. Broad based economic growth is vital for progress towards the MDGs. Further, the chapters provide evidence that donors and NGOs are not focusing on the poorest parts of the countries which actually exacerbate the problem. Explanations for this finding include concerns regarding security and aid projects and programmes being less cost effective in remote areas. However, the poor living in remote communities must be reached for the MDGs to be achieved, making it important for donors to address law and order concerns and improve rural infrastructure to make aid interventions more cost effective.

The three countries are also classified by the donor community as fragile states. Consequently, a large proportion of the foreign aid they receive is in the form of technical assistance (TA). There are often concerns regarding the quality of this assistance and TA, in general, has a relatively poor track record of improving capacity in developing countries. It is often viewed as being donor-driven and costly. Donors must therefore ensure that TA is led by aid recipients who are able to define their own capacity development needs.

While PNG, Cambodia and the Solomon Islands are not on track to achieve many of their MDGs targets by 2105, excellent progress has been made by Thailand. In fact the Thai government has set itself more ambitious MDG targets than those contained in the original schedule. Thailand's *MDG Plus* approach either shortens the time frame in which the original targets are to be achieved or increases those targets to be achieved across the range of goals. However, the country still faces the challenge of assisting those groups which have not benefitted from the country's excellent economic record.

3   International aid and NGOs

So have international aid donors really responded to the MDGs? For donors to fully commit to the MDGs, it is important that the goals are fully integrated into the design, implementation and evaluation of their aid programmes. Arguably, this has not been the case for many donors although the UK and Scandinavian countries are examples which have more formerly adopted them into the programmes. Many NGOs have included the MDGs in their advocacy activities although their programming activities are unlikely to have changed much since most were already aligned (at least partially) to the MDG targets.

Donors also need to honour their commitments to scale up their aid. However, the latest statistics reveal that international aid donors are already reneging on their commitment to scale up their aid programmes. Recent but provisional figures suggest ODA fell by more than 8 per cent (in real terms) in 2007 (OECD, 2008a). While the fall was expected due to extremely high debt relief granted in recent years, it does indicate that donors are falling short of their 2005 commitments to scale up aid by 2010. The gap is an estimated US$38 billion in 2007. Unless these commitments are met, progress towards the achievement of the MDGs will be hampered due to inadequate resources. The threat of a global recession is another factor which threatens the volume of aid required for MDG achievement. As economies falter government budgets shrink and there is a real danger that foreign aid budgets will be revised downwards. If donor governments are to maintain a true commitment to the MDGs then it must be other (domestic) sectors which bear the cost of a global economic downturn. Moreover, donors must commit to providing additional aid flows to countries making little progress towards the MDGs. Increasing aid budgets by providing aid in the form of debt relief to a select few countries will have little impact on global development.

As noted in the Financing for Development held in Monterrey, 2002 scaling up foreign aid was just one way industrialised countries should assist with MDG achievement. Developed countries must also relieve debt and improve access to their markets. Unfortunately, progress in the Doha Round of trade negotiations has stalled with some developed countries resisting calls for reductions in the agricultural subsidies. This is seriously hampering progress towards the MDGs in many developing countries. Further, the viability of some Pacific islands is increasingly being questioned. Some Pacific islands are experiencing high rates of population growth but have very limited domestic employment opportunities. This has resulted in very high unemployment rates and increasing social tensions. Developed countries could greatly assist these countries by opening up their labour markets.

At the same time a number of other related issues are presenting serious threats to the achievement of the goals. These issues include climate change, oil prices hikes and energy and food security. Climate change poses a huge threat to MDG achievement. The impacts of climate change include a loss of land, an increase in natural disasters, a loss of food security, reduced water supplies, and an increase in disease. The whole Asia-Pacific region is vulnerable to climate change. In Asia, millions live on or near the coast and there is a danger that many Pacific islanders will become so-called environmental refugees if sea levels continue to rise. In addition to signing up to policies to reduce carbon emissions and investing in research into innovative technologies, developed countries must adopt policies to assist developing countries cope with climate change. Climate change needs to be integrated into all international donors development activities and foreign aid for climate change should go beyond the 0.7 per cent of Gross National Income target for aid committed to by donor countries before the issue of climate change emerged as a serious global threat.

International organisations such as the Global Environment Facility and the World Bank's Investment Framework for Clean Energy and Development are helping to fund the transfer of clean technologies and establish renewable energy projects but more assistance is very likely to be required. Foreign aid donors can assist with climate change adaptation through measures such as disaster preparedness planning, and improving food and water security.

Sustained increases in oil prices are also impacting on progress towards the MDGs. Many people believe that the world is close to peak oil where the rate of production cannot keep up with demand. Continuing high demand from India and China is likely to keep the price high. Not only does this have major implications for economic growth and energy security but higher oil prices lead to higher food prices. Combined with other factors such as high population growth, a change in consumption habits, climate change and the increasing use of land for biofuels, many Asia-Pacific countries are experiencing a food crisis. At a 2008 summit in Rome, donors responded to the food crisis by pledging further increases in foreign aid. However, it appears that these increases are from existing aid budgets, rather than being additional aid. This further jeopardises the achievement of the MDGs. The robustness of successes thus far achieved will be tested within this new environment. People that have moved above the poverty line may remain vulnerable to even small external shocks, such as food and fuel price increases. NGOs may have to increase both their advocacy and programming efforts to ensure that gains to date are not quickly lost.

4 Conclusion

Given the failure of some countries to achieve the MDGs by 2015, there is likely to be some resistance for another round of development targets. However, the existence of well designed development goals is important. Let's not forget the MDGs have already been successful in raising global awareness of development issues and led to virtually all aid donors pledging to increase their levels of foreign aid. Moreover, international donors and governments have become more accountable for their performance at reducing poverty. NGOs and civil society can monitor progress towards the goals, identifying failures and areas needing greater attention. The question is what these goals should look like?

Lessons learnt from the global effort to achieve the MDGs must be applied to the next round of development goals. Based on country experiences with the MDGs, there are a number of guidelines that the international community should follow in devising the next round of goals. Firstly the goals must be country specific and devised by the countries themselves. True ownership of any new development goals will be a key to their success. In devising the goals, governments must ensure genuine participation from civil society. This is vital to ensure they receive wide support. Secondly, as discussed above, the goals must be ambitious but realistic and incorporated into medium and long term development plans. Governments and donors must have at least a rough idea of the financial costs of achieving them, which can be incorporated into annual budgets. Thirdly, goals and targets may need to change if the circumstances of the country changes. For example civil conflict or a major natural disaster will imply that goals and targets will need to be revised downwards to ensure they remain realistic. Fourthly, the goals must be measurable. There is little point setting development targets if developing countries do not have the data or resources to track and monitor progress. Finally, development goals should never been viewed as ends in themselves but as steps towards continual improvements in human well-being.

References

Abbott, D. and S. Pollard (2004) 'Hardship and Poverty in the Pacific: Strengthening Poverty Analysis and Strategies in the Pacific', Pacific Department, Asian Development Bank, Manila.

ACFID (2006) Program/Projects in Papua New Guinea Implemented by ACFID Members with their Local Partners, Australian Council for International Development, Canberra, Australia.

Acharya, A., A.F. de Lima and M. Moore (2004) Aid Proliferation: How Responsible are the Donors?, IDS Working Paper 214, Institute of Development Studies, Sussex.

Agg, C. (2006) 'Trends in Support for NGOs', Civil Society and Social Movements Programme Paper No. 23, Geneva, UNRISD.

Alesina, A. and B. Weder (2002) 'Do Corrupt Governments Receive Less Foreign Aid?', *American Economic Review*, Vol.92, No.4, pp.1126–37.

Alesina, A. and D. Dollar (2000) 'Who Gives Foreign Aid to Whom and Why?', *Journal of Economic Growth*, Vol.5, No.1, pp.33–63.

Allen, M. (2005) 'Greed and Grievance: The Role of Economic Agendas in the Conflict in Solomon Islands', *Pacific Economic Bulletin*, Vol.20(2).

Anheier, H., M. Glasius and M. Kaldor (eds) (2001) *Global Civil Society 2001*. Oxford: Oxford University Press.

Asia Development Bank (ADB) (1999) *Fighting Poverty in Asia and the Pacific: The Poverty Reduction Strategy*, Manila: ADB.

Asia Development Bank (ADB) (2000) *A Pacific Strategy for the New Millennium*, Manila: ADB.

Asia Development Bank (ADB) (2003) *Millennium Development Goals in the Pacific: Relevance and Progress*, Manila: ADB.

Asia Development Bank (ADB) (2004a) *Bring Water to the Poor: Selected Case Studies*, Manila: ADB.

Asia Development Bank (ADB) (2004b) *Country Strategy and Program Update (2005–2006): Solomon Islands*, Manila: ADB.

Asia Development Bank (ADB) (2004c) 'Technical Assistance to Solomon Islands for Diagnostic Assessment of Inter-island Transport', Manila: ADB.

Asia Development Bank (ADB) (2005a) *Asia Development Outlook 2005*, Manila: ADB.

Asia Development Bank (ADB) (2005b) *Private Sector Assessment for Solomon Islands*, Manila: ADB.

Asia Development Bank (ADB) (2005c) *Remittances in the Pacific*, Manila: ADB.

Asia Development Bank (ADB) (2006a) *PNG: Governance in Papua New Guinea – A Thematic Assessment*, ADB Strategy and Program Assessment, Manila: ADB.

Asia Development Bank (ADB) (2006b) *Solomon Islands: Country Information*, Manila: ADB.

Asian Migrant Centre (AMC) (2002) *Migration Needs, Issues and Responses in the Greater Mekong Subregion*, Hong Kong: Asian Migrant Centre.

Australian Agency for International Development (AusAID) (1999) *PNG Cluster Evaluation of Three Institutional Strengthening Projects*, Evaluation No.3, Canberra: Australian Agency for International Development.

AusAID (2004) *Governance in PNG: A Cluster Evaluation of Three Public Sector Reform Activities*, Evaluation and Review Series No.35, Canberra: AusAID.

AusAID (2000a) *Assisting Local Communities: Evaluation of Government Funded NGO Projects in Vietnam*, Quality Assurance Series, No. 18, Canberra: AusAID.

AusAID (2000b) *Evaluation of Australian Government Funded NGO Projects in Africa*, Quality Assurance Series, No. 25, Canberra: AusAID.

Avert (2008) *The History of HIV and AIDS in Thailand*, http://www.avert.org/aidsthai.htm, accessed June 11, 2008.

Baker, C. (1997) *Thailand*, Oxford: Oxford University Press.

Ball, C. and Dunn, L. (1996) 'NGOs Defined', in The Commonwealth Foundation (ed.) *Non-government Organisations: Guidelines for Good Policy and Practice*, London: The Commonwealth Foundation.

Banerjee, A. and R. He (2003) 'Making Aid Work', Unpublished manuscript, Massachusetts Institute of Technology, Cambridge, MA: MIT.

Banerjee, A.J. (2007) *Making Aid Work*, Cambridge, Massachusetts: MIT Press.

Bately, J. (2005) 'The Role of RAMSI in Solomon Islands: Rebuilding the State, Supporting Peace', speech presented at the *Peace, Justice and Reconciliation Conference*, 31 March–3 April, 2005, Brisbane.

Belton, S. (2005) *Borders of Fertility: Unwanted Pregnancy and fertility management by Burmese women in Thailand*, Unpublished Doctoral Thesis, University of Melbourne: Melbourne. http://www.ilo.org/public/english/region/asro/bangkok/child/trafficking/downloads/tia-1-revised-2004.pdf

Bennett, J. (2002) 'Roots of Conflict in Solomon Islands', *State, Society and Governance in Melanesia Working Paper 2002/5*, Australian National University, Canberra.

Berthélemy, J.-C. and A. Tichit (2004) 'Bilateral donors' aid allocation decisions: A three-dimensional panel analysis', *International Review of Economics and Finance*, Vol.13, pp.253–74.

Brinkerhoff, J. and D. Brinkerhoff (2002) 'Government-Nonprofit Relations in Comparative Perspective: Evolution, Themes, and New Directions', *Public Administration and Development*, Vol.22(1): 3–18.

Bulir, A. and A. Hamann (2001) How Volatile and Unpredictable are Aid Flows, and What are the Policy Implications?, IMF Working Paper WP/01/167, IMF, Washington DC.

Bulir, A. and A. Hamann (2003) 'Aid Volatility: An Empirical Assessment', Vol.50(1), pp.64–89.

Burnside C. and D. Dollar (1997) Aid, Policies, and Growth, World Bank Policy Research Working Paper No.1777. Washington DC: The World Bank.

Burnside, C. and D. Dollar (2000) Aid, policies and growth, *American Economic Review*, 90: 847–68.

Castle, L. (1980) 'The economic context', in R. Ward and A. Proctor (eds) *South Pacific Agriculture: Choices and Constraints*, Canberra.

CDC (2007) *The Cambodia Online ODA Database*, Council for the Development of Cambodia, Phnom Penh.

CDRI (2006) Cambodia Development Review, Volume 10, Issue 2, Cambodia Development Resource Institute, Phnom Penh.

Chambers, R. (1992) 'Spreading and Improving: A strategy for Scaling-Up', in M. Edwards and D. Hulme (eds) *Making a Difference: NGOs and Development in a Changing World*, London: Earthscan.

Chapman, J. and T. Fisher (2000) 'The Effectiveness of NGO Campaigning: Lessons from Practice', *Development In Practice*, Vol.10(2), pp.151–65.

Chapman, J. and A. Wameyo (2001) *Monitoring and Evaluating Advocacy*, London: Action Aid.

Chatfield, C. (1997) 'Intergovernmental and Nongovernmental Associations to 1945', in J. Smith et al. (eds) *Transnational Social Movements and World Politics: Solidarity Beyond the State*, Syracuse: Syracuse University Press.

Chauvet, L. and P. Guillaumont (2002) Aid and Growth Revisited: Policy, Economic Vulnerability and Political Instability, paper presented at the Annual Bank Conference on Development Economics, ABCDE-Europe, *Towards Pro-Poor Policies*, Oslo, June 24–26, 2002.

Clark, J. (ed.) (2003) *Globalizing Civic Engagement: Civil Society and Transnational Action*, London: Earthscan.

Clarke, M. (2002) 'Achieving Behaviour Change: Three Generations of HIV/AIDS Programming and Jargon in Thailand', in *Development in Practice*, Vol.12, No.5, pp.625–36.

Clarke, M. (2007a) A Qualitative Analysis of Chronic Poverty and Poverty Reduction Strategies in Solomon Islands, report prepared for Overseas Development Institute, London.

Clarke, M. (2007b) Over the Border and Under the Radar: A Review of Selected Migrant Burmese Community Projects, report prepared for World Vision Foundation of Thailand, Bangkok.

Clarke, M. (2008) 'Raising the Funds – Spending the Funds: A case study of the effectiveness of BOTH roles of NGOs', in A. Renzaho (ed.) *Measuring Development Effectiveness*,New York: Nova.

Clarke, M. (forthcoming) 'Over the Border and Under the Radar: Can Illegal Burmese Migrants be Active Citizens?', *Development in Practice*, forthcoming.

Clarke, M., T. Fry and S. Mihajilo (2007) 'Aid Allocation and Volatility to Small Island States', in *WIDER Research Paper No. 2007/18*, WIDER/UNU, Helsinki.

Clarke, M. and J. Shaw (2008) 'Genuine Progress in Thailand: A Systems-Analysis Approach', in P. Lawn and M. Clarke (eds) *Sustainable Welfare in the Asia-Pacific: Studies Using the Genuine Progress Indicator*, London: Edward Elgar.

Clemens, M., S. Radelet and R. Bhavnani (2004) Counting Chickens when they Hatch: The Short-term Effect of Aid on Growth, Centre for Global Development Working Paper No. 44, Centre for Global Development, Washington DC.

Clemens, M., C. Kenny and T. Moss (2007) 'The Trouble with the MDGs: Confronting Expectations of Aid and Development Success', *World Development*, Vol.35, No.5, pp.735–51.

Collier, P. and J. Dehn (2001) Aid, Shocks, and Growth, World Bank Policy Research Working Paper No.2688, Washington: World Bank.

Collier, P. and A. Hoeffler (2004) 'Aid, Policy and Growth in post-Conflict Societies', *European Economic Review*, Vol.48, Issue 5, pp.1125–45.

Collier, P. and D. Dollar (2002) 'Aid Allocation and Poverty Reduction', *European Economic Review*, Vol.26, No.8, pp.1475–1500.

Collins, C., Z. Garoyo and T. Burdon (2001) 'Jubilee 2000: Citizen Action Across the North South Divide', in M. Edwards and J. Gaventa (eds) *Global Citizen Action*, London: Earthscan.

Costello, T. (2007) 'Preface – Education for the End of Poverty', in M. Clarke and S. Feeny (eds) *Education for the End of Poverty: Implementing ALL the Millennium Development Goals*, New York: Nova.

Cox, J. (2006) *Gutpela Tingting na Sindaun: Papua New Guinean Perspectives on a Good Life*, World Vision Australia Policy Research Paper No.1, WVA, Melbourne.

Cox, J. and S. Feeny (2007) *Well-being and Development Goals in Papua New Guinea*, RMIT University, mimeo.

Cox, M. (2006) 'What Structures and Processes are Emerging at Country Level to Support a More Effective and Accountable Development Partnership?: Cambodia case Study', paper presented at the 2006 Asian Regional Forum on Aid Effectiveness: Implementation, Monitoring and Evaluation, Manila, October 2006.

Dalgaard, C-J. and H. Hansen (2001) On aid, growth and good policies, *Journal of Development Studies*, 37(6): 17–35.

Dalgaard, C-J., H. Hansen and F. Tarp (2004) On the Empirics of Foreign Aid and Growth, *Economic Journal*, 114: 191–216.

de Senillosa, I. (1998) 'A New Age of Social Movements: A Fifth Generation of Non-Governmental Organisations in the Making', *Development in Practice*, Vol.8(1), pp.40–52.

Devarajan, S., M. Miller and E. Swanson (2002) Goals for Development: History, Prospects and Costs. World Bank Policy Research Paper No.2819, Washington: World Bank.

Dinnen, S. (2003) 'Guns, Money and Politics: Disorder in the Solomon Islands', in R. May (ed.) *Arc of Instability? Melanesia in the early 2000s*, State, Society and Governance in Melanesia, Australian National University, Canberra.

Dixon, C. (1996) 'Thailand's rapid economic growth: causes, sustainability and lessons', in M. Parnwell (ed.) *Uneven Development in Thailand*, Avebury: Aldershot.

Dixon, C. (1999) *The Thai Economy: Uneven Development and Internationalism*, London: Routledge.

Dollar, D. and V. Levin (2004) The Increasing Selectivity of Foreign Aid, 1984–2002. World Bank Policy Research Working Paper 3299. Washington, D.C.

Duncan (2007) Key Governance Issues in Mobilizing Support for the Goals in Pacific, Human Development Report 2006, University of the South Pacific, forthcoming.

Easterly, W., R. Levine and D. Roodman (2004) Aid, Policies and Growth: A Comment, *American Economic Review*, Vol.94, No.3, pp.781–4.

Easterly, W. (2006) *The White Man's Burden: Why the West's Efforts to Aid the Rest Have Done So Much Ill and So Little Good*, Oxford: Oxford University Press.

Edwards, M. and J. Gaventa (eds) (2001) *Global Citizen Action*, London: Earthscan.

Edwards, M. and D. Hulme (1992) '"Scaling-Up" NGO Impact on Development: Learning From Experience', *Development in Practice*, Vol.2(2), pp.77–90.

Edwards, M. and D. Hulme (1995) 'Too close for comfort? The impact of official aid on nongovernmental organisations', *World Development*, Vol.24(6), pp.961–73.

Feeny, S. and M. Clarke (2006) *G-20 Scorecard: Are the G-20 helping to Make Poverty History?*, mimeo, Make Poverty History Campaign, Melbourne, November.

Feeny, S. and M. Clarke (2007) 'What Determines Australia's Responses to Emergencies and Natural Disasters', in *Australian Economic Review*, Vol.40(1), pp.24–36.

Feeny, S. and M. Clarke (2008) 'Achieving the Millennium Development Goals in the Asia-Pacific Region', *Asia-Pacific Viewpoint*, Vol.49(2), pp.198–212.

Feeny, S. and M. McGillivray (2008) 'Scaling Up Foreign Aid: Will the Big Push Work?', RMIT University, mimeo.

Fielding, D. and G. Mavrotas (2005) 'On the Volatility of Foreign Aid: Further Evidence', paper presented at the UNU-WIDER projecting meeting for *Development Aid: A Fresh Look*, Helsinki, 16–17 September.

Fien, J. and P. Hughes (2007) 'Education for Sustainable Development', in M. Clarke and S. Feeny (eds) *Education for the End of Poverty: Implementing ALL the Millennium Development Goals*, New York: Nova.

Fisk, E. (1982) 'Development and aid in the South Pacific in the 1980s', *Australian Outlook*, Vol.36, pp.30–5.

Foster, J. and P. Wells (2004) *'We the peoples: A Call to Action for the UN Millennium Project*, North-South Institute and World Federation of United Nations Associations, Ottawa.

Fowler, A. (1991) 'The role of NGOs in changing state-society relations: perspectives from Eastern and Southern Africa', *Development Policy Review*, Vol.9.

Fowler, A. (1997) *Striking a Balance*, London: Earthscan.

Furniss, E. (2007) 'Education and Social Exclusion', in M. Clarke and S. Feeny (eds) *Education for the End of Poverty: Implementing ALL the Millennium Development Goals*, New York: Nova.

Gemmell, N. and M. McGillivray (1998) 'Aid and Tax Instability and the Government Constraint in Developing Countries', *CREDIT Research Papers 98/1*, Centre for Research in Economic Development and International Trade, Nottingham: University of Nottingham.

Global Footprint Network (2006) *Ecological Footprint and Biocapacity*, Oakland: Global Footprint Network.

Godfrey, M., C. Sophal, T. Kato, L.V. Piseth, P. Dorina, T. Saravy, T. Savora and S. Sovannarith (2000) 'Technical Assistance and Capacity Development in an Aid-dependent Economy: The Experience of Cambodia' Cambodia Development Research Institute Working Paper 15, Cambodia Development Research Institute, Phnom Penh.

GoPNG (2004) *Medium Term Development Strategy 2005–2010: Our Plan for Economic and Social Advancement*, Government of Papua New Guinea, Port Moresby, Papua New Guinea.

GoPNG and UNDP (2004a) *Millennium Development Goals: Progress Report for Papua New Guinea 2004*, Government of Papua New Guinea and the United Nations Development Program, Port Moresby.

GoPNG and UNDP (2004b) *Papua New Guinea and the Millennium Development Goals: A Comprehensive Report on the Preparatory Work by the MDG Technical Working Group, underpinning the First Millennium Development Goal Report for Papua New Guinea*, Government of Papua New Guinea and the United Nations Development Program, Port Moresby.

Gounder, R. and V. Xayavong (2001) 'Globalisation and the Island Economies of the South Pacific', *UNU-WIDER Discussion Paper No. 2001/41*, UNU-WIDER, Helsinki.

Grenier, P. (2003) 'Jubilee 2000: Laying the Foundation for a Social Movement', in J. Clark (ed.) *Globalizing Civic Engagement: Civil Society and Transnational Action*, London: Earthscan.

Guillaumont, P. and L. Chauvet (2001) 'Aid and Performance: A Reassessment', *Journal of Development Studies*, Vol.37, No.6, pp.66–87.

Hansen, H. and F. Tarp (2000) Aid effectiveness disputed, *Journal of International Development*, 12(3): 375–98.

Hansen, H and F. Tarp (2001) Aid and Growth Regressions, *Journal of Development Economics*, 64: 547–70.

Hansmann, H. (1987) 'Economic Theories of Nonprofit Organisation', in W. Powell (ed.) *The Nonprofit Sector: A Research Handbook*, New Haven: Yale University Press.

Hearn, J. (2000) 'Aiding Democracy? Donors and Civil Society on South Africa, *Third World Quarterly*, Vol.21(5), pp. 815–30.

Hudson, A. (2000) *Linking the Levels: The Organisation of UK Development NGOs' Advocacy*, Research Report for DifD, Milton Keynes: The Open University.

Hudson, J. and P. Mosley (2001) 'Aid, Policies and Growth: In Search of the Holy Grail?', *Journal of International Development*, Vol.13, No.7, pp.1023–38.

Hunt, J. (2004) 'Aid and Development', in D. Kingsbury, J. Remenyi, J. McKay and J. Hunt (eds) *Key Issues in Development*, New York: Palgrave.

IMF (2005) *Solomon Islands: 2005 Article IV Consultation – Staff Report and Public Information Notice on the Executive Board Discussion*, IMF Country Report No. 05/365, IMF, Washington DC.

IMF (2006) *Cambodia: Rebuilding for a Challenging Future*, International Monetary Fund, Washington DC.

IndianNGOs (2007) 'What is a NGO?', http://www.indianngos.com/ngosection/newcomers/whatisanngo.htm accessed 14 May, 2007.

Intrac (1999) *The Danish Impact Study*, Oxford: Intrac.

Islam, M. (2003) 'Political Regimes and the Effects of Foreign Aid on Economic Growth', *Journal of Developing Areas*, Vol.37, pp.35–53.

Jansen, K. (1997) *External Finance in Thailand's Development*, London: Macmillan.

Jourdan, C. (1995) 'Stepping-stones to National Consciousness: The Solomon Islands Case', in R. Foster (ed.) *Nation-Making: Emergent Identifies in Post-colonial Melanesia*, Ann Arbor: University of Ann Arbor Press.

Kabutaulaka, T. (2001) 'Beyond Ethnicity: The Political Economy of the Guadalcanal Crisis in Solomon Islands', *State, Society and Governance in Melanesia Working Paper 2001/01*, Canberra: Australian National University.

Kabutaulaka, T. (2002) 'A Weak State and the Solomon Island Peace Process', *Pacific Islands Development Series No. 14*, East-West Center Working Papers, University of Hawaii, Honolulu.

Kabutaulaka, T. (2005) 'Australian Foreign Policy and the RAMSI Intervention in Solomon Islands', *The Contemporary Pacific*, Vol.17(2), pp.283–308.

Kaimowitz, D. (1993) 'The role of nongovernmental organisations in agricultural research and technology transfer in Latin America', *World Development*, Vol.21(7), pp.1139–50.

Kakwani, N. and M. Krongkaew (1997) *Thailand's Generational Accounts*, Discussion Paper 14, School of Economics, The University of New South Wales, Sydney.

Korten, D. (1990) *Getting to the 21st Century: Voluntary Action and the Global Agenda*, Connecticut: Kumarian Press.

Lawn, P. and M. Clarke (2008) 'Genuine Progress Across the Asia-Pacific Region: Comparisons, Trends, and Major Influences', in P. Lawn and M. Clarke (eds) *Sustainable Welfare in the Asia-Pacific: Studies Using the Genuine Progress Indicator*, London: Edward Elgar.

Leader, N. and P. Colenso (2005) Aid Instruments in Fragile States, PRDE Working Paper 5, Poverty Reduction in Difficult Environments Team, Policy Division, UK Department for International Development.

Lensink, R. and O. Morrissey (2001) 'Aid Instability as a Measure of Uncertainty and the Positive Impact of aid on Growth', in *Journal of Development Studies*, Vol.36, pp.31–49.

Lensink, R. and H. White (2001) 'Are There Negative Returns to Aid?', *Journal of Development Studies*, Vol.37, No.6, pp.42–64.

Levin, V. and D. Dollar (2005) 'The Forgotten States: Aid Volumes and Volatility in Difficult Partnership Countries', paper prepared for DAC Learning and Advisory Process, OECD, Paris.

Levine, R. and the What Works Working Group (2004) *Millions Saved, Proven Successes in Global Health*. Washington: Center for Global Development.

Lewis, D. (1998) *Bridging the Gap? The Parallel Universes of the Non-Profit and Non-Governmental Organisation Research Traditions and the Changing Context of Voluntary Action*, Centre for Civil Society, International Working Paper No. 1, London: London School of Economics.

Maizels, A. and M.K. Nissanke (1984) 'Motivations for Aid to Developing Countries', *World Development*, Vol.12, No.9, pp.879–900.

Makoba, J. (2002) 'Nongovernmental Organisations and Third World Development: An Alternative Approach to Development', in *Journal of Third World Studies*, Vol.19(1), pp.53–63.

Mamaloni, S. (1985) 'A Political Struggles for Rural Development', in B. Kinika and S. Oxenham (eds) *The Road Out: Rural Development in Solomon Islands*, Suva: University of South Pacific.

McGillivray, M. and M. Clarke (2006) *Understanding Human Well-Being*, Tokyo: United Nations University Press.

McGillivray, M. and O. Morrissey, (2001) A Review of Evidence on the Fiscal Effects of Aid, Research Paper No.01/13, Centre for Research in Economic Development and International Trade, University of Nottingham, Nottingham.

McGillivray, M., S. Feeny, N. Hermes and R. Lensink (2006) 'Controversies over the Impact of Development Aid: It Works, It Doesn't, It Might, but that Depends ...', *Journal of International Development*, Vol.18, No.7, pp.1031–50.

McIlwaine, C. (1998) 'Contesting Civil Society', *Third World Quarterly*, Vol.19(4), pp.651–72.

McKinlay, R.D. and R. Little (1979) 'The US Aid Relationship: A Test of the Recipient Need and the Donor Interest Models', *Political Studies*, Vol.27, No.2, pp.236–50.

Médecins Sans Frontières (MSF) (2006) 'MSF Welcomes Move to Overcome Patent On Aids Drug In Thailand', media release, MSF, Geneva, 30 November.

Médecins Sans Frontières (MSF) (2007a) The Second-Line AIDS Crisis: Condemned to Repeat?, http://www.msf.org.au/stories/twfeature/2007/163-twf.shtml accessed 17 May.

Médecins Sans Frontières (MSF) (2007b) 'MSF: Abbott should reconsider its unacceptable decision to not sell new medicines in Thailand', media release, MSF, Geneva, 23 March.

Melnick, G. (2007) 'From Family Planning To HIV/AIDS Prevention to Poverty Alleviation', *Health Affairs* 26(6), pp.670–7.

Meltzer, A.H. (2000) *International financial institutions reform: Report of the International Financial Institution Advisory Commission*, International Financial Institution Advisory Commission, US Congress.

Micklewright, J. and A. Wright (2004), 'Private Donations for International Development', in A. Atkinson (ed.) *New Sources of Development Finance*, Oxford: Oxford University Press.

Moore, C. (2004) *Happy Isles in Crisis: The Historical Causes for a Failing State in Solomon Islands, 1998–2004*, Canberra: Asia Pacific Press.

Mysliwiec, E.L. (2004) 'Envisioning a New Paradigm of Development Cooperation in Cambodia', Cambodia Development Research Institute, Phnom Penh.

National Economic and Social Development Board (NESDB) (1996) *Eighth Five Year Plan*, Bangkok: NESDB.

National Economic and Social Development Board (NESDB) (2000) *Ninth Five Year Plan*, Bangkok: NESDB.

NGO Forum (2002) *NGO Forum Annual Report*, Cambodia: NGO Forum.

NGO Forum (2006) *NGO Forum Annual Report*, Cambodia: NGO Forum.

NSO (2006) *Papua New Guinea Census 2000*, National Statistics Office, Papua New Guinea.

OECD (2003) *Policy Coherence: Vital for Global Development*, OECD Policy Brief, Paris: OECD.

OECD (2004) *Draft Report On Aid Effectiveness For The Second High-Level Forum: Review of Progress, Challenges and Opportunities*, Paris: OECD Working Party on Aid Effectiveness and Donor Practices, Organisation for Economic Cooperation and Development.

OECD (2006) International Development Statistics Online Database, Paris: OECD.

OECD (2007a) *DAC Development Cooperation Report 2006*, Paris: OECD.

OECD (2007b) *International Development Statistics Online Database*, Paris: Organisation for Economic Cooperation and Development.

OECD (2007c) Aid Effectiveness: The 2006 Survey on Monitoring the Paris Declaration, Paris: OECD.

OECD (2008a) *Debt Relief is down: Other ODA rises slightly*, Paris: OECD, http://www.oecd.org/document/8/0,3343,en_2649_34447_40381960_1_1_1_1,00.html [accessed June 11th 2008].

OECD (2008b) *International Development Statistics Online Database*, Organisation for Economic Cooperation and Development, Paris.

Ottaway, M. and T. Carothers (2000) *Funding Virtue: Civil Society Aid and Democracy Promotion*, Washington: Carnegie Endowment for International Peace.

Oxfam (2006a) *Bridging the Gap between State and Society*, Melbourne: Oxfam Australia and Oxfam New Zealand.

Oxfam (2006b) *Conflict Prevention or Promotion? An Analysis of Economic Planning and Performance in Solomon Islands*, Oxfam International Solomon Islands, Honiara.

Oxfam (2006c) *Perspectives on natural resources development as the foundation for economic growth in Solomon Islands*, notes from a discussion seminar hosted by

Oxfam International and the Environmental Concerns Action Network of the Solomon Islands, Honiara, 4 May.

PDP Australia (1991) *The Solomon Islands Economy: Prospects for Stabilisation and Sustainable Growth*, AIDAB, Canberra.

Perks, C., M. Toole and K. Phounthonsy (2006) 'District Health Programs and Health-Sector Reform: Case Study in the Lao People's Democratic Republic', *Bulletin of the World Health Organisation*, Vol.84, pp.132–8.

Phongpaichit, P. and C. Baker (1995) *Thailand: Economy and Politics*, Oxford: Oxford University Press.

Placid, G. (2003) 'The Experience of Sahayi: Capacity-Building for Sustainable Development', in M. Sharma (ed.) *Improving People's Lives: Lessons in Empowerment from Asia*, New Delhi: Sage.

Plan Bangladesh (2005) *Technical Report of the Community Learning Assistance Project (CLAP)* Dhaka: Plan Bangladesh.

Population and Community Development (PDA) (2008) http://www.pda.or.th/eng/ accessed on April 4, 2008.

Prasad, S. and D. Snell (2004). '"The Survival of Justice": South Pacific Trade Unions and NGOs during a Decade of Lost Development', *Development in Practice*, Vol.14(1–2).

Radelet, S. (2004) Aid Effectiveness and the Millennium Development Goals, Center for Global Development Working Paper Number 39, Washington: Center for Global Development.

Rajan, R. and A. Subramanian (2005a) *Aid and Growth: What Does the Cross-Country Evidence Really Show?*, IMF Working Paper No.127, International Monetary Fund, Washington.

Rajan, R. and A. Subramanian (2005b) *What Undermines Aid's Impact on Growth?*, IMF Working Paper 126, International Monetary Fund, Washington.

Ramsay, K. (2007) 'The Community Learning Action Project (CLAP): A Bangladeshi Model for Change', in M. Clarke and S. Feeny (eds) *Education for the End of Poverty: Implementing ALL the Millennium Development Goals*, New York: Nova.

Remenyi, J. and B. Quinones (eds) (2000) *Microfinance and Poverty Alleviation*, London: Pinter.

Renzaho, A. (2006) *End of Project Evaluation: Community Mobilisation for Comprehensive Approach to HIV and AIDS in Murrain town, Tanzania*, mimeo, Melbourne: World Vision Australia.

RGC (2005) *Achieving the Cambodia Millennium Development Goals: 2005 Update*, Ministry of Planning, Royal Government of Cambodia, Phnom Penh.

RGC (2007) *The Cambodia Aid Effectiveness Report 2007*, Cambodia Rehabilitation and Development Board and Council for the Development of Cambodia, Royal Government of Cambodia, Phnom Penh.

Riddell, R. and Robinson, M. (1995) *Non-Governmental Organisations and Rural Poverty Alleviation*, Oxford: Oxford University Press.

Rofeta, J. (1985) 'Self Reliance', in B. Kinika and S. Oxenham (eds) *The Road Out: Rural Development in Solomon Islands*, Suva: University of South Pacific.

Roughan, J. (2002) Mobilising domestic resources for the 'better life' in Solomon Islands', *Development Bulletin*, Vol.58, pp.85–7.

Roughan, J. (2004) 'The Villager, Poverty reduction and NGO Links', paper presented at the *Solomon Islands Government Development Partners Consultative Talks*, Honiara, 15–19 November.

Rutherford, S. (2000) *The Poor and Their Money*, Oxford: Oxford University Press (for DfID).

Sabur, M. (2007) 'The Total Sanitation Revolution', presented at *Water, Sanitation and Hygiene – Let's Come Clean Conference*, Deakin University, World Vision Australia and WaterAid Australia, Melbourne, 8 June.

Sachs, J. (2005) *The End of Poverty: How We Can Make It Happen In our Lifetime*, London: Penguin Books.

Save the Children Fund (SCF) (2007) *State of the World's Mothers Report*, London: Save the Children Fund.

Scott, C. (2005) Measuring Up to the Measurement Problem: The Role of Statistics in Evidenced-Based Policy-Making, Report for PARIS21 Partnership in Statistics.

Sharma, M. (ed.) (2003) *Improving People's Lives: Lessons in Empowerment from Asia*, New Delhi: Sage.

Sodhi, G. (2008) 'Five out of Ten: A performance Report on the Regional Assistance Mission to the Solomon Islands', Centre for Independent Studies, *Issues Analysis No. 92*, 31 January.

Solomon Islands Government (SIG) (1989) *Program of Action 1989–1993*, Honiara: SIG.

Solomon Islands Government (SIG) (2005a) *Vision 2020: A Brighter Future for Solomon Islands*, Honiara: SIG.

Solomon Islands Government (SIG) (2005b) *National Economic Recovery Reform and Development Plan: Implementation Report*, Honiara: SIG.

Solomon Islands Government (SIG) (2006b) *Household Income and Expenditure Survey (HIES) Results – Announcement*, Honiara: SIG. http://www.pmc.gov.sb/?q=node/760, accessed 9 November, 2006.

Solomon Islands Government (SIG) and United Nations Development Program (UNDP) (2002) *Solomon Islands: Human Development Report 2002. Building a Nation*, Honiara: SIG.

Solomon Islands Statistical Office (SISO) (2006a) *Household Income and Expenditure Survey 2005/6 – National Report*, Department of Finance and Treasury, Honiara.

Solomon Islands Statistical Office (SISO) (2006b) *Household Income and Expenditure Survey 2005/6 – Provincial Report*, Department of Finance and Treasury, Honiara.

Svensson, J. (1999) Aid, Growth and Democracy, *Economics and Politics*, 11(3): 275–97.

Toole, M. (2004) *Evaluation of Sayaybouray Primary Health Care Project, Phase IV Lao People's Democratic Republic*, mimeo, Save the Children Australia January/February.

Transparency International (TI) (2003) *National Integrity Systems: Transparency International Country Study Report Papua New Guinea*, Transparency International.

UK House of Commons International Development Committee (2007) 'Evidence 323 From World Bank – Sanitation: from South Asia to Global Innovation', Sixth Report of Session 2006–07, Vol.II Oral and Written Evidence of April 2007, UK House of Commons, London.

UNAIDS (2006) *UNAIDS Annual Report – Making the money work*, UNAIDS, Geneva.

Union of International Associations (UIA) (2007) '*Yearbook of International Organisations*', Union of International Associations and KG Saur Verlag, Munich.

United Nations (UN) (2002) *Common Country Assessment: Solomon Islands*, Office of the United Nations Resident Coordinator, Suva.

United Nations (UN) (2005) *Investing in Development: A Practical Plan to Achieve the Millennium Development Goals*, United Nations Millennium Project Report to the UN Secretary-General, London: Earthscan.

United Nations (UN) (2008) The Millennium Development Goals http://www.undp.org/mdg/goallist.shtml

United Nations Development Program (UNDP) (1997) *Governance for Sustainable Human Development*, A United Nations Development Program (UNDP) Policy Document, New York.

United Nations Development Program (UNDP) (2005a) *Human Development Report*, New York: United Nations Development Program.

United Nations Development Program (UNDP) (2005b) *MDG-Plus: A Case Study of Thailand*, Bangkok: UNDP.

United Nations Development Program (UNDP) (2006) *Human Development Report*, New York: United Nations Development.Program.

United Nations Development Program (UNDP) (2007a) *Human Development Report 2007/2008: Fighting Climate Change: Human Solidarity in a Divided World*, New York: United Nations Development Program.

United Nations Development Program (UNDP) (2007b) *Cambodia Human Development Report 2007*, New York: United Nations Development Program.

United Nations Economic and Social Commission for Asia and the Pacific (UNESCAP) (2003) *Promoting the Millennium Development Goals in Asia and the Pacific: Meeting the Challenges of Poverty Reduction*. New York: United Nations.

Uvin, P. and D. Miller (1994) *Scaling Up – Thinking Through The Issues*, The World Hunger Program, Washington DC.

Upton, M. (2006) 'Strengthening Civil Society in Solomon Islands: Organisational and Network Development in Development Services Exchange', *State Society and Society in Melanesia Working Paper No. 3*, Research School for Pacific and Asian Studies, The Australian National University, Canberra.

Urbano, M. (2006) *Shadows of the Kingdom: Thailand as a Trafficking Risk Factor for Burmese Migrants*, unpublished Masters Thesis, Melbourne: RMIT University.

Vandemoortele, J. (2002) Are the Millennium Development Goals Feasible? New York: UNDP.

Vandemoortele , J. (2006) Are the Millennium Development Goals Feasible?, in R. Black and H. White (2006) (eds), *Targeting Development: Critical Perspectives on the Millennium Development Goals*, New York: Routledge.

Vines, D. and P. Warr (2000) *Thailand's Investment-Driven Boom and Crisis*, Working Paper No. 00/11, Asia Pacific School of Economics and Management, Australian National University, Canberra.

Wallace, H. (ed.) (1996) *Developing Alternatives: Community Development Strategies and Environmental Issues in the Pacific*, St. Albans: Victoria University of Technology.

Watkins, K. (1998) *Economic Growth with Equity: Lessons from Asia*, Oxford: Oxfam.

Webber, R. (1985) 'Health and Development', in B. Kinika and S. Oxenham (eds) *The Road Out: Rural Development in Solomon Islands*, Suva: University of South Pacific.

Weisbrod, B. (1975) 'Toward a Theory of the Voluntary Non-Profit Sector in a Three-Sector Economy', in E. Phelps (ed.) *Altruism, Morality, and Economic Theory*, New York: Russell Sage Foundation.

White, H. and R. Black (2006) Millennium Development Goals: A Drop in the Ocean? in R. Black, and H. White (eds) (2006) *Targeting Development: Critical Perspectives on the Millennium Development Goals*, New York: Routledge.

World Bank (1991) *Pacific Island Economies: Towards Higher Growth in the 1990s*, World Bank, Washington DC.

World Bank (1995) *Working with NGOs*, Washington DC: World Bank.

World Bank (1999a) *Civil Service Reform: A Review of World Bank Assistance*, Operations Evaluation Department, Report No. 19599, Washington: World Bank.

World Bank (1999b) *Thailand Social Monitor: Challenge for Social Reform*, Bangkok: World Bank.

World Bank (2004a) *Papua New Guinea: Poverty Assessment*, Washington: World Bank.

World Bank (2004b) 'Cambodia at the Crossroads: Strengthening Accountability to Reduce Poverty' Report Number 30636-KH, Washington: World Bank.

World Bank (2006a) *Cambodia – Poverty Assessment 2006*, Washington DC: World Bank.

World Bank (2006b) *World Development Indicators*, Washington DC: World Bank.

World Bank (2007a) About Governance, http://go.worldbank.org/8CHK6P24S0 [accessed October, 2007].

World Bank (2007b) World Bank Governance Indicators: 1996 to 2006, http://go.worldbank.org/ATJXPHZMH0 [accessed October, 2007].

World Health Organisation (WHO) (1995) '1992–1993 Progress Report Global programme on AIDS', Geneva.

World Health Organisation (WHO) (2006) *World Health Statistics 2007*, France: World Health Organisation.

World Resources Institute (WRI) (2005) *Climate Analysis Indicators Tool (CAIT) Version 3.0*, Washington DC: WRI.

World Vision Bangladesh (undated) *Girl Scholarship for University*, mimeo, Dhaka: World Vision Bangladesh.

World Vision Foundation of Thailand (WVFT) (2003) *Prevention of HIV/AIDS Among Migrant Workers in Thailand – Subproject Grant Agreement*, Bangkok: WVFT.

World Vision Foundation of Thailand (WVFT) (2007) *World Vision Foundation of Thailand Annual Report 2007*, Bangkok: WVFT.

Zaidi, S. (1999) NGO Failure And the Need to Bring Back the State', *Journal of International Development*, Vol.11, pp.259–71.

Zedillo, E. and others (2001) Recommendations of the High-Level Panel on Financing for Development. UN General Assembly Document A/55/1000. New York: United Nations.

Index

Note: Page numbers with 'f' denote figures, whereas those with 't' denote tables